Dust that Breathes

Dust that Breathes

Christian Faith and the New Humanisms

William Schweiker

A John Wiley & Sons, Ltd., Publication

Library of Congress Cataloging-in-Publication Data

Schweiker, William.
  Dust that breathes : Christian faith and the new humanisms / William Schweiker.
      p. cm.
  Includes bibliographical references and index.
  ISBN 978-1-4443-3535-4 (hardcover : alk. paper)
  1. Christianity and religious humanism. I. Title.
  BR128.H8.S39 2001
  261.2–dc22

                                                        2010011932

A catalogue record for this book is available from the British Library.

Set in 10/12 pt Sabon by Toppan Best-set Premedia Limited

Printed in Malaysia by Ho Printing (M) Sdn Bhd

1 2010

To friends and colleagues who labor in the world of thought for the sake of the humane expression of religious convictions

Contents

Preface

Like every book, this one is the result of much thought and a lot of labor. And like other books, the pages that follow have etched into them the life of their author, even when the etching is seemingly concealed. How could it be otherwise? Only human beings write "books" and in the writing convey a temperament, sensibility, a bent of mind. I make no excuses about this fact. But what does it mean? A few words by way of a preface might be helpful to convey a bent of mind reflected in the chapters that follow.

This book charts engagements with various thinkers and topics that have in the course of time helped to solidify a specific theological and ethical outlook. I have always been deeply interested in and concerned about the range of human cultural activities. I came to theology from English literature rather than the study of religion or philosophy, and while I grew up in the church I have never been especially focused on the Church somehow removed from other human realities. Some of my most profound memories are of the destructive use of religious beliefs by those who, in the name of Christ, shamed and harmed people my family loved and deeply admired. Some believers obviously insist that purity of dogma is what matters most. As a youth I could never figure out how doctrine should trump love or justice. On that point, I was and I remain a Methodist. John Wesley, the founder of Methodism, ardently believed that a life without love is loss, but to be subject to error in our opinions, our doctrines, is the price of being mortal, finite. We cannot escape fallibility; we can responsibly labor for justice and for love.

During my ministerial training I was fortunate enough to spend a year as a World Methodist Intern at Wesley's Chapel, the mother church of Methodism. Interns were selected to help renew the ministry and re-open the Chapel which had been closed for an extensive renovation. Along with the other interns and the pastoral staff, I engaged in mission work, did the daily offices, and tried to carry on something like what the Wesley brothers called the Holiness Club. I also found myself heading to the University of London, working with the poor in the East End, making friends with folks in the city's library system who had little interest in the Church. By temperament and piety, I have always been inside and outside the religious community.

In the writing of the essays and articles that resulted in this book I have tried to name the temperament and piety of the insider/outsider. During my graduate studies at the University of Chicago, where I now teach, my professors introduced me, in very different ways, to the idea of "hermeneutics," a form of thought interested in human understanding through the arts of interpretation. A "hermeneut," to use the odd term, is someone who moves between the known and the obscure, present and past texts, the ambiguous and the relatively clear for the sake of understanding the wide and wild range of religious, cultural, and social activities. The term is taken from the Greek "Hermes," the messenger between the gods and human beings. I liked the term and the form of thinking it designates. It fit me well. It is how I specify the demands of theological and ethical work in a complex and dynamic global world, especially given my experience working in London. I adopted the name. I have tried to practice hermeneutical reflection ever since, including in this book. Hermeneuts cross boundaries and inhabit many "worlds."[1] Thinking is an adventure; it is a journey of discovery aimed at understanding. I hope the reader of the book gets this sense of adventure.

Over the last decade or so I have come to realize that while "hermeneutics" is an apt description of a way of thinking, it does not capture completely the temperament and piety that I struggle to live. Another term was needed in order to capture that kind of life. Much to my surprise, I came to realize that historically the best term for this outlook was Christian humanism, a legacy steeped in a love of learning, the examination of life, a practical take on Christian faith, and open to truth wherever it can be found. The Christian humanist is a hermeneutical thinker, to be sure. But her or his focus is wider since it is not only about understanding but also about the complex and joyous challenge of rightly orienting human existence. As the reader will also come to see, I have decided that a decisive *revision* is needed within Christian humanism in order to speak to our global age. What we have to interpret and the lives we have to orient are more complex, more diverse, and more global than previously imagined by the legacy of Christian humanism.

In light of the needed revision, I now designate the temperament and kind of piety that I try to inhabit as Christian theological humanism or, in a more cumbersome way, as theological humanism drawn from Christian sources. This is meant to get at a temperament and piety steeped in my specific religious tradition but lived on the global scene. Like it or not, we have to move between social, cultural, and even religious communities. More precisely, we inhabit many "worlds" and our identities are complex. In this light, one could be a theological humanist drawn from Jewish or Hindu or Islamic or Buddhist sources. In an age when too many religious and secular people remain ardently dedicated to drawing sharp distinctions between the insider and the outsider – building walls around their precious identities in order to protect themselves from global flows and global inter-actions – some of us live in-between, some of us relish the movement between social spaces, some of us work for complex identities. We do so in the service of the integrity of life, as I call it. This book is written from the stance of the believing insider/outsider – the Christian theological humanist – in the hope of helping others with a similar temperament and piety to claim the outlook for themselves and to live it freely and hopefully in our global times.

Most of the chapters that follow originated as lectures, essays, or requests for chapters. I am thankful to be able to collect them in this volume and so I want to express my deep gratitude for the invitations to speak and to write. This book is also the result of untold hours of conversation with colleagues, friends, and students. I cannot name them all, but a few are important to note. I especially thank Svend Andersen, Maria Antonaccio, Harlan Beckley, Don S. Browning, Aimee Chor, Kelton Cobb, Kristine Culp, John de Gruchy, Jean Bethke Elshtain, Michael Fishbane, Franklin I. Gamwell, Carl-Henric Grenholm, W. David Hall, Philip Jackson, David Jaspers, David E. Klemm, Paul Mendes-Flohr, Lewis Mudge, Thomas Ogletree, Wendy Olmstead, Richard Rosengarten, Andreas Schüle, Max Stackhouse, Per Sundman, Klaus Tanner, Günter Thomas, Dale Wright, Michael Welker, and Glenn Whitehouse. Over the last several years, the topics, problems, and thinkers engaged in this book have appeared in classes and seminars. I have learned deeply from students. I thank them for their insight and labor. I also want to thank my assistants for their considerable help with the production of the volume: Elizabeth Sweeny Block and Bruce Rittenhouse. Finally, I thank my son, Paul, and Maria for care of life and mind.

WS
Chicago, Illinois

Note

1   Interestingly enough, Thomas Aquinas, in *Summa Theologiae* 1a q.91 art. 1, notes that human beings are "little worlds" because other parts of "reality" are found in human existence.

Introduction

1

In one creation story of the Bible, God is pictured as stooping down, sweeping together a pile of dust, and breathing life into it. A human being is created. It is a quaint story, perhaps. Consider its meaning within the texture of Christian thought.[1]

Adam: the name means "earth" or "dust" creature. Symbolically, human beings are dust that breathes. Made of the earth, "humus," human beings are also enlivened by "spirit," the breath of life. Christians are taught to remember these realities of human existence. On Ash Wednesday, the traditional beginning of the season of Lent, ashes are imposed on one's forehead in the sign of the Cross with these words: "Remember that thou art dust and to dust thou shall return." And yet, Christians also believe in the resurrection of the body. While human beings are embodied, finite, creatures – beings of dust – we are dust that breathes. To be human is to participate in the life-giving power of God's spirit. The glory and the fragility of life – breath and yet also dust – are permanent features of existence within which persons and communities must navigate their lives. The hope of Christian faith is for new life, a renewal of spirit that enlivens our dust. Can these ancient symbolic and conceptual resources speak anew in the global age? Can they provide insight into our lives and how we can and ought to orient the life of faith? This book aims to reclaim resources for current thought and life.

Dust that Breathes: the title signals several things about the book. Some of its meaning indicates *forces* that shape human life around the world. The title is also about specific *challenges* and *possibilities* open for Christian thought and life. The chapters that follow try to get at these forces, challenges, and possibilities from the perspective of a Christianly shaped vision of human existence.

Dust that Breathes, by William Schweiker © William Schweiker 2010.

I live in Chicago and have the joy – and agony – of jogging along the city's beautiful lake front. Away from my home, through the tree-lined neighborhood streets of Hyde Park and towards the lake, eventually I reach the Point and then trudge along the path northward to the city until my legs and lungs fail and I turn to make the trip back home. Chicago is called the windy city. Runners and joggers know this well. We have to brace ourselves against the fierce wind coming off Lake Michigan that at times stops one from running. Along the lake to turn into the wind is to experience a deep and profound sense of the limits on our lives from forces beyond us – the natural environment, structures of the urban world, and other forces that can bring life to a standstill. In the chapters that follow I try to confront, analyze, and respond to the *forces*, the winds, which rush upon people of faith and limit our lives. These forces remind us that while we breathe, while human beings are enlivened spirit, we are also dust. There are forces that resist our striving. Realism is demanded in our religious and moral lives and just as much in theological and ethical thinking about our lives.[2]

The title of this book has other meanings as well. One of my deepest joys as a young man was to learn to sail. My family never owned a sailboat, but thanks to friends I was able to learn to sail. There is a rush of power that sweeps up from within the sails when skimming across the water and hiking-out to keep the boat pitched just right. One comes about, and so turns into the wind. There is resistance. The boat trembles and rockets forward in a fold of air. The tell-tails laced to the sails whip back against the canvas and flicker like flames. Their darting signals the direction of the wind. To sail is to feel power within strain; it is to know that sometimes we are sustained by forces that we cannot master but which we are nevertheless challenged to navigate. These challenges embolden resolve. This experience is also part of the chapters that follow. Each of them tries to discern the spiritual and moral *challenges* at work in our world and how we might navigate them responsibly in ways that invigorate and embolden human existence. We need to learn to navigate the age in which we live. That is one moral and religious task facing people of faith around the world.

There is a third and most obvious meaning of the title of this book, at least for Christian readers. The image of "breath" is deep within the Christian imagination. In the creation story, God's spirit moves over the face of the deep. The rhythm of human breathing is a sign of spirit. Christ teaches that the spirit blows where it will, just as the wind. At Pentecost, the birth of the Church, the Spirit enters the place where the apostles had gathered like the rushing of the wind. The image of wind symbolically presents the vitality and movement of the divine spirit in creation, in teaching, in the gathering of the church and thus in new and transformed life. To think about human existence as "dust that breathes" is, accordingly, to think in terms of how the divine spirit is alive, bringing forth renewed life and even new forms of life. The chapters that follow explore the *possibilities* now open for human existence, and, accordingly, how we can and should live responsibly within those possibilities.

These meanings of the title of this book – forces, challenges to navigate, divine spirit and the possibilities for new life gathered together in an image of human beings as "dust that breathes" – run through the chapters that follow. These meanings denote the structures, the dynamics, that give form to current human life, or so I claim. Yet these forces, challenges, and possibilities gather within a specific *dynamic* afoot in our time. It is a surprising one, actually. This global dynamic resists Christian faith and yet is also a challenge that can invigorate faith, if rightly navigated. This dynamic is a possibility for the divine and human spirits in our age. And what is that dynamic? It is new and diverse expressions of human-ism. How can Christian thinking about human beings as "dust that breathes" engage the new humanisms? That is the founding question of this book.

My suggestion about "humanism" as a global dynamic that is a force, challenge, and also a possibility will seem odd to some readers. Many Christians think in terms of an absolute opposition between Christian faith and humanism. Strident secular humanists agree. They cannot imagine any connection between religious faith and humanistic convictions. A lot of people, religious and secular, have been taught that humanism is a relic of the past. They believe that humanism is basically at odds with current sensibilities, especially ecological ones. The idea is that belief in a distinctive human dignity is somehow demeaning to non-human life. That is not the case from a Christian perspective. Whatever else Christian faith means, it is a way of life rooted in the conviction that God was in Christ, a full human being, reconciling the world to God's self. The divine does not despise the human lot. Given this truth, Christians can and must always and everywhere think about what it means to be and to live as a human being. Of course, many forms of humanism have rightly passed into obscu-rity, especially ones that celebrate unbridled human power and the absolute worth of human beings and no other form of life. Nevertheless, around the world and in many cultures and traditions there are stirrings for a kind of humanism that conceives of human responsibility within and not against other forms of life. Faithful people have to decide how to interpret, understand, and live their religious conviction in an exceedingly com-plex global age.[3] New humanisms pose the possibility and challenge of freedom *within* religion. The purpose of this book is to outline a vision of Christian faith and freedom that can navigate forces and possibilities for new life.

2

Christian Faith and the New Humanisms: by the subtitle of the book I mean to show that the chapters that follow try to map some of the current discussion about humanism and to engage a variety of positions from a specific account of Christian life. The book builds on some of my earlier work, and especially a volume recently co-authored with my friend and colleague, David E. Klemm.[4] The chapters of the present book were originally written in response to requests for a lecture or an essay. The origin of the chapters clarifies why I have engaged specific thinkers and topics linked together through a concern to survey and engage the relation between Christian faith and new humanisms. I have made revisions in the essays for the sake of coherence in the book. Hopefully there is some wisdom in collecting them within one volume. Perhaps it is a vice to believe that one's thoughts bear repeating. Sometimes one must sin boldly (as Martin Luther would put it). The theologian's responsibility is to speak as clearly as possible about the religious and moral questions of the age.

Throughout the book the reader will encounter a vision of Christian faith and life that runs decidedly against the winds of contemporary theology and ethics. It does so in several ways. A good deal of current Christian thought, especially among North American Protestants, is markedly particularistic, that is, it is concerned with the particular character of Christian thought and practice and the supposedly unique reality of the Church in the world. These thinkers draw on many ideas to develop their account of the Christian life. They focus on the formation of Christian virtues in light of the narrative character of human understanding and the story of God's action in Christ. Often, they are stridently against modernity and "The Enlightenment." They insist on obedience to Christian authorities. Finally, Christian particularists are suspicious of any demand that Christians show the truth of their convictions within the rough and tumble of public discourse. These positions have thankfully taught us a lot about the distinctive shape of the Christian life and also the problem with overly general, even universalistic, claims on behalf of a Christian vision of the moral life. That being said, this book presents a decidedly different account of Christian existence. This account is focused on responsibility and the cosmopolitan conscience, insistent about the interpretive character of human understanding in its many forms, appreciative of modern advances in thought and life while mindful of their problems and ambiguities, ardent in its defense of religious and political freedom, and one that insists on the public task of Christian thinking in the global age. In this light, one could see theological humanism as a new form of liberal theology or a version of Christian realism, although I do not think those labels capture in detail the outlook of theological humanism.[5] Besides, I fear that "liberal theology" is so grossly misunderstood and misrepresented that it is best to drop the term. And while I develop a type of moral realism in this book and others, its resources are not limited just to Christian sources.

Labels do not matter as much as outlook. What theological humanism shares with those pastors, theologians, and believers who stand in the lineage of "liberal" theology is the conviction that the truth of faith must be stated in terms that people can understand and actually live, and, further, that there is a proper liberty, freedom, *within* the religious life in terms of how one understands and lives out Christian commitments. But this freedom is not the fancy of the isolated individual driven by his or her own desires and greed; this freedom is also not a mindless relativism where there is no truth but simple preferences. Despite the many and proper criticisms of those faulty ideas of freedom – ideas too obvious in current social life – there is another and true conception of freedom rooted in the Christian message. Here "freedom" designates a way of living faithfully amid the actual realities that sustain and also limit contemporary existence. Nowadays we cannot honestly live or think as if the Enlightenment did not happen; Christians cannot sincerely act as if the massive advances of the sciences are simply not true; we cannot pretend that the teachings of the Church remain unchanged from the dawn of time. Christians cannot really claim that it is possible to inscribe social reality – the reality of other peoples, other faiths, other civilizations – within the flow of the biblical story. If they claim to do so, it is not obvious what that would mean for actual life. We can only live in the age we are given to live and that is why the task of navigating forces, challenges, and possibilities is the permanent responsibility of Christians. That is the freedom of responsibility. And that responsibility has been the mighty cause of liberal theology. Seen in this way, St Paul, Augustine, Aquinas, Luther, as well as many others, were, in fact, "liberals." They sought to speak truthfully to their age for the sake of life within the Spirit. That remains the task today.

Admittedly the voices of Christian particularism have a certain attraction in an uncertain and complex age. A good deal of the attraction, it seems, is that they paint a clear picture of Christian thought and life that relieves believers of the burden of current reality. Social life is neatly boxed into the "Church," where Christians are to live in peace, and the "World," which is violence and war. The task of the Church is to be the Church. The background of this picture is a rather grim account of modern thought and life and also a deep longing somehow to dwell in a pre- or post- or anti-modern world. This kind of clarity can bring consolation to believers and certainly it gives them confidence about the virtues of their faith. That is the strength of this kind of theology. In other words, these theologians speak powerfully to the anxiety of Christians in wealthy and increasingly secularized nations about the meaning and relevance of faith. By the same token, they risk playing into the need among people in complex cultures to have some unique "identity." Theology becomes a kind of sociology or politics and faith is understood in terms of identity formation. But Christian faith is not really about Christian identity. It is about God's action in Christ and the power of new life. In my judgment, the real task of theology is to grasp and be grasped by the daring insights of Christian faith into human beings as "dust that breathes."

That is not all. The major weakness of church-centered theology in a particularist mode is that it is unrealistic either about goodness found outside of the Church or about the forms of distortion within the Church. And in this respect, as noted above, theological humanism is a version of what used to be called "Christian realism," and in a number of ways. First, it is a bit silly to contend that everything outside of the "church" is a realm of sin and death and war and so to deny the obvious good will, insight, intelligence, creativity, and peace of other cultures and religions, many of whom – if we are honest – are more peaceful than Christian communities. Christians cannot live in the Church sealed off from the world. "Church" and "World" are complex, interrelated, and ambiguous realities of forces, challenges, and possibilities. Yet believers are supposed to denounce the world and retreat into the church while their daily lives rely on developments in modern science, technology, medicine, social existence, communication, and education (to name a few) that characterize our global age. Theological and ethical thinking should not force faithful people into hypocrisy. What is more, the dismissal of the "world" is a dismissal and scorn for the very reality Christ came to reconcile unto God. In this light, the advance of knowledge, freedom, and equality around the world is something Christians should celebrate and seek to further. Christians are called to live into the reign of God and not to long to return to a pre-modern social order on the assumption that it can be re-adopted as though time has not marched on. We are to walk in the ways that *lead* to life, as scripture puts it. For Christians, the future is about being fully alive with God and with others. No period of history, no philosophical outlook, and no figure of thought can claim to signify without remainder the reality of the living God.

The argument of this book is cast against prevailing winds in Christian theology in yet another important way that carries forward insights of Christian realism. If anything characterizes the various stripes of current theology and Christian ethics it is that human problems are primarily social ones and, what is more, theology itself must be seen as a form of sociology. Christian morals are conventional; they are a reflection of custom and inherited Church authority. Redemption is liberation from oppressive structures or a transformation of character through one's resocialization into the life of the Church. The human "fall" is not turning from God or from our "true" nature; it is not about a struggle *within* human life between the "flesh" and the "spirit," as St Paul calls it. Rather, the "fall" and the struggle take place between human beings and their institutions. Everywhere we look, the claim is that life would be better if we had better institutions; oppression would vanish from the earth if only we joined the right community (e.g. the Church). The idea, as Irving Babbitt noted, has its roots in the thought of Jean-Jacques Rousseau and "has tended not only to substitute sociology for theology, but to discredit the older dualism [i.e., spirit/flesh] in any form whatsoever."[6]

I do not agree with most of Babbitt's ethical and religious position. I do believe he is right on this point. Any Christian realist would as well, like Reinhold Niebuhr and others. In the rush to avoid invidious dualisms of "body and spirit" or "mind and body," dualisms that are said to be non-biblical and somehow the result of Greek thought and Western patriarchy, there has been a wholesale embrace of Rousseau's main idea that the human problem is between persons and institutions, whether those institutions are various "isms" (sexism, racism, colonialism, etc.) or whether the conflict is between Church and world. Now, I too want to champion in every way possible the liberation of human beings from forces of oppression. And I have no desire to deny the depth of human sociality. We are social and relational creatures through and through, as the various chapters constantly attest. Yet in the pages that follow one will find the dogged insistence that we confront with honesty and humility the problem of our inmost being, the struggle for integrity in our lives and communities. This is not only a social problem. I seek to articulate and to examine the complexities of human existence from a theological perspective for the sake of orienting social and personal life realistically and responsibly. The human problem is deeper and more intractable than current forms of Christian theology and ethics admit. It is *inside* of each of us as well as in the institutions that shape, sustain, but also corrupt human existence. This conviction has drawn me to engage certain themes and thinkers in the chapters of the book. It is what renders the outlook humanistic and realistic and not just a new version of theological liberalism.

We can only think in the age in which we actually live even if we strive and long for new life. I have tried to think honestly and responsibly in the pages that follow. It has meant exploring Christian faith from an angle of vision called theological humanism. I understand that this way of thinking runs headlong against many of the winds of current theology in terms of the kinds of claims one can make, how to show the truth of Christian convictions, an understanding of the relation of person and community, and also in matters of moral theory. The aim of the book is to make a case for this outlook in the hope of convincing others to inhabit Christian convictions freely as theological humanists and therefore dedicated to what respects and enhances the integrity of life.

3

The main theme of this book is the relation between Christian convictions about human existence and the widespread debate about humanism. I enter this debate because of a shared concern held by humanists: for the sake of orienting life rightly, we must explore and assess the fault, tragedy, folly but also hope and aspiration inscribed in human existence. I want to clarify the idea of theological humanism by setting it in context. This means two things that are important to have in mind when reading this book. First, various themes important for my account of theological humanism will arise in the course of the chapters, ideas about conscience, responsibility, the integrity of life, faith, transcendence, and so on. These themes are not treated at just one point in the book. The same is true of humanism. I do not devote a chapter to its meaning and history; that would be better done in a single volume on its own. What this book does is to allow a distinctive Christian moral and religious sensibility to come to expression in and through engaging themes and thinkers.

Of course, this strategy of thought is important in itself. Come what may, human thought about practical matters arises within the ongoing conversation and debate with others for the sake of understanding and orienting existence. While some philosophers and theologians write their books by presenting clean and direct lines of argument, my thought is circuitous, engaged, and multidimensional. I try to think along with and yet beyond other thinkers, religious and not, based on a belief about the entanglement of thought and life. I am aware that this makes my arguments "difficult," as it is put by my friends and critics. The theologian Bernard Meland supposedly said that "we live deeper than we think." I agree. Theological and ethical thinking is always trying to get as deep as we actually live; it aims to bring to expression and to understand the structures and dynamics of lived reality for the sake of orienting faithful and responsible existence. That is the kind of thinking practiced in this book. I invite the reader to join in this adventure.

The second thing to bear in mind when reading this book is that there will be, by the nature of the case, some repetition. This is partly because the various chapters were originally developed in response to specific requests for an essay or lecture that circled around the topic of Christian conviction and humanism. It is also the case because, as the product of one man's mind, every chapter is going to reflect my concerns. But there is a deeper reason for repetition. Just as thinking is bound to the dynamics of human living, so also theological and ethical reflection can never grasp reality *in toto*. Mortals that we are, the human mind can never get everything in focus at once, to have a God's eye perspective on any topic, let alone reality itself. We only see in part and then darkly. We inhabit various and limited perspectives, and thus are forced to use our imaginations to fill out what we cannot completely grasp. One should never confuse one's perspective with the whole of things, as if we somehow got it all. We should never confuse our best and most faithful attempts to speak of the living God with the living God. Whatever we can say about human existence will be limited, partial. Yet this fact about the inherent limits on human thought also means, on my account, that we can attain a more complete understanding, a better grasp of any topic or question, when we see it from multiple perspectives and dimensions. By engaging various thinkers and topics, I am, accordingly, trying my best to assess perspectives on the question of Christian convictions about human existence and the new humanisms in order to understand forces, challenges, and possibilities and thereby to present a more adequate response to them. This fact about my style of argument demands patience on the reader's part. Given the limitations of the human mind, I cannot imagine another way to carry out the complex task of theological and ethical reflection.

Theological humanism is then a stance and orientation in religious thinking and life. The term is meant to designate an approach often neglected in strident times when the advocates of kinds of orthodoxy vie for power both inside the academy and within religious communities. Precisely because spiritual truths are held by human beings, they are vulnerable to human fallibilities and therefore must be interpreted in terms of their bearing on human and non-human life. Theological humanism denotes a deep religiosity, but one that gains critical distance from one's home tradition, which in my case is Christian faith. A theological humanist finds within the insight of others, even those who deny one's own faith, a human connection that ought not to be wantonly violated but rather treasured. Yet because theological humanists insist that one's beliefs and practices must be tested by their impact on life, there is normative weight to the task. Not everything that appears under the guise of religion counts as spiritual insight. Not all claims or actions or practices of a religious community, one's own or that of others, can be or must be endorsed. There are judgments to be made. Over the last years thinkers in various religious traditions have been pursuing something like theological humanism. There is not much at stake in a name, in any case. What matters is the stance and orientation, the bent of heart and mind, which characterizes an approach to religious and moral thinking.

There are differences among those who are thinking about theological humanism.[7] For my part, I have tried to plumb and compare decidedly religious symbols, texts, and practices in order to grasp the ways they display a lived structure to reality and intimate how responsibly to orient life. I do this in the chapters that follow. Others have pursued different ways into theological humanism and expressed different concerns and sensibilities. Whether or not a theological humanist takes an ethical focus, a more speculative one, works with non-religious thinkers and texts to grasp their religious significance, examines resources in non-Western and even non-theistic traditions, or seeks to understand the import of the arts, is a matter of temperament and expertise. I hope my reader recognizes herself or himself in the range of work that falls within theological humanism and joins this venture.

Theological humanism is, further, a hermeneutical enterprise insofar as religious disclosures traverse realms of culture and thus human meanings. These disclosures of meaning demand to be interpreted – the work of hermeneutics – because they are not self-evident revelations of God nor are they so odd and strange that they fail to make any connection to the everyday job of human living. For a theological humanist of my stripe, the demand for interpretation arises partly because one understands the religions as cultural realities, but also because there is no reason to limit disclosers of truth to the explicit texts, symbols, and practices of historic religions. Almost everyone has some religious longings, and so one can be less concerned with structures of authority and the need for obedience to those in the know. Religious meanings can even appear in the self-overturning of explicit authoritative religious forms. As an orientation in thought and life, theological humanism insists on interpreting human spiritual longings. This is why, again, I have engaged the various thinkers: because each of them seeks to probe and understand our condition, morally and religiously.

One needs to grasp the force of these moves. My strategy of interpretation is, in part, to use religious resources diagnostically, that is, to deploy religious ideas, concepts, symbols, texts, and the like to decode meanings in what are supposedly non-religious realms of life. This is to suggest that a purely non-religious hermeneutics is finally unable to grasp the full texture of human experience or cultural practices. Yet the tactic is also, dialectically, to apprehend distinctively religious orientations anticipated or announced in cultural realms that can thereby fund creative religious and theological thinking and revision.[8] Where this differs from previous kinds of theological reflection on culture is at least twofold: one makes no assumption that this venture is necessarily undertaken within the context of Christian theology, and, further, its criterion of validity is linked to a concern for the integrity of human and even non-human life. Theological humanism is a decidedly religious orientation and not a secular one; it likewise wrestles with human foibles and flourishing, rather than trying just to bolster the authorities of some tradition.

4

With some sense of the aim of the book and its distinctive outlook, what about its organization? I have structured the chapters under two headings: topics and thinkers. This order gives structure to the book even though it does not have the strict coherence that characterizes the usual single volume. A reader can dip into this chapter or that chapter without fear of missing the larger point. And like a piece of music, themes and variations appear and reappear throughout the volume in order to provide the fullness and complexity of the whole. In this respect, the organization under the headings "Topics" and "Thinkers" too easily gives the impression of a neat distinction between the book's parts. So, beware: the organization of the chapters is not what matters so much as the themes and their variations that appear in the context of engaging different topics and thinkers.

Part I, "Topics," explores various forces that sweep around the world. The chapters of Part I move from the general to the more specific: they show how a Christian theological humanist, as I call myself, draws on religious resources in order to address shared human challenges and concerns. More specifically, three big topics are treated in Part I: religious identity in our global times (Chapters 1–2), the idea of conscience as a means to articulate the most basic mode of moral existence (Chapters 3–4), and current versions of humanism, including Christian humanism (Chapters 5–6).

Part II, "Thinkers," engages some prominent contemporary philosophers and theologians on the relation between faith and humanism. However, these chapters are not simply studies of the specific thinker. They are written in order to clarify theological humanism by developing and contrasting it with other types of humanism on some shared point of reflection. The movement of this part of the book is also from the general question of humanism to specifically Christian works. Part II also has some rough and ready divisions of labor, much like Part I of the book does. Chapters 7–8 engage two current philosophers important in recasting the question of humanism, specifically Paul Ricoeur and Iris Murdoch. This is followed, in Chapters 9–10, with reflections on the theme of the integrity of life important for theological humanism. *Conscience* is crucial for thinking about the human mode of moral being (Chapters 3–4). *The integrity of life* is the norm and measure of conscience and so for theological humanism as well. Recent work by Jürgen Moltmann and also the Danish philosopher and theologian Kund Løgstrup is helpful in clarifying the topic of "life," theologically and ethically. Finally, Part II, in a way parallel to Part I, returns to the theme of "Christian humanism" with discussion of Paul Tillich's idea of ecstatic humanism (Chapter 11) and John W. de Gruchy's recent work on Christian humanism (Chapter 12). There are then connections between the parts of the book – themes and their variations that weave through the book – even if I have not been slavish in trying to fit everything into a neat and tidy box. The topics and thinkers, themes and variations, hang together within a capacious outlook.

This book seeks to make a simple point, really. Despite what some might think, it is possible to articulate the meaning, significance, and truth of a Christian outlook on life that does not involve special pleading – saying that Christian faith cannot be tested by other ways of knowing and living – or triumphalism, the grisly idea that only Christians know the truth and the whole truth. On the contrary, this book outlines an approach to Christian existence fully engaged with shared human concerns and yet meant to show the force and truth of convictions for meeting the practical challenges and possibilities of our age. In ways often not seen, God's Spirit is at work in the world empowering persons and communities to respect and enhance the integrity of life. The divine breath enlivens dust.

Notes

1   Christians are not the only ones to make these kinds of claims. Similar ideas can be found in other cultures and traditions. For instance, Marcus Aurelius, the Stoic philosopher and Roman Emperor, notes in his *Mediations*: "A little flesh, a little breath, and Reason to rule all – that is myself." So the point is not the uniqueness of the Christian vision so much as a distinctively Christian interpretation of finite human being. I aim to clarify that distinctive vision throughout this book, but especially in Chapters 6 and 12, below. See Marcus Aurelius, *Meditations*, trans. M. Staniforth (New York: Penguin, 1964), Bk II, p. 2.
2   In other works I have explored these matters in terms of kinds of realism important for theological ethics, especially moral realism, as a claim about the nature of norms and the good, and also hermeneutical realism, a theory about the character of human moral understanding. On this point see William Schweiker, *Responsibility and Christian Ethics* (Cambridge: Cambridge University Press, 1995). For a related account see Robin W. Lovin, *Christian Realism and the New Realities* (Cambridge: Cambridge University Press, 2008). Lovin helpfully distinguishes, and relates, political, moral, and theological realism. The point being, for realists, that human beings do not dwell only within a "world" of their making (their "cultures"), but are always interacting with, responding to, forces, challenges, and possibilities beyond their powers that limit, sustain, and further human activity. It is popular nowadays to deny these claims of realism. But the denial does not finally succeed. While we cannot know completely or with certainty all of the reality which limits, sustains, and furthers our existence, we practically confirm it in everything we do – unless, of course, one is lost in delusion.

3 For examples among religious thinkers see *Humanity Before God: Contemporary Faces of Jewish, Christian, and Islamic Ethics*, ed. William Schweiker, Michael A. Johnson, and Kevin Jung (Minneapolis: Fortress Press, 2006). For a non-religious argument see Luc Ferry, *Man Made God: The Meaning of Life*, trans. D. Pellauer (Chicago: University of Chicago Press, 2002).

4 See David E. Klemm and William Schweiker, *Religion and the Human Future: An Essay on Theological Humanism* (Oxford: Wiley-Blackwell, 2008).

5 I realize, of course, that Christian Realism is often seen as opposed to the legacy of liberal theology because, as Reinhold Niebuhr would put it, the "liberal" outlook seems too positive in its evaluation of human capacities for genuine moral action and is often inattentive to the forces that resist every attempt to refashion the social order around the ideals of justice and Christian love. While that difference is certainly true, Christian Realists and Liberal theologians seek to make the Christian faith intelligible and meaningful within the conditions of contemporary life and thus seek to respond to shifts in personal and social life rather than adhere to traditional formulations alone. The disagreement arose in terms of how to understand contemporary conditions of life and also the dynamics of personal and social life. In any case, my concern is not with the similarities and differences among these theological movements, but, rather, with what can be learned from them and their critics for the sake of advancing a vision of Christian existence today.

6 Irving Babbitt, "What I Believe" in *Irving Babbitt: Representative Writings*, ed. George Panichas (Lincoln: University of Nebraska Press, 1981), p. 5.

7 For a nice summary of the options, see the volume dedicated to theological humanism in the journal *Literature and Theology: An International Journal of Religion, Theory and Culture* 18:3 (2004).

8 See William Schweiker, *Theological Ethics and Global Dynamics: In the Time of Many Worlds* (Oxford: Blackwell, 2004).

Part I
Topics

Chapter 1

The Specter of Religious Identity

1

In the first two chapters of this book I want to explore the idea of "humanizing religion." This chapter looks at actual conflicts found in religious life on the global scene, what can be called "the specter of religious identity." I isolate three responses to it, namely, religious terrorism, moral particularism, and theological humanism. The next chapter steps back in order to take a more general approach to the topic, one that also explores how we ought to think ethically about the life of faith and the relation of theological ethics to other forms of thought. Both chapters introduce the idea of theological humanism, but through different forms of inquiry. The chapters ask: how ought we to inhabit and to think about our religious convictions?

What I mean by the specter of identity is quite simple. People in our global times live with multiple identities. For example, I am male, white, a citizen of the USA, a Protestant Christian, a father, a fan of the Chicago Fire soccer team, a political progressive, and so on. My "identity" is a bundle of more specific ways of identifying who I am, and it is hard to imagine how just one of these attributes (father, Fire fan, Christian) could subsume the rest, so that I would be, for instance, only a Fire fan. Our lives are multidimensional and complex. Is the complexity of actual life a good thing or is it a problem? Maybe my identity should be unified under just one, absolute identity, say, that I am a Christian. Since religious convictions claim to be about what is most real and important, as we explore in the next chapter, it is not surprising that they are usually believed to trump other ways of identifying a community or a person. That is the argument of moral particularists, as we will see. Their contention is that one's identity should be formed by the beliefs and practices of one particular community, say the Church. Oddly enough, that is also an idea driving a good deal of religious conflict, including religious terrorism.

Dust that Breathes, by William Schweiker © William Schweiker 2010.

Theological humanism, conversely, thinks that the complexity of identity is a good thing, morally and religiously. It is a good thing partly because it is crucial for individuals and communities to have the freedom to fashion different kinds of lives, but it is good also because this complexity enables kinds of self-criticism that are important in our age. The freedom for self-criticism is at the root of the human problem *inside* of every human life. People tend to want to justify themselves, that is, to show that they are right and righteous. Of course, more will be said later about these options in current religious life, but again, the basic question is whether or not the complexity of identity is a problem or a possibility, religiously and morally. Theological humanism thinks it is a possibility; others see it as a problem.

The very idea of "theological humanism" might sound odd, or at least confusing. Tzvetan Todorov has noted that humanists believe that "freedom exists and that it is precious, but at the same time they appreciate the benefit of shared values, life with others, and a self that is held responsible for its action."[1] The point of "theological humanism" is to understand religious identity in relation to commonalities of human existence and the responsibility we have to respect and enhance the integrity of life with and for others. It denotes a third way beyond the usual divide between secular humanistic outlooks and those forms of belief and practice that seek to enfold life into one particular religious community.[2] The great Renaissance humanist Petrarch wrote that "theology is a poem, with God for [its] subject."[3] The task of Christian thinking is to understand and orient human existence within a divine poem. When we think about the moral life within a theological perspective, we interpret the divine poem in terms of human needs and meanings. So, I will use religious texts and stories not just to know those stories or somehow to try to live within them alone. These texts are a prism, the spectacles, in and through which one can grasp the actual structures of lived reality.[4] By the end of this chapter I hope to have shown the importance of theological humanism as a way of inhabiting religious identities in our age.[5]

2

It is important to realize that one decisive feature of our global age is that human identities are *internally complex*. After all, there are German Muslims in Berlin, south Chinese Christians as well as women Hindus who cheer for (say) Italy in the World Cup. The reasons for this complexity are many: migration of people due to war or economic plight, worldwide communication processes and the flow of cultural symbols and commodities that enable people to envision new identities, the global spread of the religions, and so on. Of course, this fact is not new in world history. People have always moved around for various reasons, especially due to the forces of empire, colonization, and war. Nevertheless, a feature of global dynamics is the re-fashioning of traditional identities on a scale not previously seen.[6] This fact poses a problem to the religions.

Any religion includes many things: rituals, stories and myths, communal organizations, and ideas for how to live rightly. Religions also claim to be about what is unsurpassably important *and* real that connects human beings to "sacred" or "divine" powers.[7] For Christians the living God revealed by Christ is what is most real, most important. Yet if a religion is about what is of unsurpassable importance and reality, then the complexity of identity would seem to be *a problem*. It would mean that people's lives are wrongly formed if they are shaped by what is not unsurpassably important and real, say, around political beliefs, ethnic connections, or sexual identities. On this reasoning, in order to be religious one ought to fashion lives that unify existence under one dominant identity. One should just be a Christian or only a Jew or be prepared to stand before Allah on judgment day as a devout Muslim. In other words, it appears that the religions *require* that one's identity be unified under one category that designates what is unsurpassably important and real. My Christian identity must trump my cultural or political or ethnic identity, if I am to be faithful to the living God.

If this is true of religious convictions, then how can one live in a society where the authority that backs one's identity is not recognized as absolute? How can the religions avoid conflict since my Christian identity must be at odds with, say, your Buddhist identity? The Nobel Prize winner in economics Amartya Sen has wisely written that "many of the conflicts and barbarities in the world are sustained through the illusion of a unique and choiceless identity." The problem is "the presumption that people can be uniquely categorized based on religion or culture."[8] After 11 September 2001, the rhetoric was extreme, at least in the USA. We heard about "the Islamic Nation" or "international infidels," the "Christian" West, or the "axis of evil," terms which classify people under one description. Sen has put his finger on what I am calling the "specter of identity." Is it a good thing that people's identities are complex, and, further, how ought we to live with that complexity?

The specter of identity is a clue to the inner-meaning of terrorism used in the name of religion. In the attempt to protect an identity from criticism by others or from being polluted by other ideas and values within the flow of global reflexivity, some religious communities seek to enfold existence within one description and thus one way of reading their community's divine poem, as it were. They want their identity to become their destiny, a reality about which they have no choice. More precisely, they want to force an either/or choice: either one is a real Christian or a true Buddhist or a genuine Muslim, or one is unfaithful, untrue. This *can* lead to conflict, even terrorism. And that is because terrorism is a way to form people's identities through violent means.

In order to get this point about terrorism and identity formation one needs to be clearer about terrorism and, more specifically, "religious terrorism." As it happens, the Bible is a great text to study in order to understand terrorism. (Texts of the other great religions could also be used, but that is another matter.) Recall two biblical stories as we proceed through the rest of this chapter. They are the lenses, the spectacles, the "divine poem," in and through which we are trying to get at the lived structure of contemporary reality. They are what the biblical scholar Phyllis Trible once called "texts of terror."[9]

The first text is the various plagues God sends upon Egypt in order to free the Israelites from slavery to Pharaoh. God tells Moses that the people need to leave Egypt and go into the desert and worship. Pharaoh sees this request as a threat to his political power and also a religious challenge because he is the head of Egyptian state religion. After locusts, frogs, a bloody Nile and other horrors, God finally slaughters the first-born of Egypt, human and non-human. Then we read (Exod. 12:30–1):

> Pharaoh rose in the night, he and all his officials and all the Egyptians; and there was a loud cry in Egypt, for there was not a house without someone dead. Then he summoned Moses and Aaron in the night, and said, "Rise up, go away from my people, both you and the Israelites!"[10]

Later, in Deuteronomy 26:5–11, the Israelites are told to repeat this story, to see themselves within this divine poem, and so God's salvation of Israel. This is part of Passover celebration.

The second text is the slaughter of the innocents in Matthew's Gospel. Remember that King Herod gets wind of the birth of a king of the Jews, and in order to stop this "messiah" he sends his soldiers to slaughter all male children aged 2 years and younger. The prophet Jeremiah is quoted in Matthew's Gospel about the terror of the people:

> A Voice was heard in Ramah, wailing and loud lamentation, Rachel weeping for her children; she refused to be consoled, because they are no more.

But, in fact, Jesus escapes. His father Joseph is warned in a dream and he takes Mary and Jesus down to Egypt. To this day, Christians celebrate this flight of Jesus as part of the Christmas season. What about the slaughtered children?

These texts of terror portray horrific, even genocidal, violence and the death of innocent children that destroys the future of people. They shape the way the people in the stories see reality in and through a clash between political powers, a king or a pharaoh, and divine power. They form identities: the people of Israel versus the Egyptians; those who worship the messiah against Roman might. But, of course, religious terror is not a thing of the past. The reality of terrorism is hard to miss in our current world. It fills the daily newspapers. While usually associated with fanatical Islam, terrorism is found among most of the world's religions. It is not just the monotheistic religions that are involved in terror, although it is very popular nowadays to think that somehow monotheism is uniquely linked to terror. For instance, Buddhist monks in Sri Lanka who are part of the National Heritage Party have been fighting a war against Hindu and Christian separatists. Buddhist monks, usually thought of as peaceful, have in fact stood by kings and fought wars for centuries.[11]

Part of the problem is what one means by "terrorism." What looks like an act of terrorism from one perspective is seen by someone else as an act of faith or martyrdom or liberation. Further, terrorism does not denote just specific violent acts, say, a car-bomb, a suicide bomber on a city bus, or even acts of genocide. More profoundly, terrorism is a psychological reality. It is a way of shaping how people see and experience the world by forming their identities through pain and fear. Jonathan Glover in his book *Humanity: A Moral History of the Twentieth Century* cites a memo written in 1918 by Lenin about the suppression of an uprising and how it was to be crushed. The memo is graphic but important to cite. It helps us grasp the meaning of terrorism. Part of the memo reads:

1) Hang (and I mean hang so that the *people can see*) *not less than 100* known kulaks, rich men, bloodsuckers.
2) Publish their names.
3) Take *all* their grain away from them.
4) Identify hostages. ... Do this so that for hundreds of miles around the people can see, tremble, know and cry: they are killing and will go on killing the bloodsucking kulaks ...

Yours, Lenin.[12]

Lenin and Stalin engineered the Soviet terror, but notice that features mentioned in this brief memo are found in most forms of terrorism, including the biblical texts: horrific violence, publicity, economic deprivation, hostage taking, and systematic, widespread and public action – killing the kulaks or every first-born in Egypt or all the male children aged 2 years or younger around Bethlehem. The effect of terror is to create a situation of ongoing fear and complacency. The purpose is to make people victims of force and thereby more easily subject to control. It is to form a unified identity through subjugation to one power and one description.

Religious terrorism is a *form* of terrorism. What *religion* adds to this business is a motivation for terrorist action. One is to be a prophet or a martyr or is somehow being faithful to God and will be rewarded for one's faithfulness. Religious terrorism is psychologically powerful, because, remember, the religious are about what is *unsurpassably* important and real. There is supposedly nothing more important or more real for a Christian than the God known in Jesus Christ; there is nothing that is more real and more important for a Jew than the God of Israel known through Torah. Religious terrorism sanctions physical and psychological violence in the name of what is believed to be most important and most real, that is, the divine. In doing so, it forges an identity under only one description in relation to divine authority. Recently, the Saudi author Wajeha al-Huwaider wrote a poem titled "When." It powerfully makes the point about Islam, but it could be applied to other religions, such as fundamentalist Christianity, Judaism, or Hinduism, as well. A few lines: "When you see people living in the past with all the trappings of modernity – do not be surprised, you are in an Arab country. ... When religion has control over science – you can be sure that you are in an Arab country. ... When fear constantly lives in the eyes of the people – you can be certain you are in an Arab country."[13]

The point here is not about fanatical Islam or Christian fundamentalism. The point, rather, is that religious terrorism often erupts because of a conflict over what ought to form people's identities. The attacks on reason and democracy we see around the world in militant forms of religion go together, of course. What is being challenged is the idea that one's identity can and ought to be formed by anything other than obedience to absolute authority. And the debate about religion, reason, and political authority is being played out in the popular media, in religious institutions, and also in think-tanks in the United States and elsewhere. It surfaces, for instance, in the question about the relation between "Europe" and Christianity hotly debated in the framing of the constitution of the European Union. Daily we see the tensions between traditional and secular "Jews" in Israel. The question is whether or not democratic states can accept the idea that some people will form their identities through obedience to divine authority, rather than secular political authority, and, conversely, whether or not religious people can accept and live by political institutions that have no religious backing or purpose.

The global debate about religious identity is really two-sided and this is part of the structure of contemporary social and global reality. On the one side is the question of whether or not religion requires identity to be categorized under just one description – say, that one is just a Buddhist, just a Christian, or just a secular humanist – and if that is so how then does one avoid conflict with others? The other side of the question is the relation of religious identity to political organization and freedom. These two sides of the question of identity seem to be on a collision course. If religion demands that one's identity be unified under just one description, say, a Christian identity, and yet modern politics demands the freedom to question identities and to choose which one to live, then we should expect to see the conflicts we are now in fact seeing around the world. It makes us think that we are living in the midst of a "clash of civilizations," as Samuel Huntington famously put it.[14]

What then are we to do? It depends on how religious people read the "divine poem" in which existence is to be understood. There might be ways to see human existence religiously, to interpret the divine poem, which respect and enhance, rather than demean and destroy, the integrity of life. We could even identify types of religious freedom and reason. I will come back to those possibilities later. They are, obviously, important for theological humanism. Now we need to step back and dig deeper into the idea of identity itself and, more specifically, what is meant by a *religious identity*. That will enable us to isolate with more precision the problem that must be addressed.

3

I have isolated some features of current social existence. People's identities are being challenged and refashioned within various global cultural, economic, political, and religious dynamics. Around the world, people are increasingly interacting with each other; those who were distant are now near, either through immigration or communication. This is sometimes called "global reflexivity." The term designates the ways in which we increasingly know ourselves in terms of how we are seen by others and the capacity to adjust to that information. The perception of others bends back, reflects on us, and we must respond to that perception and recognition. Sometimes people respond violently to how they are perceived by others, as when, for instance, Muslims around the world reacted to the publication of political cartoons of the Prophet or when Catholics protested the showing of *The Da Vinci Code*. In these cases, people seek to shield their identities from those forces that would criticize and change them. In other situations, people fashion new identities, sometimes called "hybrid" identities, through immigration or because of freedom from previous colonial powers.

One needs to slow down and take stock of ideas. What, really, does *identity* mean? In order to answer that question, we have to engage in conceptual analysis and also careful description of experience. And this will be important for the conclusions I want to draw about theological humanism.

Most basically, to have an "identity" is to be able to be designated as someone distinctive and to be recognized as such. People fashion identities in a number of interrelated ways. One way is to possess some attribute or collection of attributes – like race, class, or gender – that enables oneself and others to indicate, to recognize, and to identify someone as an individual and a member of some group. If you can imagine a middle-aged white male college professor typing away at his computer and looking forward to the Fire game, then you have a way of identifying me. I can also identify myself as that man. So, first of all, social recognition and particular attributes are important in identity.[15]

Next, at a linguistic level, we identity ourselves with "names": I am William Schweiker; you are designated by yourself and by others with your name, whatever it is. This is important because in many cultures names situate us within some family lineage; a name "identifies" an individual as distinct, our first names, and yet related, family names. But even that is not all, at least on the linguistic level. We also use pronouns as linguistic markers of identity. I am me. I can say that I am myself – but I cannot say that I am you. But you can (ironically) say the same thing, that is, you can say, "I am me," too. Oddly, these pronouns are reversible; both you and I can say you and me, but we designate someone different in the use of those pronouns. What I mean by you, you designate as "me," and vice versa. This linguistic fact shows us that there is something common between us: we can each refer to ourselves as individuals. It also shows us what is different: we cannot refer to each other in the same way we refer to ourselves. On the simple linguistic plane, there is human commonality and also difference.

There is even something more in terms of language use. Strangely, "I" can refer to "me." That is, I can in some respects make myself an object of description; it is me who is the white male college teacher now struggling with the computer. And I can, of course, make you an object of description. Importantly, when I identify me, it is not at all clear who that "I" is making the description of "me." While I can make myself an object of description, in another way I cannot. Curiously, "I" am different than "me," at least linguistically. "I" transcend the "me" that is an object of various descriptors: male, white, long-winded. Philosophers call that "I" the "transcendental ego" whereas the "me" is my concrete, embodied self. Given the reversibility of pronouns, I need to realize that you too transcend the various descriptions I can make of you. None of us is merely the sum total of descriptions. Something about a human being escapes complete description. That is part of the reason Christians believe that human beings are made in the image of God. Like God, there is something about human beings that escapes control, description, complete knowledge. It is why we are social creatures, but also something more.

Notice, then, that there are various ways we create and sustain an identity: through the use of linguistic markers, through the practice of name-giving, and through social recognition. There is one more way we fashion an identity. This is through acts of fidelity or infidelity.[16] Part of who I am, my identity, is due to the commitments I make and to which I am true through time, some commitment of love, political loyalty, membership in a church, or, most profoundly, to God. My identity can be shattered by infidelity, either my own or when someone is unfaithful to me. This dimension of trust or fidelity is important because our sense of the world, our ability to be responsible for our actions, and the nature and purpose of our social and political communities require ways of identifying someone or some community through time and in patterns of fidelity. Acts of fidelity provide reasons to sacrifice immediate wants and desires because those acts represent higher, greater goods. These insights let us grasp the special connection between responsibility and identity that is absolutely crucial for theological humanism, as we will see later. Who I am, my identity, is profoundly tied to my actions and my relations within which I faithfully or unfaithfully bear responsibility. Our identities orient us in the world and find expression in our actions and relations; our actions and relations bend back, as it were, and help to shape our identities.

Now we can understand why identity is so important to any religion. In the world's major religions adherents are always uniquely identified. A Buddhist seeks refuge in the Dharma. A Jew is part of the people of Israel. A Christian is one who follows Christ. Muslims submit to the will of Allah. Whatever is common among the religions or among certain religions, say the great monotheistic faiths of Judaism, Islam, and Christianity, they are also particular ways of life. Each religion shapes life in a distinctive way. If I say I am a Christian, that means trust and loyalty in Christ and his way. I see and evaluate the world and others in a certain way. At least I ought to assess and see the world and others in a specific way. That is why the Israelites had to separate themselves from the Egyptians in order to worship their God, as we have it in the text noted earlier.

What is more, the religions form identity in the ways we just explored. In some religions, say Judaism, one becomes a member through lineage, birth. In religions not bound to blood-ties, like Christianity, there is the need for a symbolic or ritual birth, in baptism as a new birth into the Church. Names are involved. God changes Abram's name to Abraham; Saul becomes Paul after his conversion; Adam and Eve name their children; a Christian is given a Christian name; in other religions one can also be given special names. Even the linguistic markers are important in some religions. When asked who he is, God answers to Moses, "I am who I am." God is also called LORD. Of course, Moses can say the same thing; he can say "I am who I am," but it means something different than when uttered by God. It is not reversible because only God is the LORD. But, interestingly, a Hindu can say that the deepest insight and liberation is to see that the "I," my innermost self, and Atman are one. St Paul, to use a Christian example, can say that it is not he that lives, but Christ in him. So too with the idea of trust or fidelity: one must practice the Dharma, a Jew must keep the Law, a Christian must have faith in Christ and follow his way.

Religions have ways to re-identify people. They endow members with a new identity that is laid-over and transforms other identities. This religious identity shapes the way the person sees existence and how they conduct life with others. A Muslim and a Buddhist might do the same action – say help someone in need – and yet in an important and real way they are not the same actions. Christian love, to use another example, is different from other acts of love because the identity of the Christian is defined by faith in Christ.[17] What makes a religious identity different from some other identity is that it claims, again, to be rooted in what is unsurpassably important and real. For a Christian nothing is more important and more real than the God whose grace is revealed in Jesus Christ. For the Hindu it is Atman, while for a Jew it is the God revealed at Sinai who is in covenant with Israel. This seems to mean, again, that a religious identity *ought* to trump other identities: one's gender, family, political, or ethnic sense of self and community. That is the logic, as it were, of certain forms of religious terrorism, as we have seen. But is there a way to have one's religious identity formed just through one description and avoid fanatical religion? This question brings us to Christian particularism and to the next step in these reflections.

4

Importantly, there are positions that think that identity should become destiny, but these take a different tactic than religious fanaticism. I want to explore these arguments, at least briefly. They are a contrast position to theological humanism. I will do so by looking at Christian churchly theologians, although one can find similar arguments in other religious traditions. They are forms of what is called "moral particularism." The core idea is that moral norms, values, and identities are particular to the community that holds them.[18] But Christian particularism is flawed, and, therefore, we need to pick up the banner of theological humanism. On the way to that conclusion, it is necessary to examine the Christian particularist argument in terms of what we know about the problem of identity.

Some current Christian thinkers argue that the point of the Christian life is to have one's identity enfolded within the story of Jesus and to develop the virtues and traits of character needed to live out that identity. The Church is to be a kind of counter-community to empire. As the biblical scholar Walter Brueggemann writes:

In the Christmas story we remember that Jesus was born just as "Caesar" (the emperor) sent out a decree. On Good Friday we participate in the echoes of the crowds, "We have no King but Caesar [the emperor]." Caesar is everywhere in the narrative. The emperor is highly visible and powerful. But the community gathered around Jesus dares to commit itself to that alternate narrative that "he was crucified/ he is raised to new life/ he will come again in power."[19]

The Church is a people formed by the story of Jesus and God's action with Israel, who, surprisingly, have knowledge of mercy unknown by those in the "empire." The nations of the contemporary world, and especially Western nations, are the new empire, driven by violence and war. Christians offer the way out of that lethal condition.

On this account, the threat to Christian existence is that one's identity might be strung between political commitment to a modern democratic nation and one's proper Christian identity. Christian particularists draw an exceedingly sharp line between the Church as a people of peace, and the world, a domain of violence. What is more, the Christian story – the divine poem – only makes sense once you are on the inside, as it were. It is not the case, they argue, that we have something called "reason" that is shared by human beings and that we can use to figure out political policy, scientific theorems, or ethical norms and values. Our ability to see and understand and evaluate the world is utterly dependent on the stories that have shaped our lives. If Christians have learned their story correctly, they will just see things differently than others. They will help people, tend to the sick, promote peace, but Christians do those things for different reasons than others who are doing the same actions. A Christian is to re-narrate their life in terms of the story of Jesus and gain the virtues necessary to see their life within the Christian story.

On this account, the Church is to enfold Christian identity within the poem of God's actions in Jesus Christ, and that poem alone. Identity ought to become one's destiny. The Church's ethical task is the business of identity formation, and, further, faithfulness is to have one's identity bounded by just one description. Theology becomes sociology. This means, in the thought of Stanley Hauerwas, that Christians do not have much at stake in democracy because that demands a different identity. As he writes:

> To be saved is to be grafted into a body that constitutes us by making us part of a history not universally available. It is a history of real people whom God has made part of the Kingdom through forgiveness and reconciliation. Only a people so bodily formed can survive the temptation to become a "knowledge" in the name of democracy.

And after challenging both knowledge and democracy in the name of a saved people, he adds the chilling words: "Only such a people deserves to survive [as the Church]."[20] This is just what we would expect once religion is linked to identity formation. If the story of Jesus is unsurpassably important and real, then one's identity should be refashioned within that story, and no other. When religion has control over science, you can be certain you are in the church!

One might puzzle over this argument in terms of whether or not its basic features are really any different from fanatical religion. How is it going to help us avoid the conflict between Christians who have their identity over-against the world and other religious believers who have different, but no less absolute, identities? One might also wonder about the oddity of assuming that only Christians know about mercy and that somehow the Church is not responsible for all the forms of violence and terror done in its name throughout history. These questions would miss the point of Christian particularism. Actually, these thinkers are trying to provide a picture of Christian existence that can stop Christian complicity with political violence. They are trying to provide a specific way to read the divine poem, as it were.

Their argument hinges on two points. First, for these thinkers the problem with modern forms of political thought is the belief that human beings are really the same and therefore democracy rejects real difference. That is what democracy is supposedly all about, namely, human *equality* before the law, stripped of particular and unique identities. This rejection of specific different identities, the particularist argues, is the background for violence since the nation must now stop deviance from its vision. Their second claim is that political communities are willing to use war and violence to assert their authority and unsurpassable importance. The church has a different story. It is not the story of God slaughtering Egyptian children or God saving Jesus while the boy children of Bethlehem die at the hands of Herod's soldiers. It is a story of peace and one that accepts difference, loves the other and even the enemy. Christians therefore need to be resocialized – grafted into the body of the church as Hauerwas put it – and one task, therefore, is to get clear about the radical distinction between that story and any other story. Only in that way will Christians avoid being drawn into the violence of the political world. In other words, these thinkers are trying to show Christians how to inhabit their faith in ways that challenge any form of religious or political violence and terror.

What is wrong with that argument? The problem is this: the Christian particularist argument defuses texts of terror by insisting on just one description of identity and in utter difference to other human communities. Its strategy of Christian self-criticism requires the rejection of truth that might be found in other communities. The human problem is a social one and theology is really a form of sociology: truth and identity are a function of membership. Theological humanism seeks another way to inhabit religious beliefs and practice, another way to read human existence within the divine poem, and other grounds for self-criticism.

5

In our global times people's identities are too often circumscribed within one description and this fosters the "illusion of destiny." Strategies of identity-formation arise in part because of the reflexive interaction among peoples on the global field.[21] No community is free from interaction with others that shape its own context of life; no one is sovereign over all forces, natural and social, that shape her or his existence. The failure to control the formation of identity readily leads to harsher and even more violent means to retain the boundaries or to reassert the right of self-formation.[22] Is it really surprising that when interactions among peoples increase in our global age, so too do conflict and violence? Through the media system hatred has gone global. In terms of the religions, the question, as I have put it, is how one can and ought to inhabit a religious identity, read human life within the divine poem. What is needed is a vision of the internal complexity of identities and the various ways one can and ought to live with that complexity in self, in community, and in the world.

The nub of the issue is this, really: is the complexity of actual human identities a religious *problem* or a religious *possibility*? While religious fanatics and Christian particularists reach very different conclusions, for both of them – and for many other people – the complexity of identities in our global times is the *problem*. The answer to that problem is to have one's identity unified within *one* description defined by a community's belief about what is unsurpassably important and real. Theological humanism takes a different stance. It sees the complexity of identity as a *possibility*. People have choices to make about their identities and the real job is to form them in a way that respects and enhances the integrity of life. Recall Amartya Sen one more time. He writes,

> The point at issue is not whether *any* identity whatever can be chosen (that would be an absurd claim), but whether we do indeed have choices over alternative identities or combinations of identity, and perhaps more importantly, substantial freedom regarding what *priority* to give to the various identities we may simultaneously have.[23]

Theological humanism is a distinct way to inhabit a religious identity. It involves a choice about how to integrate one's identities, living simultaneously with an actual religious identity and some humanistic identity while orienting one's existence by what respects and enhances the integrity of life.

Humanists have long held that there is a role for choice and reasoning in shaping human lives.

This brings us, at last, to the crucial point. There is a decisive connection between *responsibility* and *identity*. Christian particularists make moral responsibility a subset of identity. That is, moral responsibility is delimited by one's Christian identity. A Christian theological humanist insists, conversely, that *responsibility is the condition for and purpose of identity*. The claims of responsibility reach across the bonds of human existence and find their roots deep in freedom, reason, and conscience which testify to human dignity. One's responsibility is the capacity for an identity and that identity can and ought to serve the integrity of life rather than the unity of identity itself. The "good" of one's identity is not something bounded by just one description; if it is genuine it is not forced but rather the outcome of a lifetime of self-labor. This means – shockingly – that one's identities can and ought to serve a good beyond themselves. The troubling assumption of particularism from this perspective is that an identity is an end-in-itself rather than being oriented by the good of the integrity of life that transcends our dear selves, our identities.

Acts of horrific violence require seeing another human being *as lacking humanity*.[24] The strategies to dehumanize others, the social mechanism needed to engender ongoing violence, are many, sadly. Tribalism, revenge, terror, racism, the eroticism of violence and power in the media, and the will of God (to name but a few) have all been used, are being used, to dehumanize others and thereby to drive social life into fury and unending violence. In our world of global reflexivity what is most important, then, is the capacity to see the other as a human being with multiple identities, some of which are shared. This means that no specific identity, including one's religious identity, can trump the whole of existence and claim exclusive right to orient action. In some contexts I need to see myself as a human being who faces death, who loves his family, and who bleeds *just like, in principle, every other human being*. And I need then to see that the one suffering before me is also a human being. In this case, more distinct identities (say, Indian or Communist or White or Christian) are set in the background and are only judged valid when believed to support shared humanity. That commonality can and must delimit the scope and extent of violence, because, again, unending conflict requires the *dehumanization* of the other. Of course, there will be other situations where one must stress more particular identities, say, in the midst of theological debate with fellow Christians or among members of one's political group. Yet even in those cases, something shared is the condition for cooperation and persuasion and also limits coercive interaction.

Notice two things about this argument regarding responsibility and identity. It actually entails a practical rule and, more importantly, a specific stance towards oneself, one's community, and the identities of others. First, at each point of encounter with others the task is to find the relevant *commonality* that is the condition for cooperation and the limit on coercive interaction. This is a procedural rule for decisions about what priority to give to one's various identities in specific situations. It requires that no specific identity be deified as the singular description of one's existence because one's life can and ought to be dedicated towards responsible relations with and for others. This is true of the religious community as well. The Church, for instance, is not only the gathered body of believers or the body of Christ (as Christians believe), it is also a human community, a treasure in *earthen* vessels.[25] Put otherwise, because our identities are complex, we can be self-critical; we can challenge parts of our lives that lead to conflict by other parts that bind us to others. That is the nature of moral freedom, we can say. And that freedom is why we can never completely describe ourselves or another human being. It is, we might say, the image of God in human beings.

Second, this rule implies and enacts a more basic stance possible in our time. The various beliefs, values, and traditions that shape identities are enlisted in the project of fashioning social existence dedicated to what respects and enhances the integrity of life with and for others. The rule for decision-making implies a moral and spiritual stance. Someone who accepts the stance ought also to abide by this rule. Anyone who can grasp the intelligibility of the practical rule thereby endorses, at least implicitly, the co-ordinate stance in life. Both the rule and the stance would seem to apply to individuals and to communities insofar as the idea of "identity" is analogically applied to persons and communities.

Theological humanism arises out of and provides orientation to the complexity of life: one is a religious person (of some sort) and a humanist (of some sort) and has other identities, too. Human beings are bound together in their mortality, their fleshliness, but also because we are social creatures and persons who seek some meaning in our lives, reflexive goods. These are all embedded in the aspects of "identity" isolated earlier. There is no justification for the charge made by Christian particularists that if a situation demands priority of one's humanity (or one's Christian identity) that is somehow a betrayal of the Christian confession (or humanistic convictions). Confessions, like identities, find their *point* in a way of life. One can and must treasure a life dedicated to responsibility rather than the particularities of our identities and the convictions one embodies. Later in this book we will isolate scriptural backing for this stance and thus counter the horrific "texts of terror" (see Chapters 3 and 4).

A possible misunderstanding of theological humanism needs quickly to be corrected. I am not saying that in all situations with all people one must find commonalities and only commonalities. Part of the joy of life is to share in our differences. Further, there are situations in life when one must resist connection with others, resist – even the use of force – when actions and policies threaten utterly to demean and to destroy the integrity of life. Unlike Christian moral particularists, a theological humanist does not believe that pacificism is the one and only norm of the life of faith. That is because a theological humanist seeks to respect and enhance the integrity of life, a commitment that requires one to resist forces that demean and destroy the integrity of persons' and communities' lives as well as the fragile integrity of our planet's ecosystem. The point is that these acts of resistance – which can take a variety of forms – are a last resort when other means of communication, understanding, and concord have broken down. But the theological humanist is not committed to accepting works of destruction and evil in the name of a love of peace.

Theological humanists inhabit their particular religious, ethnic, gendered, cultural, and racial identities deeply and yet freely. While shaped by these identities we are not slaves to them. And it is that freedom, that capacity to take responsibility for the integrity of life, that is the inner-meaning of the divine poem, I suggest. This kind of freedom makes possible faithfulness as the religious meaning of responsibility. We should read the texts of terror not only to see the workings of violence and terrorism in the formation of identity. We can and must and may read those texts as a challenge to forms of oppression in the name of the freedom to be faithful in responsibility for the integrity of life.

6

In our global times it is possible to inhabit religious identities in ways deeply religious but also humane. The freedom to take responsibility for choices about priority in our identities is actually a form of faithfulness to the integrity of life. If we grasp that insight, then the divine poem is more than just the story of the Christian tribe or a text of terror.

Notes

1   Tzvetan Todorov, *Imperfect Garden: The Legacy of Humanism*, trans. Carol Cosman (Princeton, NJ: Princeton University Press, 2002), p. 4.
2   For a non-religious option, see again Luc Ferry, *God Made Man: The Meaning of Life*, trans. D. Pellauer (Chicago: University of Chicago Press, 2002).
3   Cited in Morris Bishop, "Petrarch," in *Renaissance Profiles*, ed. J. H. Plumb (New York: Harper Torchbooks, 1961), p. 14.
4   In other texts I have called this approach "hermeneutical realism." See William Schweiker, *Power, Value and Conviction: Theological Ethics in the Postmodern*

Age (Cleveland, OH: Pilgrim Press, 1998). The idea of scripture as "spectacles" is taken from John Calvin's *Institutes of the Christian Religion*.

5 Similar arguments have been made by prominent intellectuals in various traditions. See the Palestinian-American literary critic Edward W. Said, *Humanism and Democratic Criticism* (New York: Columbia University Press, 2004); the Indian-American economist Amartya Sen, *Identity and Violence: The Illusion of Destiny* (New York: Norton, 2006); as well as the Chief Rabbi of the United Hebrew Congregations of the British Commonwealth, Jonathan Sachs, *The Dignity of Difference: How to Avoid the Clash of Civilizations* (New York: Continuum, 2002); the philosopher of African thought Kwame Anthony Appiah, *The Ethics of Identity* (Princeton, NJ: Princeton University Press, 2004); and John W. de Gruchy, *Confessions of a Christian Humanist* (Minneapolis: Fortress Press, 2006). Also see *Humanity Before God: Contemporary Faces of Jewish, Christian and Islamic Ethics*, ed. W. Schweiker, M. Johnson, and K. Jung (Minneapolis: Fortress Press, 2006).

6 On this see Arjun Appadurai, *Modernity at Large: Cultural Dimensions of Globalization* (Minneapolis: University of Minnesota Press, 1996); and Manfred B. Steger, *Globalization: A Very Short Introduction* (Oxford: Oxford University Press, 2003).

7 For a related if different treatment see Martin Riesebrodt, *Cultus und Heilsversprechen: Eine Theorie der Religionen* (München: C. H. Beck, 2007).

8 Sen, *Identity and Violence*, p. xv.

9 Phyllis Trible, *Texts of Terror: Literary-Feminist Readings of Biblical Narratives* (Minneapolis: Augsburg Fortress, 1984).

10 At points throughout the text, extracts from the Bible are used. New Revised Standard Version of the Bible, copyright 1952 by the Division of Christian Education of the National Council of the Churches of Christ in the United States of America. Used by permission. All rights reserved.

11 "Sri Lankan Government Finds Ally in Buddhist Monks" by Somini Sengupta (*New York Times*, February 25, 2007) can be read online by TimesSelect subscribers at: www.nytimes.com/2007/02/25/world/asia/25lanka.html?_r=1&oref=slogin. Also see Martin E. Marty, "Killing for Buddha?" on *Sightings*, March 5, 2007, at http://divinity.uchicago.edu/martycenter/publications/sightings/archive-2007/0305.shtml.

12 Jonathan Glover, *Humanity: A Moral History of the Twentieth Century* (New Haven, CT: Yale University Press, 2000), pp. 241–2.

13 Cited by Thomas L. Friedman in his editorial "The Silence that Kills" in *The New York Times*, March 2, 2007, A21. The poem was also posted on the Arab reform site (www.aafaq.org) and also the MEMRI translation site (www.memri.org). Even more pointed is the recent book by the Somali-born author Ayaan Hirsi Ali. For years she has been forced to live in hiding and under constant threat. An anti-Qur'an script that she wrote provoked the assassination of filmmaker Theo Van Gogh. Her recent book *Infidel* is about the movement from religion to reason, as she put it. In the name of reason she attacks Islamic culture as "brutal, bigoted, [and] fixated on controlling women." See Ayaan Hirsi Ali, *Infidel* (New York: Simon and Schuster, 2007).

14 Samuel Huntington, "The Clash of Civilizations," *Foreign Affairs* 72:3 (Summer 1993), 22–49.
15 On this see Paul Ricoeur, *The Course of Recognition*, trans. David Pellauer (Cambridge, MA: Harvard University Press, 2005); and Charles Taylor, "The Politics of Recognition," in *Multiculturalism*, ed. Amy Gutman (Princeton, NJ: Princeton University Press, 1994), pp. 25–73.
16 On this see William Schweiker, *Responsibility and Christian Ethics* (Cambridge: Cambridge University Press, 1995); Paul Ricoeur, *Oneself as Another*, trans. Kathleen Blamey (Chicago: University of Chicago Press, 1992); and H. Richard Niebuhr, *The Responsible Self: An Essay in Christian Moral Philosophy* (Louisville, KY: Westminster John Knox Press, 1999).
17 On this see Edward Collins Vacek, *Love, Human and Divine: The Heart of Christian Ethics* (Washington, DC: Georgetown University Press, 1994).
18 These arguments find expression in political theory in terms of what is called communitarianism. The argument here is that modern democracy requires that people bracket their deepest beliefs about the meaning of life or what is ultimately good and true. These must be held at bay when deciding norms of justice and public policy. Norms for justice must be defined without reference to comprehensive doctrines, as John Rawls calls them. But if that is so, then, the communitarians argue, it is hard to see how someone would hold any political convictions at all. Thinkers like Michael Walzer distinguish between thick and thin moralities. A "thin" conception of what is good and just is one that supports broad, but minimal, requirements for justice within pluralistic societies. In fact, a "thick" outlook is what everyone really inhabits, that is, a set of beliefs and practices about what is good and right and just. Without those commitments, it is hard to imagine why citizens would abide by the requirements of procedural justice. The question then is whether or not those "thick" commitments define social identity in terms of a process of realization rather than the long labor of conscience and choice. As Sen put it, if identity becomes a destiny, then we are trapped by who we are and how we have been shaped rather than being able to criticize and refashion identities.
19 Walter Brueggemann. "Alien Witness: How God's People Challenge Empire," *The Christian Century* 124:5 (March 6, 2007), 31.
20 Stanley Hauerwas, *Dispatches from the Front: Theological Engagements with the Secular* (Durham, NC: Duke University Press, 1994), p. 106. Also see his *A Community of Character: Toward a Constructive Christian Social Ethics* (Notre Dame, IN: University of Notre Dame Press, 1988).
21 On the problems and possibilities of constructing new identities, see Charles Spinosa, Fernando Flores, and Herbert L. Dreyfus, *Disclosing New Worlds: Entrepreneurship, Democratic Actions and the Cultivation of Solidarity* (Cambridge, MA: MIT Press, 1997); and Régis Debray, *Transmitting Culture*, trans. Eric Rauth (New York: Columbia University Press, 2000).
22 See Saskia Sassen, *Globalization and its Discontents* (New York: New Press, 1998).
23 Sen, *Identity and Violence*, p. 38.
24 For a powerful statement of this point see Pumla Gobodo-Madikizela, *A Human Being Died That Night: A South African Woman Confronts the Legacy of Apartheid* (New York: Houghton Mifflin, 2003).

25   This point has been made by many Christian theologians, thankfully. See E. Troelstch, *The Social Teachings of the Christian Churches*, 2 vols (Louisville, KY: Westminster/John Knox Press, 1992); H. Richard Niebuhr, *Christ and Culture* (New York: Harper, 1975); James M. Gustafson, *Treasure in Earthen Vessels* (Chicago: University of Chicago Press, 1985); Thomas W. Ogletree, *The World Calling: The Church's Witness in Politics and Society* (Louisville, KY: Westminster/John Knox Press, 2004); and Kristine A. Culp, "The Nature of Christian Commuinity," in *Setting the Table: Women in Theological Conversation*, ed. Rita Nakashima Brock, Claudia Camp, and Serene Jones (St Louis, MO: Chalice Press, 1995), pp. 155–76.

Chapter 2

Humanizing Religion*

1

The previous chapter addressed a vexing problem in contemporary religious life. How ought believers to understand their religious identities? How are Christians to live their faith freely and faithfully within the whirl of global dynamics? Christians navigate these forces with the conviction that God's spirit is active. The last chapter sought to outline some ways of navigating those forces and to outline a Christian form of theological humanism. The present chapter continues the discussion but now with more specific and detailed reflection on assumptions and patterns of thought. It also introduces themes and thinkers that will be addressed in more detail throughout the remainder of this book.

The title of this chapter names two interlocking worries about religion and the human future. How can the religions be humanized so that they might help to forge a viable future rather than reduce the world to violence and ignorance? Conversely, how, if at all, are the religions humanizing forces that invigorate the human spirit in a time when existence seems increasingly flattened and drained of depth? The idea of "humanizing religion" designates then a double movement of thought that can be undertaken in different ways within diverse traditions and communities. However, it must be admitted that the idea of humanizing religion marks contested ground. Religion and humanism are often at odds and sometimes violently so. The interactions among humanism and religion are the topic of this chapter. And we will also see how this relates to reconstructing the shape and purpose of Christian theological ethics.

* This chapter was originally delivered as the Edward L. Ryerson Inaugural Lecture and first published in the *Journal of Religion* 89:2 (2009), 214–35. Copyright William Schweiker.

If one wants to grasp what is revealed and concealed in the debate about religion and humanism, then the connections, if any, between religious and humanistic outlooks need to be articulated and analyzed. The French philosopher Paul Ricoeur, whom I will engage more deeply in another chapter, enables us to get at some of these connections. His words help us to grasp what Christians mean by saying that human beings are dust that breathes, as I put it in the Introduction. Ricoeur wrote:

> Man is man when he knows that he is *only* man. The ancients called man a "mortal." This "remembrance of death" indicated in the very *name* of man introduces the reference to a limit at the very heart of the affirmation of man himself. When faced with the pretense of absolute knowledge, humanism is therefore the indication of an "only:" we are *only* men. No longer "human, all too human:" this formula still shares in the intoxication of absolute knowledge; but "only human."[1]

This quote draws us into modern and classical thought about death, the will-to-power, creativity, the human attestation to being and, most radically, the question of the good human power is to serve. Can sustained attention to that oft silenced remembrance of death limit the illusions of human power and knowledge and also signal the religious impulse? This remembrance of death, I will argue later, is indeed at the origins of our sense of responsibility.

However, the remembrance of death – the fact that we are *dust* – fails to specify the good which we can and ought to respect and enhance, a good revealed, I contend, in the *love of life* intertwined with death's remembrance. We are dust that *breathes*. Yet Ricoeur also obscures the fact that the tensions among life and death are etched not only into our being, but also, and importantly, within the social and natural environments, the structures of experienced reality, in which we dwell and for which people are increasingly responsible. The tensions between remembrance and love, death and life, or dust and breath, give rise to different outlooks on human existence, both religious and humanistic. Mortality inscribed *within* a love of life lays open as well how we can and ought to relate to realms of life endangered in our age, or so I contend. The complex relation of love of life and the remembrance of death gives rise to various sensibilities and dynamics of existence. I will explore some of these in other chapters, such as spiritual conviction (Chapter 3), the claim of conscience and moral empowerment (Chapter 4), reverence and respect for life (Chapter 9), and freedom, boundedness, and aspiration (Chapter 5). But this chapter explores the most basic and dynamic feature of the structure of lived human existence, the interlacing of the remembrance of death and the love of life.

The tensions between love and remembrance within our being and found in the social and natural environments are given expression in the religions. In Christian faith the tenacious ambiguity of our being and the reality of the world is articulated in symbols, narratives, and doctrines from different perspectives. Most profoundly, God can only be conceived without absurdity, St Augustine once put it, when one "thinks of Him as life itself."[2] God is pure life graciously animating the whole of creation, yet a creation which is, nevertheless, constitutively finite, "dust." God's spirit is the spirit of life. Yet, the reality of death and the desire for continued life can – and, tragically, does – fuel in human beings the celebration of power at war with finitude. When it does, it becomes a structure of experience, an environment within which we dwell, and it is depicted in scripture as the law of sin and death, a bondage to the social machinery of violence and injustice under which creation groans even while human beings paradoxically mistake slavery for real life. But the problem of human existence is not just within the social realities driven by the law of sin and death. The problem is, more profoundly and more ambiguously, *inside* of human existence. Redemption is liberation from illusion and servitude into the freedom of new life – new creation – under the power of Christ's spirit. The Christian community witnesses to this new life and passes it along, but is not and cannot be the source of new life. The source of new life is God's action in Christ made active in the Spirit. How can Christian theological ethics make sense of those symbolic resources and their power of new life for the sake of orienting responsible existence? The complex modalities of life captured in religious discourse – Christian or some other – disclose the deepest questions posed by thinking about "humanizing religion."

I intend to explore humanizing religion in a few steps already intimated and which enact different but related strategies of thought: history and social diagnosis, the critics of religion and humanism, systematic reconstruction of theological ethics, and existential reflection that connects the steps of the argument. The argument of this chapter is then a bit complex even as it is crucial to the rest of this book. I turn first to the wild and confusing debate about religion and humanism in history and current life.

2

The origin of humanism is often traced back to the second century CE in the West and also the concern for good Latin usage. Further, *humanitas* is sometimes linked to Greek ideas about *paideia*, or education, and training in the arts. Yet the idea of humanizing religion, as I have coined it, aims to reclaim some other insights of ancient thinkers, Hellenistic and biblical, that are lost if we just focus on the history of the idea of humanism. Indeed, the connection between the formation of human life, as the core of any conception of humanism, and discourse about "God" reaches far back into Western thought. The renowned classicist Werner Jaeger noted that the Greek idea of *paideia* found expression not only in sophistic and rhetorical terms, in Protagoras' insistence that "man is the measure," but also in Plato and Aristotle's claim that "theology," or rational reflection on the divine, is in fact first philosophy. God is the measure of all things, the "unconditioned" as Plato put it.[3]

The grand enterprise of a rational theology was meant to articulate the divine norm of human existence and the means, if any, of forming human life so measured. Strategies of formation are many, ranging from ascetic practices to the struggle for virtue and also devotion and obedience to the divine. Yet among classical thinkers the labor of self-formation did not set religious devotion and education in opposition. Stoics, Platonists, Aristotelians, as well as Christian and Jewish thinkers, in different ways agreed that human life is only rightly formed, or educated, through disciplines that link human beings to what exceeds finite being. Life is a struggle of self-transcending towards what is most high, most real, most divine. As Aristotle puts it in his *Nicomachean Ethics* X, 7, 1077 b 31: "Man must not, as the poets tell us, strive for human things nor, because he is mortal, attend only to mortal things, but he should make himself divine as far as possible." That idea returns in an inverted form in the nineteenth century with Friedrich Nietzsche's proclamation of the *Übermensch*, the self-overcoming of man.

The idea of humanizing religion succinctly captures other historic strands of thought outside Hellenistic philosophy. Rather than designating the apotheosis of human striving, here religion itself humanizes. The Sabbath was made for man and not man for the Sabbath, we have Jesus teach after healing a man. The Hebrew prophets and Abraham demanded that the divine too is called to justice. There is, as Hans Dieter Betz has noted, something of an ancient humanism around the theme of the treatment of the enemy.[4] Humanizing religion designates then not only the agenda of Hellenistic first philosophy but also convictions about justice and care of the oppressed and thus the critique of and liberation from structures of bondage. These ideas arise mainly within strata of the biblical texts and so signal another side of our civilization's legacy. "Humanizing religion," historically speaking, denotes, then, different strands of thought and social life that have shaped Western discourse.

These ancient strategies of thought and evaluation about human striving for perfection and overcoming structures of bondage are buried in the cultural memory of the West. Two opposing movements seem to characterize much modern thought, as Luc Ferry has noted: the humanization of the divine where religious convictions are increasing understood and judged by their impact on human beings, and, conversely, the divinizing of the human, making human existence the sacred object of love.[5] That is too simple, of course. But the larger point is that that ancient conception of perfection and also freedom from bondage now seems lost. Humanism nowadays usually means an outlook on life in which human flourishing is of central concern and in relation to which other ways of construing the world are interpreted and evaluated. Humans are the "center" of value and other forms of life derive their meaning and purpose from human needs and capacities and not the human relation to the divine. What is more, the operative powers in the world, and so the makers of history, are human beings no matter what other "powers" might be operative, divine or social. Modern humanism insists, as Tzvetan Todorov puts it, that "man *alone* (and not only nature or God) decides his fate. In addition, it implies that the ultimate end of these acts is a human being, not suprahuman entities (God, goodness, justice) or infrahuman ones (pleasures, money, power)."[6]

This kind of humanism, we can say, encodes a specific way of seeing and evaluating the world, a mentality or sensibility, and thereby forms part of the structure of lived reality within which people dwell. Its hallmark is the creative self-formation of human beings.[7] The best expression of this outlook, as scholars note, is found in the Renaissance thinker Giovanni Pico della Mirandola. In his famous *Oration on the Dignity of Man*, Pico depicts the deity speaking to human beings:

> The nature of all other creatures is defined and restricted within laws which We have laid down; you, by contrast, impeded by no such restriction, may, by your own free will, to whose custody We have assigned you, trace for yourself the lineaments of your own nature.[8]

Humanistic *paideia* is nothing else, in this exalted form, than the formation of human "nature," the core of which is the strangely wonderful and yet also vulnerable power of will. Human beings are subject to nothing beyond their kind, not even the divine, and the norm or measure of existence must arise within the will itself. Renaissance and modern humanism, converse to much classical humanism, holds that the right orientation of human life is the *creative* exercise of power to shape one's existence. It draws together a vision of the good as finite flourishing with the drive to liberate human beings from ignorance and want.

Within the emphasis on human agency and flourishing among modern humanists there is a deeper philosophical claim about knowledge. Edward W. Said made the point extremely well.

> The core of humanism is the secular notion that the historical world is made by men and women, and not by God, and that it can be understood rationally

... [and] that we can really know only what we make or, to put it differently, we can only know things according to the way they were made.[9]

The scope of human understanding is linked to the artifacts of human imagination, theory, and labor and in the domains of history, science, and language. This makes the productive sciences, or *poiesis* as Aristotle would call it, basic to human knowing in ways Aristotle and other ancients would not have understood. If Said's claim is right, then all we can know are the products of human making, the reservoir and legacy of cultural products. That "making," while an affirmation of creative power, also denotes a limit to knowledge rooted in human finitude.

From this perspective, "humanizing religion" could mean an inquiry into the penchant of the human imagination to create deities in human, all too human, form and yet to mistake the creative power behind those ideas. The ancient satirists rightly noted that if animals had gods, they would look like them. Gods usually look like their worshippers. Wander through the "spirituality" section of a local bookstore and you will get the point. Humanizing religion, accordingly, would engage religious symbols, myths, and practices – even in their most blatant anthropomorphic forms – as indirect expressions of the human quest for meaning and thus inscriptions of spirit. It would mean decoding ideas and stories about the "gods" as nothing more than projections of human ideals, human hopes, fears, and dreams. One of the most penetrating humanistic critics of religion, Ludwig Feuerbach, explored this linguistic and psychological point, namely, that ideas about deities or heavenly realms are projections of the human essence and thus the alienation of human beings from themselves.[10] Once this is seen, he reasoned, alienation might be overcome. The followers of Feuerbach are many, often unknowingly, and they rarely note the historical roots in the biblical texts of their protest against human servitude and illusion. Still, there is a strategy of humanizing religion that is conjoined to the modern critique of religion. Man is not to strive for divinity, as Aristotle or Plato claimed, but, rather, the "gods" are to be decoded as expressions of human alienation.

Here we find, I suggest, one of the conceptual roots of the current global debate about religion and humanism. At the level of structures of perception and frameworks of experience the present tendency, unlike that of the ancients, is to draw the distinction between a humanistic outlook and a religious one in terms of the scope of human knowledge. Humanists explore the domain of human making, and so history, language, culture, in which we fashion and seek meaningful individual and social lives. Reality exceeds human makings, yet knowledge centers on our creative powers and finite limits (as Immanuel Kant first insisted in his *Critique of Pure Reason*). The humanist account of knowledge thus requires the denial of any other higher, sacred, or revealed meanings. The religions, conversely, are believed to present a different observation of the world that transgresses or exceeds the limits of human knowledge. Lived social reality on a global scale is being structured by a debate about the creation of meaning and the nature of knowledge. The debate comes to a head in disputes about posting the Ten Commandments at State Houses or riots and deaths over political cartoons of religious figures, and, more subtly, in theories about language and the scope of knowledge.[11] I will return to this theme in other chapters of this book.

We have now isolated one of the structures of current lived reality – the environment of our moral lives – rooted in debates about knowledge. If we shift from an account of humanism to the idea of religion, and so continue to probe the title of this chapter, other dynamics structuring contemporary life come to the fore. What do I mean?

Debates about how to define, analyze, and assess "religion" are of course longstanding. Theories of religion abound and multiply daily, or so it seems. As noted in the previous chapter, a practice, symbol, story, community, tradition, is "religious" if it requires some belief, sense, or construal about what is unsurpassably important *and* real that invigorates life and enables people to meet, endure, relish, or surmount intractable features of existence through contact with some power or powers. Whatever else religion involves, it is about life and death, creation and destruction, peace and conflict, damnation and redemption, suffering and enlightenment, vulnerability and access to power, or, conversely, the escape from the illusion of those powers. The world's religions conceive and orient human existence in radically different ways, but always with respect to modalities of being and worth irreducible to finite existence or the products of human making. The point of religious existence is *conformity* to sacred realities, that is, the formation of a way of life shaped by non-human powers and agents.

In this light, the idea that religion might be humanized is attacked by many religious people. Around the world religious leaders decry secular humanism, rant against the godlessness of modern science, and lament what they see as mounting moral decay. Within the academy there are thinkers, like Charles Taylor, who worry about "exclusive humanism" and its loss of a sense of transcendence and also how this form of humanism is driven by a "rage for order" to transform and control all facets of life for human benefit. Mystery seems drained from life, Taylor complains.[12] Some Christian theologians challenge humanistic claims in the name of a theocentric outlook meant to thwart anthropocentrism. Others want to draw a strict line between the Christian community, as a community of peace, and the "world" as a domain of violence. They cannot imagine that truth might be found outside the walls of the Church. Conversely, the so-called new atheists of Richard Dawkins and company find laughable or lamentable the idea that religion might elevate, invigorate, and ennoble human dignity and destiny. It is inconceivable to them that some truth might be encoded in the myths, symbols, and practices of the religions. Religious claims to authority, deference, and even obedience sound to these critics like nothing but crass authoritarianism and priest-craft. Feuerbach speaks anew, even if in much less sophisticated form.

Another dividing point between religion and humanism now becomes clearer. Typically, the religions, whether indigenous, primitive, or axial (to use some standard and blunt distinctions), conceive of reality as the inter-action of agencies or powers that can and do act on and in human existence and to which human beings ought to conform. What is most important and real cannot be grasped within the framework of human actions, but must be seen within a wider, if more chaotic, field of forces, often conceived as deities, spirits, or the One God. Religion implies the animation of self, community, and world from what is beyond the self or community or the world. God breathes life into dust and a human being is created, to use the biblical image. The debate about religion and humanism is not then just over knowledge and perception but also power and agency.

We have probed the title of this chapter. Having done so, we are back to the nub of the human problem. Is the purpose of human power to form existence, our own and the environment in which we exist, a creative over-coming of mortal being in order to make "man" as divine as possible, as Aristotle argued? Maybe the good is to increase the will to power and overcome "man" into a new form of life, as Nietzsche thought. Conversely, we might agree with Todorov or Said that the aim of life is our responsibil-ity for other human beings. Or is the purpose of human life, as religions say, conformity of self and community to some divine force, reality, power, or being which might invigorate but, we have to admit, also diminish human worth and finite life?

Looking briefly at debates about religion and humanism and drawing on a range of classical and modern thinkers, I have tried to articulate and also analyze animating sensibilities of our age around the themes of knowledge, power, and value. These sensibilities motivate social life, religious and political conflict, academic dispute, and deep anxiety among people around the world. What has the diagnosis uncovered?

3

The themes of knowledge, power, and value found in the global debate about religion and humanism shape current lived reality. Let us briefly explore each of them and in doing so isolate salient criticisms which must be addressed. This is important for how we think about orienting life in a Christian perspective and, so, the work of theological ethics. Only in the final step of the chapter will diagnostic, critical, and systematic levels of reflection be brought together through more existential concerns.

First, consider the theme of knowledge. Humanists, like Said, link knowledge to the domain of human making and so the realm of history, language, culture. Human action forms the "center" around which the rest of reality is observed, known, and valued. The religions, conversely, are taken to present a different observation of the world. What is real, ultimately, is sacred, holy, or divine powers that interact with and on human beings, and what is ultimately important is the right relation between human beings and these suprahuman powers. Humanism and religion seem to encode different structures of perception through which knowable reality is organized. As we saw in the previous chapter, part of the global conflict between humanism and religion is about which encoding of perception and knowledge ought to orient social life.

Yet one has to ask a question. Given the condition of the global age, is either account of knowledge possible and pertinent? The German sociologist Niklas Luhmann notes,

> Modern society is a polycentric, polycontextual system. It applies completely different codes, completely different "frames," completely different principled distinctions according to whether it describes itself from the standpoint of religion or the standpoint of science, from the standpoint of law ... from the standpoint of economics.[13]

Contemporary high-modern global societies are not ordered around one center, whether divine or human. We cannot grasp reality from just one frame of reference; there is no single center to knowledge or society. Of course, a specific discipline of thought might have a definable "center." Social systems, such as an economy, a political system, or a media system, have their own central norms and values. Yet knowledge and the social system as a whole are polycentric; they are the intersections of diverse frames and systems.

Some thinkers find this situation terrifying and retreat into strident humanistic or fanatical religious outlooks centered on man or God. They hope to control the whirl of the age. Others see the polycontextual space of social life backing a free play of meaning and the destruction of inherited binary options (God/man) that are encrusted in traditional thought forms (religion/humanism). Yet for some thinkers, myself included, our global polycontextual condition invigorates a search for more complex and yet also coherent accounts of knowledge in order to orient life. Knowledge is multidimensional, I contend, and is constituted by the interaction among codes and frames rather than being organized through a single "center," whether that "center" is the man of humanism, the god of traditional religion, or the deconstruction of those binaries. Ironically, it seems that both religionists and strident humanists want to push back on the complexity of contemporary societies and champion simpler modes of thought, and yet in doing so risk a reduction, not a gain, in understanding.

This critique of knowledge exposes the theme of power as well. There are thinkers who decry both religious and humanistic outlooks as illusory, on the one hand, and, on the other, dangerously naïve. The problem is not that religion and humanism offer *different* observations of reality, but, rather, that they *share* too much, namely, a focus on "agents," human or divine, who exercise power and shape reality for their own ends. Thinkers as diverse as Niklas Luhmann, Martin Heidegger, and Michel Foucault, to name a few, see the obsession with "agents" who make reality as part of a metaphysical and "technological" outlook. The extension of power shapes human subjectivities, as Foucault put it, but also endangers the future or the very fate of Being, in Heidegger's terms. If we are to understand the world in which we dwell, then the quaint idea, nicely put by Todorov, that "man *alone*" makes his fate must be jettisoned root and branch and so too ideas about divine providence. The criticism is redoubled when we recognize that both "humanism" and the religions have blinded us to the moral status of endangered non-human life.[14]

These points lead to a third one that has emerged from this investigation: the theme of value. If the accounts of knowledge and power rooted in conceptions of human or divine agents are no longer plausible – that is, if humanistic and also traditional religious outlooks seem incapable of grasping the structures of current lived reality – what is to serve as the measure or norm for evaluating individual and social existence in relation to the whole realm of mortal life? Where, we might say, does the good reside and can it orient responsible existence? The search for the norm or measure of life hounds our age no less than ancient Greek philosophy, the biblical witness, modern humanists or current critics of humanism and religion. Worldwide, people are asking about the forces structuring reality and whether ideas about goodness and justice have relevance and truth at all. Are we at the mercy of non-human and non-divine powers, the "fate of Being," and therefore must endure our fate devoid of appraisal? Is there no ground for confidence that convictions about what is good have some purchase on the world in which we dwell, a confidence that can well up from the human love of life?

Siding with either humanism or religion in order to respond to this global situation is a false option. These outlooks do not address the challenges posed to their basic assumptions: first, the assumption that reality is structured by agents; second, an account of knowledge from the perspective of the favored agent; and, third, that the good is defined either in terms of human flourishing or in terms of conformity to sacred powers. It is not surprising, then, that the humanities, religious studies, theology, and ethics seem at a loss for how to orient their work. Their operative assumptions about knowledge and acting agents are widely rejected by various social and natural scientists but also by dominant strands of philosophy and cultural analysis.

4

Can Christians reclaim the task of humanizing religion as an enduring religious and cultural project buried deep within the social and cultural legacy of the Church but along lines intimated by the critics? That would seem to be the task now facing any Christian who believes, as I do, that we need to humanize religion. One has to start with one's own community and hope and pray that others will do the same within their communities of faith and practice. How to do so?

Humanizing Christian conviction requires, at its most profound level, escaping forms of thought systematically dominated by the idea of a "center," either a human or divine agent, or the deconstruction of those binaries still tied to that logic. Freedom to think beyond the logic of a "center" has profound ramifications for theological ethics. Most forms of Christian theology and ethics in our day have been dominated by that logic; they have been theocentric, Christocentric, or ecclesiocentric. Stanley Hauerwas, as noted in the previous chapter, claims that to say something theological is to say "Church." Karl Barth and other "neo-Orthodox theologians" insisted on a Christocentric orientation in thought and life. And still other theologians, notably H. Richard Niebuhr and James M. Gustafson, have insisted on radical monotheism, a theocentric outlook. What would it mean, then, to think otherwise?

At the level of knowledge we need to conceive of disciplines, and so theological ethics, as multidimensional in shape. The philosopher Mary Midgley has noted,

> We exist, in fact, as interdependent parts of a complex network, not as isolated items that must be supported in a void. As for our knowledge, it too is a network involving all kinds of lateral links, a system in which the most varied kinds of connection may be relevant for helping us to meet various kinds of questions.[15]

Attending to the debate about humanism and religion as encoded yet intractable perspectives on lived reality is important because it alerts us to the multidimensionality of knowledge and thus the demand to develop disciplines of thought which resist reduction to one form or one center. Any discipline so conceived must clarify lateral links within the network of knowledge and how it brings its resources to bear within the wider field of inquiry. Knowledge is a reflexive space of reasonable claims advanced and redeemed in response to basic questions. The field of knowledge, as noted above, is polycentric and polycontextual; it is created by multiple interactions among disciplines. These links are then important in order to establish the cogency, scope, and validity of a "discipline."

This multidimensional idea of knowledge bears fruit in a reconstruction of theological ethics.[16] In very different ways we can now see that the "religions" in fact provide guidance for human living not simply with reference to a "center," but by answering a range of questions elaborating the complex interactions among these questions. The questions demarcate a "space" or environment of human existence determined by the problem of how one ought to live, say, as a Protestant Christian or a Reformed American Jew, a Shi'ite Muslim or a Tibetan Buddhist. "Morality" is a name for the placement and right conduct of human existence, an outlook and way of life. "Ethics" is the critical, comparative, and constructive thinking about this "moral" space by answering the question "how should one live a good life?" and the various sub-questions that problem poses. The validity of ethics is determined by the scope and intensity of its ability to intersect with other disciplines and redeem the pertinence of its claims. An ethics that can intersect with and engage a wider scope of outlooks and positions will attain greater validity than rival options for guiding human lives. That criterion dictated that I explore the structure of current lived reality and engage various thinkers. It is why this book engages a wide array of thinkers and themes.

This leads to the question of the forces or agencies structuring lived reality. The moral space of contemporary life is increasingly a polycontextual field of forces, some human and some supra-human, whether conceived religiously or not. That fact has been a reason for interest by Christian theologians, myself included, in responsibility. An ethics of responsibility insists that human beings exist within patterns of interaction, or environments, to which they must respond and in which environments and agents reflexively shape each other. The capacity to have actions imputed or ascribed to an "agent" is with respect to the power to respond to environments – some composed of other agents – which sustain but also limit action. Imputing and ascribing responsibility and so identifying "agents" are of course exceedingly complex processes. I explore them in other chapters, including the previous one on religious identity. Still, responsibility is about the exercise of power in response to other powers, human and non-human.[17] The "world" is a concept for the complex ecology of reflexively interacting environments. As human power grows through technological means, so too does our responsibility and also, interestingly, the "world."

The current attacks on human agency in the name of the fate of being, like Heidegger, or non-personal social forces, in different ways by Luhmann and Foucault, are wide of the mark. The increase of power expands rather than effaces agency and responsibility; it creates new worlds, for good or ill. The work of ethics is to provide a normative discourse of power and responsible agency linked to the articulation and analysis of the lived structure of reality. The religions and the legacy of humanism were right to explore agents who fashion worlds.

The reconstruction of theological ethics requires, in terms of knowledge, replacing "making" with a multidimensional network of lateral connections. In terms of power, it replaces concern for unbridled forces with the relation between power and responsibility in world creation and orienting human life. What then ought to form the normative conviction of a theological and ethical vision? If we jettison here as well monocentric approaches, if we insist that we cannot define the good just around "man" or just around the "divine," if we try to tread a path in and through but finally beyond anthropocentrism and theocentrism or ad hoc postmodernism, what do we have? This returns us, I think, to the elusive and tenacious ambiguity of human life that comes to expression in both religious and humanistic outlooks.

If anything characterizes our age it is the many endangerments to and alterations of life in all forms from the genetic to the planetary. In this situation, some thinkers insist that we need a heuristics of fear about the possible end of nature and also to focus on human mortality in order to evoke a sense of responsibility. Jacques Derrida puts this forcefully in his book *The Gift of Death*.

> My irreplaceability is therefore conferred, delivered, "given," one can say, by death. It is the same gift, the same source, one could say the same goodness and the same law. It is from the site of death as the place of my irreplaceability, that is, of my singularity, that I feel called to responsibility. In this sense only a mortal can be responsible.[18]

Yet that is not quite right. While showing the *origin* of the consciousness of responsibility – that is, in the singularity of being towards death, my own or that of others – the focus on mortality, our being mere dust, by Derrida and others as well cannot clarify the *purpose* of responsibility, that is, the good human power is to serve. At best, death discloses that we ought not to do harm, the demand of non-maleficence. Ethical reflection on how we ought to live too often dodges the question why we ought to affirm life, our own, that of others, and also the wider compass of life on this planet. The theologian or philosopher thereby fails to grasp what St Augustine profoundly understood, namely, that the remembrance of death is inscribed within the love of life, and, therefore, one can bring this vitality to articulation in terms of the good of moral responsibility. We are not just dust. We are dust that breathes. How then are we to articulate the purpose of responsibility beyond the claims of a modern, humanistic orientation, man as the measure, but also beyond theocentrism?

Recall that the great insight of the Hellenistic and early Christian humanists, as Werner Jaeger recounted it, was to think through the opposition. As he noted, "Theology was intended from the very beginning to transcend humanism but at the same time it was the true fulfillment of the task which humanism had formulated."[19] It implied a *paideia* or a form of education that provided orientation to individuals and societies. Further, the biblical religions and the modern critics of religion, as we saw above, advanced the insight that life, the flourishing of existence, and not death can and must orient human action. The remembrance of death is indeed at the origins of the sense of responsibility. Yet when one interrogates the complexity of religious symbols and practices along with the dynamics of mortal experience one can come to see, I submit, that the purpose of responsibility is to respect and enhance the integrity of life.

A revision is needed for our global times. It is not life *qua* life that is the norm for responsible existence. That conception would merely replace one centrism for another: biocentrism for anthropocentrism or theocentrism or ecclesiocentrism. It is, rather, the integration of many dimensions of life, the *integrity of life* we can call it, which must orient individuals and social action in our global times. And this idea – the integrity of life – is a complex one. It will occupy reflection throughout this book, and especially in Chapters 9 and 10. Within ethics this norm enables critical reflection across an array of domains of existence and the goods proposed or entailed. It also provides orientation for responsible action. Keeping our attention on humanizing religion is meant to save us from a reduction in a conception of the moral good, to insist on the complexity of goodness. From diverse strands of our cultural legacy – Hellenistic, biblical, modern – there arise the resources to render productive, rather than destructive, the tension between the limit of death and the love of life, a sense of responsibility and the proper object of responsible action, the integrity of life.

I have now sketched a reconstruction of theological ethics around a multidimensional account of moral knowledge, the place of responsibility in the moral and religious life, and, finally, the good of the integrity of life. This conception requires rejection of monocentric forms of thought, humanist, theistic, or anti-humanist, in favor of differentiated and pluralistic conceptions of knowledge, power, and value. The idea is to try to think as deeply and complexly as the structures of lived reality for the sake of orienting life responsibly. Much more could be said, of course. And, in fact, other chapters of this book will advance the position. I want to conclude this chapter with thoughts of a somewhat different order.

5

We live and think in a time when it seems that many intellectual disciplines are unsure of their task and purpose. Some scholars bemoan the listlessness of the humanities and religious studies. There are the relentless attacks, sometimes warranted and sometimes not, on things modern and Western. Of course, the question of what constitutes knowledge and a discipline is itself constitutive of the disciplines. Yet the purpose of clarifying the nature and connection of forms of knowledge is not always obvious in our time. Unconcerned with squabbles among humanists and scholars of religion, the natural sciences, such as neuroscience and genetics, and the social sciences, especially economics, daily make inroads into domains of thought previously defined as the human sciences, the *Geisteswissenschaften* (to use the German term). In this context I have proposed a reconstruction of my own discipline in order to demonstrate its place within and contribution to the wider work and purposes of the university. This proposal might have implications for other fields of study. That is a question for debate. Yet beyond the matter of how we constitute and conceive of disciplines of inquiry, I have been driving at something else in this chapter.

The remembrance of death and love of life which I have explored are in fact etched into the structures of our everyday, lived reality. Some 40 years ago in the spring and summer of 1968 riots broke out at Columbia University and other institutions of higher learning and then in May throughout the USA and Europe over the war in Vietnam. We are still at war and now on a global scale. Martin Luther King, Jr, was shot in 1968. Years ago some far-sighted people foresaw the massive danger we posed to our planet's environment and forms of life, and now we celebrate Earth Day in order to counter that danger. Every week in cities around the world there is an onslaught of murders, especially of children. The remembrance of death surrounds us. Yet this age like every age is also one of freedom and life. During Passover, Jews look back and reenact those events that led to their liberation from bondage. Christians look forward to Pentecost and the rush of new life in the spirit. People around the world struggle against the tyranny of poverty, oppression, and ignorance in the name of human dignity and the fragile goodness of finite life.

Other events, celebrations, and sorrows, religious and otherwise, could be mentioned. All of these – and much, much more – form the structures and dynamics within which people dwell and which pose the basic question of how we can and ought to orient life. How can Christian theology and ethics add its voice to the labor of respecting and enhancing the integrity of life? How can knowledge grow so that life might increase, especially in our age when so many forms of life and cultural forms are endangered? Is it possible to rejuvenate the humanities and to probe the religions in order to envision a new self-overcoming of human power and knowledge into responsibility for the integrity of life? That is the hard work of humanizing religion, I have been proposing. And when communities and disciplines respond to this task with all the vitality and resources at our disposal, then, I believe, knowledge will indeed grow from more to more and life will be increased without the illusions of power or servitude to the tyranny of idols.

Notes

1 Paul Ricoeur, "What Does Humanism Mean?" in *Political and Social Essays*, ed. D. Stewart and J. Bein (Athens, OH: Ohio University Press, 1974), pp. 86–7.
2 Saint Augustine, *On Christian Doctrine*, trans. D. W. Robertson, Jr (New York: Bobbs-Merrill, 1958), Bk I, p. ii.
3 See for example Werner Jaeger, *Early Christianity and Greek Paideia* (Cambridge, MA: Harvard University Press, 1961).
4 See Hans Dieter Betz, *The Sermon on the Mount: A Commentary on the Sermon on the Mount, Including the Sermon on the Plain (Matthew 5:3–7:27 and Luke 6:20–49)* (Minneapolis: Fortress Press, 1995).
5 Luc Ferry, *Man Made God: The Meaning of Life*, trans. David Pellauer (Chicago: University of Chicago Press, 2002).
6 Tzvetan Todorov, *Imperfect Garden: The Legacy of Humanism*, trans. Carol Cosman (Princeton, NJ: Princeton University Press, 2002), p. 30. Also see Timothy G. McCarthy, *Christianity and Humanism* (Chicago: Loyola Press, 1996); Salvatore Puledda, *On Being Human: Interpretation of Humanism from the Renaissance to the Present*, trans. A. Hurley (San Diego, CA: Latitude Press, 1997); and Corliss Lamont, *The Philosophy of Humanism*, 5th edn (New York: Frederick Ungar Publishing, 1967).
7 One undertakes this formation through a variety of strategies including the application of human power and knowledge to shape personal and social exist-ence in order to relieve human want and suffering and also the drive to make reality a symbol or organ of human intent. This was of course the way the great nineteenth-century theologian Friedrich Schleiermacher understood the nature of ethics, namely, as the science of history in which reason makes nature its organ. On this see his *Lectures on Philosophical Ethics*, ed. Robert B. Louden (Cambridge: Cambridge University Press, 2002).
8 Giovanni Pico della Mirandola, *Oration on the Dignity of Man*, intro. Russell Kirk (Washington, DC: Regnery Publishing, Inc., 1956), p. 7.
9 Edward W. Said, *Humanism and Democratic Criticism* (New York: Columbia University Press, 2004), p. 11.
10 Ludwig Feuerbach, *The Essence of Christianity*, trans. George Eliot (Buffalo, NY: Prometheus Books, 1989). One should also see Karl Marx's early essays "Economic and Philosophical Manuscripts of 1844" and "Theses on Feuerbach"

in *The Marx–Engels Reader*, 2nd edn, ed. Robert Ticker (New York: Norton & Co., 1978), pp. 66–125 and 143–5, respectively.

11 The modern humanistic account seems to entail one of three options about language and human understanding: first, the enclosure of human existence within semantic horizons, the prison house of language as it has been called, or, second, the need to see the creation of meaning through acts of deconstruction in post-structuralism, or, finally, a shift to define language in terms of intersubjective communication.

12 Charles Taylor, *A Secular Age* (Cambridge, MA: Harvard University Press, 2007).

13 See Niklas Luhmann, *Theories of Distinction: Redescribing the Description of Modernity*, ed. W. Rasch (Stanford, CA: Stanford University Press, 2002), p. 52.

14 See Mary Midgley, *Animals and Why They Matter* (Athens, GA: University of Georgia Press, 1983).

15 Mary Midgley, *The Myths We Live By* (New York: Routledge, 2003), p. 25. Also see William Schweiker, *Power, Value and Conviction: Theological Ethics for the Postmodern Age* (Cleveland, OH: Pilgrim Press, 1998); and James M. Gustafson, *Intersections: Science, Theology, and Ethics* (Cleveland, OH: Pilgrim Press, 1996).

16 See William Schweiker, "On the Future of Religious Ethics: Keeping Religious Ethics, Religious and Ethical," *Journal of the American Academy of Religion* 74:1 (2006), 135–51.

17 See William Schweiker, *Responsibility and Christian Ethics* (Cambridge: Cambridge University Press, 1985).

18 Jacques Derrida, *The Gift of Death*, trans. David William (Chicago: University of Chicago Press, 1995), p. 41.

19 Werner Jaeger, *Humanism and Theology* (Milwaukee, WI: Marguette University Press, 1943), p. 55.

Chapter 3

Conscience and Spiritual Conviction

1

The previous chapters explored some of the problems and forces now moving around the world and the challenges they pose for Christian life. Those problems mainly centered on questions of "identity," explored in Chapter 1, and the shape of Christian theological and ethical thinking in global times, the topic of the last chapter. This chapter and the next one dig deeper into the challenges facing Christians by exploring the human capacity to live freely and faithfully. The chapters center on "conscience" as a crucial idea for theological humanism insofar as it denotes the capacity of human beings, dust that breathes, responsibly to fashion and to orient their lives. Sad to say, conscience has fallen out of favor within ethics. This is due mainly to the priority of language and social institutions among philosophers of the twentieth century and the shift from the analysis of existence to narrative and the Church among Christian theologians. Language and community have dominated ethics and this has meant a lack of interest in the depth and complexity, the joy and the perplexity, of experience and existence. My argument cuts against current consensus. Along with some of the thinkers explored in Part II of the book, I want to reclaim a robust account of the travail and delight of the human condition. Of course, language and community remain important. Who could doubt that fact? Yet it is the structures of lived reality that I want to explore. Some digging into the history of thought will be needed in order to reclaim and rethink the idea of conscience for theological humanism.

On the way to the place of conscience in ethics, this chapter isolates a specific kind of experience. In our global age, we increasingly come to know ourselves in and through encounters with people from other religious traditions. That is hardly a novel insight. Yet a good deal is at stake in the way one articulates and conceptualizes that kind of self-understanding. While

Dust that Breathes, by William Schweiker © William Schweiker 2010.

most discussions of pluralism center on how we are to interpret, understand, and respond to others, I am actually reversing the line of inquiry. I am concerned to explore how others can interpret us and even disclose within the particularity of our lives some more abiding general, universal, convictions. How can one make this kind of argument?

Despite the focus on language and social communication, some thinkers, and I join them, have sought to isolate basic structures of human experience and existence by attending to events, encounters, or moods, like (say) anxiety, that strip away our usual strategies of sense-making and speaking, in order to get a glimpse of reality and the existence of human beings. The wager is that while we are profoundly social beings, we are not only social creatures.[1] Martin Heidegger, Jean-Paul Sartre, and others examined death, or what Paul Tillich called the threat of non-being. Albert Camus spoke about the Absurd. Jean Nabert and some of Paul Ricoeur's early works plumbed human fault and fallibility. Nowadays, it is popular to explore, as Emmanuel Levinas does, the encounter with the "face" of the other or, like Jean-Luc Marion, to ruminate on the phenomena of "gift." Later in this book we will explore the Danish theologian Kund Løgstrup's account of the "sovereign expressions of life," as he called them. The shared tactic, despite the profound differences, is to pierce the veil of the world, a veil cast upon things through the unrelenting human act of making reality familiar in our customary forms of language use. One seeks, then, the reality of things, their meaning and truth, in and through human cultural evaluations. Once the lived structure of existence is disclosed under the negation of the familiar or everyday, one asks, what then is required? What consequences follow from an apprehension, an insight, into the structures of life? Is it resoluteness towards death (Heidegger), the courage to be (Tillich), an infinite responsibility for the other (Levinas), or the denial of suicide in the face of the absurd (Camus)? Thinking aims to enable one to live truthfully from the familiar into the real and thereby to reclaim cultural forms beyond illusion, deception, or complacency.

My work stands within this legacy of reflexive and hermeneutical thinking, but with a difference. Later I intend to explore a parable told by Jesus in which, I contend, one grasps how the familiar patterns of religiosity – as a kind of sense-making – are shattered by a person from a radically different way of life and yet the inner meaning of one's convictions is also disclosed. The contention is that by means of an encounter with a person of integrity outside one's own communal and evaluative frameworks one can, surprisingly, experience the call of conscience. This call binds one not to the convictions of the person encountered, but, rather, to live truthfully and with greater depth and tenacity one's own convictions. This call initiates an act of radical interpretation in which one's own existence is transformed in the direction of responsibility with and for others. It opens, I contend, the possibility of new life in response to a disclosure of the goodness of the integrity of life. The encounter is what I will call an experience of *spiritual conviction*. It is, as noted in the previous chapter, one way in which the remembrance of death is inscribed within the love of life. A basic dynamic of human life comes to expression within the structure of lived reality. In the available lexicon of moral terms, spiritual conviction is best interpreted through the discourse of conscience, or so I claim. The meaning of "conscience" is also transformed from discourse about the mind's grasp of moral laws, the experience of guilt, accusation, or the fallen conscience. It is, rather, a description of the basic mode of moral being.[2]

The experience of spiritual conviction unsettles familiar patterns of life, but precisely through a disclosure of goodness that can empower a new way of life. Rather than exploring events or experiences or moods that threaten loss, like death or the Absurd, as a way to pierce the familiar, an experience of spiritual conviction, I want to show, issues forth from a claim on behalf of life. The call of conscience, then, is not resoluteness in being towards death, as Heidegger might put it. It is the call to exist and to act towards the integrity of life. It is not possible to explore further in the present chapter arguments related to mine, like Levinas's "humanism of the other man" or Tillich's ideas about an "ecstatic humanism." I return to those and other thinkers later in this book. Here I will develop my argument in contrast to other currents within ethics that focus on emotions and virtues. I adopt the language of conscience rather than trudge the well-worn path of virtue theory.

I admit that the kind of reflexive thinking I undertake might seem out of fashion nowadays in the mad rush to think about anything but ourselves and our relations. The prevailing opinion, again, is that if one were to pierce cultural forms like the stories that Christians tell, there would be nothing there behind the stories. It is community and language all the way down, we are told. Yet, in fact, before thought comes on the scene the density of experience and relations – not just some linguistic code – is already present. The lived density needs to be interpreted in order to be understood. Thinking aims to gain possession of the structures of lived experience and to provide adequate articulation of them for the sake of new orientation in life. The act of reflection therefore aims to grasp the elusive if ever dynamic lived texture of reality. Let me now begin the journey of interpretation.

2

For all of us, the wild diversity of human life and forms of culture is at least of some interest. I treasure them, at least at a distance, but, if honest, I am apt to prefer to engage "the other" in written form or through cultural artifacts that preserve some comfortable distance. Yet the question at the root of these reflections is not just about forms of culture or the written and solid monuments that we peer at, read, and excavate. It is about living human beings in actual societies. When I call to mind people known and experienced in daily life, then the challenge becomes clear to me. The sheer oddity of others' lives rubs against my professed interest in things human and I run the risk of dismissal, facile curiosity, blatant misunderstanding, or even revulsion. I cannot imagine living certain kinds of lives, even if I can admire them. I will never be a Buddhist monk or a Catholic priest or part of the London business class. Other ways of life I find repugnant and evil. I accept that they are ways of being human, but they stretch my imagination and moral sensibilities in order to keep affirming that point. In still other cases, I come to realize, like Gulliver did in his travels, that what I thought was a beast, the Houyhnhnm, is in fact the most civilized of beings, and my own community nothing but brute Yahoos. I am not sure that others pay me the same compliment. They might look at my life and culture and shake their heads, or their fists. An awareness of the bonds of human commonality is paradoxically linked to, heightened by, or confounded with difference.

In the light of these experiences there are some common and some not so common responses to pluralism. Consider some responses. One can reject the claim of others, insist that their cognitive and evaluative framework is incommensurate with one's own, pity them, live and let live, try to convert others, or wage war on them. It was popular a few years ago to deploy the idea of "dialogue" as a way to navigate pluralism. All of these responses rely on some more or less cogent account of what pluralism means. These accounts of pluralism range from seeing it as nothing more than human diversity, to ideas about the incommensurability of discourses and evaluative frameworks, isolating differentiated social structures, to the debate within theology and ethics about the possibility of a global ethics or a shared moral core to all traditions. While important and interesting, I cannot examine these various meanings of pluralism much less enter the debate about global ethics.[3]

Beyond well-known responses to pluralism, there are other nuanced accounts of the encounter with others that take a hermeneutical and humanistic angle. Professor Lee Yearley has astutely noted that there is a kind of *spiritual regret* that arises out of the fact that while we can admire another way of being religious, we also know that we can never really inhabit that kind of life.[4] There is also, it would seem, a form of *spiritual protest*, if I can call it such, which arises from witnessing religious people engaged in heinous acts of hatred and violence against the best insights of their own convictions. I think that most of us have had these moments of *regret* and *protest*, not only about adherents of other religions but much more within the many sides of our own traditions. The waves of incense I saw and smelt in the Church of the Holy Sepulchre in Jerusalem carried praises to the heavens, but I also knew, regrettably, that was not my kind of piety. The strident evangelicals in the USA denouncing women's ordination, those who harp on the teaching of creationism in public schools, or priests sexually abusing children chill my bones and evoke protest in me. They seem to miss the point of being in Christ and the Christian focus on new creation and the love of neighbor.

I could explore these experiences of *regret* and *protest* further as a way to capture the meaning of religious pluralism in its felt dimensions. The benefit would be that these experiences signal responses to the "other" and thereby focus on religious difference. Yet that tactic of thought also has its dangers. The inverse of spiritual regret is complacency; spiritual protest too often slides into pride. As important as those other experiences and their dangers might be for thinking about religious pluralism, one can isolate another kind of experience. This experience comes to light once we reverse the direction of reflection and ask how it is that we can be interpreted by others. Further, exploring that kind of experience can serve as a key to a theological humanist response to radical religious pluralism. I am going to call it the experience of *spiritual conviction* interpreted as the claim of conscience, in the very root meaning of the term: a form of knowing (*scientia*) with (*con*) another. Later I will have to explain in detail what that means and also clarify how it fits into the agenda of theological humanism.

Examples of spiritual conviction would be the impact of Gandhi on Martin Luther King, Jr, the sayings of Jesus on Gandhi, the moral force of the Dalai Lama for many people, or reading a Buddhist or Confucian or Hindi text, of whatever stripe, which does not call one away from one's own convictions, but, rather, to live more truthfully by them. Even the popular cinema enacts these kinds of encounters, as in the film *Seven Years in Tibet*. One character turns Buddhist and yet another, the movie's star, returns to his home in Austria a changed man. It is popular nowadays within ethics to speak of these as experiences of saints or moral exemplars.[5] That puts the focus on the one who has the spiritual power to exemplify the good and the need for virtues that embody excellence. More is going on in this kind of experience than is captured by ideas about saints and the virtues.

What happens in the experience of spiritual conviction is not a conversion to a different way of life. Rather, there is a deeper insight into the moral and religious truth of one's own values and commitments and renewed capacity to live them: one is *convicted* by the life of another, who may or may not be a saint, in terms of a rupture or hypocrisy in one's own life, but one is also empowered, inspired, to live out one's *convictions*. It is this double intentionality of judgment and empowerment in spiritual conviction that I want to explore. The idea of conscience articulates its moral meaning.

The experience of spiritual conviction as the call of conscience is the realization that through the encounter with a person of another religious tradition one's own life has been called into question, new resources in the depths of one's own tradition illuminated, and, accordingly, there is a deepening of self-understanding and religious conviction. One knows that one cannot become like the other, so there may be tinges of spiritual regret; one hardly protests about the other since what has been exposed is oneself and one's own convictions. How is it, we might ask, that another person can nevertheless activate a profound and interior self-examination in oneself? In an age in which the historical religions have become decidedly lacking in self-criticism even in their most erudite expressions, often bellicose in their interactions, and seemingly too ready to despise the human lot, isolating and articulating what I am calling spiritual conviction within the religions seems important. The challenge of pluralism from this perspective is a challenge to live freely the human adventure in our distinctively religious ways made possible through encounters with others.

A few more steps will thereby occupy these reflections. I want to turn next and try to isolate the lived structure of the experience of spiritual conviction as a response to pluralism. After that I can show why the language of conscience, rather than just the current interest in virtue, is important to ethics. And that will lead me, at the far end of these reflections, back to theological humanism and religious pluralism.

3

At first blush, it seems that the challenge of pluralism is simply to understand the lives, cultures, religions and societies of others. Yet, if by "pluralism" one merely means human diversity, it is rather obvious and also unhelpful. There are in fact many kinds of pluralism: normative, epistemic, social-functional. My concern will be the experience of others who contest one's basic convictions about the world, one's self, and others, and so *normative pluralism*.

The idea of normative pluralism is easy enough to grasp. As deeply social creatures, people naturally adopt some picture of life embedded in convictions about what counts as a way of life worthy of a human being. The grounds for that picture and correlate convictions are often nothing other than the evaluative habits of one's community or the stories and fairy tales one learns on a parent's knee.[6] We get on with life by inhabiting a "world" constituted through evaluative frameworks that interpret basic needs, impulses, and capacities. This is why no one is a barbarian to themselves; other people with other languages and customs and values are always the barbarians, to use the pointed and ancient Greek expression. Normative pluralism is a challenge to self-understanding and patterns of evaluation. The encounter with others either hardens normative convictions and thus makes one dig in the heels with firm resolution and then gawk at the barbarians, or it challenges one to think again and provide a different account of why one believes what one believes. Pluralism on this account means divergent, possibly incommensurable, value-systems and outlooks that shape people's daily existence. It is about the ways people render the world familiar through patterns of evaluation, some scale of value, used to orient their existence.

To live as a human being in community with other human beings demands some convictions about what is good and bad, right and wrong, just and unjust, better and worse, otherwise we simply could not get on in life. Further, those normative convictions are bound, in complex ways, to needs, capacities, and relations important for human flourishing, individually and socially. An attack on a person's normative convictions can take place through their denial, or, importantly, through inattention to or destruction of the needs and capacities basic to life. Normative beliefs and values are then not just "conflict-notions," that is, notions that one needs because sometimes one does not know what to do. To be sure, normative beliefs and values answer those kinds of quandaries, but much more they are what enable people to make sense of their lives and their world against a background of needs and capacities. That is why the normative challenge of pluralism is so deep and radical. It is not just that I use some values or norms to help me get along with those who have a different outlook. It is that their whole outlook on life cannot jar with mine or mine with theirs. The old humanist slogan that "nothing human is foreign to me" is a wonderful sentiment, but once I grasp how much my humanness is bound to valuations, the slogan loses some of its plausibility. Encounters with others can pierce the familiar make-up of my world.

There are limits on the range of viable normative outlooks simply because human beings are members of the same biological species and certain human features – call it the realm of embodiment – relate to needs and capabilities that any society must meet if it is to remain viable and existent. These needs and capacities constitute an internal demand on a society for viability and thereby limit the range of differences between societies. However one enumerates them, there are a finite number of basic or common goods that inhere in sexuality, embodied needs, sociality, reflexivity, and culture-making capacities.[7] Of course, how those features are evaluated will differ among cultures and thereby how needs and capabilities will be met, fulfilled, ranked, brought into conflict, or even denied will differ as well. Yet a society and culture must pay a debt to those enduring features of human existence. At least part of the challenge of pluralism is the divergence of human outlooks against the backdrop of shared needs and capabilities. The aspiration to grasp something more universal supposedly disconnected from needs and capacities might, depending on how conceived, blind one to the situated nature of normative commitments. If humanism means that the work of formation and cultivation is always with respect to human needs and capabilities, then some convictions might be especially opaque.

We can make some headway in isolating spiritual conviction as an experience of pluralism if we explore its articulation in textual form. But please note: the textual form is at the service of the lived reality and not the other way around. The story exists to articulate experience rather than simply to be used to re-socialize people into the Church. In fact, the parable exposes the ways in which one has not properly appropriated the convictions of a community into one's very life. This detour through a text will enable us to examine how a familiar religious world can be pierced in such a way as to disclose a consequent demand on human beings. It will also show how some, but not all, religious forms can distort the moral demand experienced in the texture of lived existence. At root, we are uncovering the meaning of religious transcendence once the familiar world of cult and piety is pierced in the event of spiritual conviction as the call of conscience. To borrow a phrase from Paul Ricoeur, I want to articulate spiritual conviction and the call of conscience as they appear in the "mirror of scripture."[8]

4

Many texts could have been chosen in order to examine spiritual conviction. A paradigmatic example of this for the Christian imagination is Jesus' parable of the Good Samaritan (Luke 10:25–37). The well-known text is surprising because it inscribes religious pluralism within the Torah teaching of Jesus such that the non-Jew, a Samaritan, discloses the inner-truth of biblical faith. What do I mean?

Samaria was the capital of Israel captured in 721 BCE by the Assyrians who then settled the land with "pagans" from other parts of their empire. According to Jewish tradition the Samaritans were descendants of those settlers who had a separate temple, at Mt Germi, and a distinct Pentateuch. The hostility between Jews and Samaritans was well known. It is remarkable, then, that in Luke 10 and 17 Jesus shows sympathy for them.[9] The Samaritan's action recounted in Luke 10 pierces the familiar world of Jewish cultic piety to disclose an inner dynamic of existence of profound consequence for the reader. Someone not of a religious world nevertheless enters that world, defamiliarizes it, and reveals the truth of existence in a way that empowers new life.[10] Consider the text in some more detail.

The parable of the Good Samaritan comes in Luke following Jesus' sending of seventy to proclaim the reign of God. They return joyous in their success. Jesus says, "Blessed are the eyes that see what you see" (Luke 10:23b) The disciples have witnessed the coming reign of God. The text of Luke places the reader outside the perception of divine power and poses the question of what is required to have that perception. The challenge to the reader is actually configured in the text itself. A "lawyer" encounters Jesus with a question that formulates for the reader the demand for spiritual perception: "what must I do to inherit eternal life?" Jesus answers by having the man recite the great double-love command: "You shall love the Lord your God with all your heart, and with all your soul, and with all your strength, and with all your mind; and your neighbor as yourself" (Luke 10:27). This formulation of the command links Deuteronomy 6:5 about proper worship of God with the command in Leviticus 19:18 about the demand of neighbor love rather than vengeance in situations of conflict. Jesus is engaged in Torah teaching; he provides a midrash on other texts. He is then asked by the lawyer to clarify who is the neighbor. The parable unfolds in response to a question about the neighbor. It is also about the conditions for eternal life in the love of God and a reciprocal love relation to another, to love the other *as* oneself. The command provides the *form* of truthful existence that orders other claims and actions.[11]

The encounter with the neighbor presented in the parable centers not on the question of a belief system, but on the correspondence between life and actions. Recall that a Priest and a Levite on the way to Jericho cross the road in order to avoid a man who had been beset by robbers. A perilous road at that time, the Priest and Levite act prudentially and religiously: they retained their safety and their purity by avoiding the man in distress. They did not soil their religious purity by caring for a "worldly" sinner. Yet a Samaritan was moved by pity for a hurt and vulnerable man. He came to the man's aid. The force of the parable is to suggest that the Samaritan's action rightly interprets the double-love command and therefore articulates the conditions of eternal life. The parable pierces the lives of the hearer exposing the gap between conviction and life. A faithful Jew would know that one is to love God and love the neighbor even if the connection between the commands had not been rightly grasped. Cultic purity cannot be separated from compassion and justice for others. The parable is the imaginative articulation of the command's meaning linking love of God and the love of neighbor. It instigates an event of spiritual conviction, in the twofold sense of the term explained above.

Even more is displayed in this text. As many have noted throughout the centuries, in the parable of the Good Samaritan the question of the "neighbor" is reversed. The Samaritan, someone despised by the Jews of Jesus' day after untold years of conflict, had compassion on a man beset by robbers. Historically, the parable is against the backdrop of a shocking attack on Temple worship. "In recent times," William Spohn notes, "Samaritan radicals had dumped a corpse in the Temple during Passover, defiling it so that the feast could not be celebrated. The shock of reversal in this parable … displays the meaning of Jesus' new commandment of love."[12] Spohn rightly notes that what is challenged is the whole machinery of Temple worship. Jesus' parables and actions pierce the religious world of cult and lay bare a claim about love, rather than purity, as the true form of righteous existence.[13] This is why, presumably, there is absolutely no suggestion that Jesus thinks the Samaritan must become a Jew in order to act as a neighbor. The loving act of the Samaritan is what constitutes him as a neighbor. Rectitude of love, not purity of cult, is the right form of faithful existence.

There is a triple piercing of the world in this text that enables us, as reflective readers, to bracket our all too human world and see the consequent claim upon us. First, the parable transgresses usual interpretation of the idea of the "neighbor" implied in the lawyer's question. It forces the judgment of whether one is or is not a neighbor to others. Next, the parable centers on the action of a man who is religiously different, a radical outsider to Jewish faith and worship, and yet this man's action displays the true meaning of biblical faith. The particularity of the Temple cult is shattered by the capacity of a man to tend to another man beyond the bounds of cult, creed, or custom. Finally, the text pierces the reader's or hearer's world insofar as the acts of the Samaritan can instigate the call of conscience in us and therefore interpret the depth and tenor of our lives.

This triple piercing of the world, as I am calling it, enables us to grasp love of God and of neighbor as the consequent claim on our existence. This consequent claim has a surprising presupposition. Jesus is not suggesting that his hearers become Samaritans. Quite the inverse is the case. The insight and the very inversion in the parable, its power to bracket the familiar and confront us with a consequent claim, rests upon Jewish beliefs about the relation between righteous action and the human being as created in the image of God. "Since human beings are created in the image of God," Menachem Kellner writes, "it is obvious that one achieves the highest possible level of perfection or self-realization by becoming as similar to God as humanly possible. This is the basis for what may be the single most important ethical doctrine of the Hebrew Bible, that of the *imitatio Dei*, the imitation of God."[14] This is a vision of biblical *paideia* and human perfection (see Chapter 2). The "imago Dei" is hardly an attribute of the mind or soul as many early and medieval Christian theologians thought. It is manifest in actions that imitate God. "Neighbor" is defined not by likeness grounded in community or memory, but by compassion. The Samaritan disambiguates a moral situation – can a Samaritan and a Jew relate? – by enacting a wider moral order reaching from humanity to the living God.

It is important to see that the normative framework of the parable is not Samaritan religion, but the beliefs and convictions of Jesus' fellow Jews. Jesus' parable, surprisingly, pictures the Samaritan as imitating the God of Israel who loves when despised and who sustains human worth. Earlier in the text, at Luke 6:35–6, we read: "But love your enemies, do good, and lend, expecting nothing in return. Your reward will be great, and you will be children of the Most High; for he is kind to the ungrateful and the wicked. Be merciful, just as your Father is merciful." This command is grounded in God as creator, the one who sustains all of life. Just as in the parable, the meaning of "neighbor" is shattered and expanded, but with respect to the actual problem of how to live beyond cycles of violence and conflict. "Neighbor" is not someone near and dear to us, but anyone who acts righteously and, more radically, who, like Christ, loves even the enemy.[15] The humanity of the Samaritan's act is seen when it imitates the living God of the Jews. The real core of Jewish faith on Jesus' account is not the ritual practices of the Temple cult as a condition for eternal life, but what is revealed in the merciful action of a non-Jew but righteous man. Simple membership in the community, socially speaking, is not enough to be genuinely faithful.

It is at this juncture that the reader's existence can be seen in the mirror of the text. The parable isolates the crossing point of two experiences long noted in ethics. The first is the phenomenon of the divided self as St Paul portrays it in Romans 7, or what is sometimes called the abyss of the will: a conflict between the law of the mind and the law of the "flesh" (as Paul puts it). The lawyer knows the divine Law and yet is driven to ask for its meaning out of his longing about eternal life. The lawyer emblematically configures the moral struggle of our own wills. As I argue throughout this book, the human problem is also and always *within* each of us and our community, the struggle for the integrity of life.

There is another phenomenon, sometimes related to conscience, which transpires in the hearing of the parable: the accuser and the accused are one. A doubleness arises in the self wherein one is both judge and the judged. Linguistically, as we saw in Chapter 1, this doubleness is denoted by the difference between "I" and "me." We are and are not at one with ourselves, but, in fact, are internally complex. In the figure of the Good Samaritan is displayed a consistency between life and conviction that nevertheless can resonate in the self as the claim of one's own being exposing one's duplicity and fault. For some uncanny reason, one knows that the Samaritan enacts the meaning of love even though this up-ends our familiar path of prudence and purity. That is why the lawyer, no less than the reader, gets the point. It is also why the "*as*" structure of the command is so crucial; the "as" in neighbor love articulates the reflexive relation of oneself to oneself in and through love of another.[16] The parable instigates the work of conscience. It ignites the radical interpretation of oneself by oneself in relation to another with respect to the question of the integrity between convictions and loves, desires, and action.

The parable thereby convicts the hearer through the righteous action of a man, the Samaritan, who abides by different and even conflicting religious beliefs and practices and yet enacts the truth of one's own convictions. The parable presents an action that pierces the rituals and beliefs that define a religious world and discloses its inner structure in terms of love. What then is required, what is consequent? "Go and do likewise" (Luke 10:37). Further, within the Samaritan's actions are presented the very conditions for eternal life insofar as a neighbor loves the other and thereby imitates God's action. The truth of eternal life is not some other-worldly mode of being. The Samaritan responds to the concrete suffering of a man beaten and beset by robbers. In the Samaritan's actions we can glimpse the capacity to perceive in the concrete suffering of another person a wider, more universal perspective formulated in the command to love the neighbor *as* oneself. It was the attack on the poor man's needs and capacities – and not his cultural "world" – that evoked the Samaritan's response. Normative commitments are held accountable to the human reality they are meant to serve. The probing insight of the parable is the assertion that a condition for eternal life is action on behalf of suffering human beings. Our usual ways of parsing out the religious and ethical are overturned. The call of conscience just is spiritual conviction. Conscience and spiritual conviction are not causally linked but they arise from within the space of experience viewed from a different perspective. Conscience, as the moral form of spiritual conviction, is one way, albeit not the only way, to experience and respond to the reality of religious pluralism, as radical as the painful conflict among Jews and Samaritans during the time of Jesus' teaching.

5

Notice the strategy of thinking. I have tried to get at a certain experience of pluralism by interpreting a parable, a cultural artifact, marked by suffering, exchange, command, and difference in which the familiar structure of a religious world – ritual purity, belief, demarcations of insider/outsider – is pierced through the righteous action of someone who inhabits a different and even conflicting religious outlook, who is a religious outsider. The text of Luke 10:25–37 folds within it the parabolic display of a person, the Samaritan, whose response to suffering counters the conflict of loves presented in the lawyer's question. Yet the Samaritan's actions can also instigate in the hearer or reader the call of conscience. The parable reveals the inner dynamics of true life under the form of the love of God and neighbor. Justice interpreted through love is at the heart of being rather than the sheer possibility of nothingness or the struggle for personal authenticity before that nothingness, as modern thinkers hold. In the acts of the Samaritan the reader or hearer is enabled to see her or his ownmost self in judgment on actual life and then bid to follow a new path of integrity. "Go and do likewise."

The moment of judgment is not and cannot be the whole of conscience. The basic claim is about life, its goodness, and the demand of a suffering man to be aided as articulating the conditions of eternal life. Of course, the language of conscience has fallen on hard times in ethics. Many theologians and philosophers now prefer the language of virtue and the emotions in order to escape what they see as the abstract nature of too much modern moral theory. Why then do I want to reclaim the language of conscience to interpret spiritual conviction? How have I altered traditional ideas about conscience? How might this help in response to religious pluralism?

Briefly put, the language of virtue is about the formation of capacities with respect to some good or end of human aspirations. It is about bringing the self to an end, telos, or achievement designated as good where the meaning of "good" is specified in the moral vocabulary of some community. One could read the text of the Good Samaritan, and encounters with moral exemplars in other religious traditions, in just this way. The Samaritan embodies human excellence and even God's mercy in such a way that one is to "Go and do likewise." He is a moral saint and exemplar. William Spohn advanced this argument and showed how it develops moral perception, dispositions, and also the transformation of identity. Further, a virtue account rooted in aspirations to excellence provides ethical meaning for what I have called before spiritual regret and spiritual protest. One sees in the figure of the Samaritan a way of life one can only partly enact for oneself. Given the presuppositions of Jewish conceptions of God in the parable, Jesus puts limits on the extent to which one can and should simply adopt another way of life. Spiritual regret is a possible response. At the same time, one can protest the failures in one's own life and one's own community. That is the force of the parable in its judgment on the Priest and the Levite. Understood through the rubric of virtue ethics, what is basic is the drive of aspiration, the movement of transformation from one way of life to another, more excellent way of life.

Granting its importance, what is missing in a virtue reading is precisely the doubleness in self that I have isolated in the parable and which, I contend, is basic to the experience of *spiritual conviction*. What is more, on a virtue account what is central is precisely the reach of human aspiration and the structure of communal valuation; but that is, so it would seem, just the engine of the human overlay on reality that is pierced in the parable. The Samaritan does not simply display human excellence in such a way that I am moved to seek it in my own life. This figure – whether real or literary – instigates a crisis wherein I am both judge and judged, accused and accuser, put on trial before a tribunal in my ownmost being under the form of the love command. What is revealed in the piercing of the familiar is that the dynamic of true life is not human aspiration but the response of love elicited by the other. I am convicted before the inner dynamics of the very conditions of true life. The force of the parable is that I do not love myself if I do not love as a neighbor loves.

In this light, the world that I inhabit – a world constructed through all too human valuations, social structures, and cultural practices – is riddled with conflict, suffering, death, and quests for purity, but it is also, surprisingly, structured by the conditions of eternal or true life. The call of conscience pierces this world and self-understandings and enables one to dwell in the goodness of life on behalf of vulnerable, finite life. There is thereby a rupture in the structure of self-love that thwarts too easy appeals to aspirations and virtues. The encounter with the Samaritan figure ignites self-examination, a radical interpretation of self, which is the work of conscience aimed at moral integrity distinct from but related to the perfection of capacities through the development of virtues. It is a sign of our times, I think, that a good deal of ethics has lost the discourse of conscience and thereby forsaken a crucial means to articulate the reflexive interrelation of self and other. The Samaritan, the other, is *in* the self even as the self is to live *as* that other lived in neighbor love.

It is vitally important to see that the account I am giving transforms some standard ideas of conscience. It does so precisely through sources that enact an experience of religious pluralism. Often in Western ethics conscience is the name for self-relatedness. As Immanuel Kant put it, "This original intellectual, and (because it represents a duty) moral capacity called conscience, has this peculiarity in it, that although its business is a business of a man with himself, yet he finds himself compelled by his reason to transact it as if the command of another person."[17] Later, Martin Heidegger would speak of conscience as the call of *Dasein* to itself. Christian theologians, like Thomas Aquinas, throughout the ages have understood conscience both as the grasp of the first principle of practical reason and the habit of moral reasoning and judgment. Protestants, for their part, explored the terrified and also the free conscience and so a claim about the entirety of a person's existence. More recently, Paul Tillich explored the "transmoral conscience" as a mode of participation in the divine that transcends obedience to the moral law. My purpose here is not to enter into a long inquiry into ideas about conscience. It is, rather, to note something important for our interpretation of religious pluralism.

The insight attained by engaging the parable of the Good Samaritan is that while conscience does in fact address the question of the integrity of the self, it can do so, if the parable is right, not through the simple and often dubious act of introspection or experience of guilt, or acting *as if* the command comes from another person, but precisely in relation to another who tends to life. The call of conscience need not issue from the self to itself, an account that too easily effaces the concrete reality of the other person. On the contrary, another person, the Samaritan, can display one's ownmost convictions in such a way that one is thereby convicted by them and empowered towards transformation and integrity. Furthermore, this appearance of conscience in the other focuses on how persons in some concrete situation ought to respect and to enhance the lives of actual suffering human beings. It is then not "transmoral" insofar as it effaces the reality of the concrete other person through participation in the divine. Quite the inverse is the case. The call of conscience manifests the transcendence of the divine in the moral encounter not with "law" but with vulnerable human beings. While a strictly philosophical account of conscience locates its *source* in reason (Kant) or *Dasein*'s being-in-the-world (Heidegger) or the thought of an ideal spectator (Adam Smith), a distinctly theological or religious account, I suggest, specifies the *source* of the call of conscience elsewhere and examines the mediation of that call in human beings.

A theological humanist account of conscience developed from an analysis and interpretation of spiritual conviction thereby finds in it not only a relation of self to self, but, also, a dynamic of transcendence. This was the insight of the old Christian theological claim that conscience is the "voice of God" resonant in the self, an idea I return to later (see Chapter 6). The *source* of conscience is not the self or the community, even if it is mediated in and through self and others and even a community. The fact that we can have moments of spiritual conviction, I am suggesting, is experiential confirmation of the insight that the *source* of the claim on existence is otherwise than oneself and yet resonates within one's own life. The parable of the Good Samaritan not only provides a surprising account of radical religious pluralism by instigating an experience of spiritual conviction. It also enables a reconstruction of our ideas about conscience in a humanistic but also theological direction. At least that is what I have been trying to show in these reflections.

6

I want to conclude this chapter by returning to the question of what the argument means for interpreting religious pluralism. We have engaged a text in which normative pluralism is inscribed in the sacred writings of a tradition in such a way that a truth claim of that tradition is disclosed by someone who is genuinely other, different – a "pagan" – and yet righteous. By attending to this kind of text, one can then, hopefully, work to curtail an invidious particularism in one's home tradition in light of a genuine human possibility and thus reach towards a more universal perspective. In a time when the religions stand in need of profound acts of self-criticism, this kind of engaged and participatory reading would seem demanded. It is one way, I judge, to engage in the labor of theological humanism. Theological humanism does not require that I deny or even escape the distinctive aspects of my home tradition. Yet it does require that I isolate within its resources the means to break open my religious world in terms of the possibility of responsibility with and for others. We have shown, paradoxically, that at the core of the Christian ideas of love and even eternal life is the action of a Samaritan, a "sinner." Building on that insight, the intent of this chapter has been to isolate an experience of religious pluralism too often neglected, articulate its moral meaning and consequence for current thought, and, finally, to show that this enacts the stance of theological humanism.

Notes

1 This seems to be the main difference among thinkers who have made the turn to language. So-called socio-linguistic thinkers, like post-liberal theologians, find the relevant structures that provide order to a social world to be the "grammar" of a community's languages and practices. Thinkers of a more phenomenological bent, like myself, are interested in exploring not simply linguistic practices but, additionally, the structure and intentionality of existence. Part of the force of my argument is to show that through a detour of interpretation we can indeed articulate some more basic dynamics in existence, the call of conscience. Yet I am acutely aware that others will disallow this move and remain satisfied to explore the linguistic practices of their community.

2 The discourse of conscience is long and complex, reaching from Hellenistic and medieval thinkers who saw it as the apprehensions of the first precepts of practical reason, as Aquinas put it, to more recent claims, by Heidegger, Paul Tillich, and others, that it is the call of human being to itself. This later interpretation, which is closer to my own, owes a good deal to the Protestant Reformation, and especially Luther, who grasped conscience as constitutive of a person's moral and religious being. However, against Heidegger and many others, I contend that conscience is not the call of the self to itself; it is not the *source* of the good of the integrity of life, but, rather, a mode of self-interpretation and examination rooted in an affirmation of that goodness as disclosed in and with the other. Conscience on this account is not just self-referential or a grasp of moral laws; it is a form of transcendence. I will have more to say on this point later in this chapter. On this argument see William

Schweiker, *Power, Value and Conviction: Theological Ethics in the Postmodern Age* (Cleveland, OH: Pilgrim, 1998), esp. ch. 5.

3   My argument in what follows accepts the longstanding humanistic assumption that human beings are always in need of learning. We escape the confines of our particularity partly through the wisdom of others. As Jean Grondin has written, universality "is something one achieves by broadening one's horizons, by going beyond the particularity of our given nature and by learning from others who have transmitted to us the wealth of their wisdom." This kind of universality is not a mathematical or logical kind; it is about a perspective, a growth in understanding, and thus hermeneutical in nature. See Jean Grondin, *Sources of Hermeneutics* (Albany, NY: SUNY Press, 1995), p. 130.

4   Lee Yearley, "Religious Virtues and the Study of Religion," The 15th Annual University Lecture in Religion at Arizona State University, February 10, 1994. Published by Arizona State University.

5   There is a mountain of literature on this topic, but see especially Susan Wolf, "Moral Saints," *Journal of Philosophy* 79 (1982), 419–39; and Robert Merrihew Adams, "Saints," *Journal of Philosophy* 81 (1984), 392–401. Also see Edith Wyschogrod, *Saints and Postmodernism: Revisioning Moral Philosophy* (Chicago: University of Chicago Press, 1990).

6   This argument from custom is found among advocates of one form of Christian humanism, although I worry that it is too easy. See G. K. Chesterton, *Orthodoxy* (New York: Doubleday, 1959). For an analogous argument, but out of Orthodox rather than Catholic sources, see Vigen Guroian, *Incarnate Love: Essays in Orthodox Ethics*, 2nd edn (Notre Dame, IN: University of Notre Dame Press, 2002).

7   The idea that there are basic human needs and capacities that various moral outlooks and social orders must meet is now important to a range of thinkers. See, for example, the works of Martha Nussbaum, Paul Ricoeur, Phillipa Foot, and Don S. Browning, and William Schweiker, *Responsibility and Christian Ethics* (Cambridge: Cambridge University Press, 1995).

8   See Paul Ricoeur, *Figuring the Sacred: Religion, Narrative, and Imagination*, trans. David Pellauer, ed. Mark I. Wallace (Minneapolis: Fortress Press, 1995).

9   See John Bright, *A History of Israel*, 2nd edn (Philadelphia: Westminster Press, 1974).

10   I suspect, but cannot argue here, that this formal structure is characteristic of religions of redemption and enlightenment, like Christianity.

11   The idea that love is the *form* of Christian ethics is longstanding. It is found in Augustine, Aquinas, Wesley, and many others. For a recent discussion of this see Oliver O'Donovan, *Resurrection and Moral Order: An Outline for Evangelical Ethics* (Grand Rapids, MI: Eerdmans, 1986).

12   William Spohn, *Go and Do Likewise: Jesus and Ethics* (New York: Continuum, 2000), p. 91.

13   I am not making a claim for the originality of Jesus on this point. It seems to me that the Hebrew prophets and also thinkers like Hillel, who claimed that a version of the so-called Golden Rule was the sum of Torah and the rest was commentary, thought likewise.

14   Menachem Kellner, "Jewish Ethics," in *A Companion to Ethics*, ed. Peter Singer (Oxford: Blackwell, 1919).

15   Hans-Dieter Betz, *Sermon on the Mount* (Minneapolis, MN: Fortress, 1995). Also see Jürgen Becker, "Feindesliebe-Nächstenliebe-Bruderliebe. Exegetische Beobachtungen als Anfange an ein ethisches Problemfeld," *Zeitschrift für Evangelische Ethik* 25 (1981), 5–17.

16   For further consideration of the structure of the command, see William Schweiker, "And a Second Is Like It: Christian Faith and the Claim of the Other," *Quarterly Review* 20:3 (2000), 233–47; Paul Ricoeur, "Ethics and Theological Considerations of the Golden Rule," in *Figuring the Sacred: Religion, Narrative and Imagination*, trans. David Pellauer, ed. Mark I. Wallace (Minneapolis: Fortress Press, 1995); *Paul Ricoeur and Contemporary Moral Thought*, ed. J. Wall, W. Schweiker, and W. D. Hall (New York: Routledge, 2002); and also H. Richard Niebuhr, "Conscience: Its Role in Ethics and Religion," unpublished paper given for the American Theological Society, New York City, April 7, 1945, manuscript held in the Andover-Newton Theological Library.

17   Immanuel Kant, *Die Metaphysik der Sitten*, Part II, par. 13, in *Werke 5* (Köln: Könemann, 1995), p. 528.

Chapter 4

Metaphors of the Soul

1

The last chapter explored one of Jesus' parables as a way to clarify the meaning of conscience as the human capacity to sense, to feel, the moral claim of others on ourselves. Conscience is, we might say, the most basic mode of moral being. It is an important idea for theological humanism because it shows us, just as the Samaritan does in the parable, that human existence, while profoundly social, is not just the product of social formation. There is an *inside* to human life, a depth, freedom, and sensibility that is part of the struggle and the joy of life. In this chapter I want to explore various metaphors of the soul, and, so, different images of human existence and the struggle and joy that our lives involve. Of course, "soul" is an outdated word for many people, a quaint reminder of days gone by. But the idea of the "soul" captures something that seems lacking in contemporary forms of thought. It might be best, then, to begin this chapter with the actual problem I am trying to get at in the following pages.

If one looks at contemporary Western cultures and also many forms of thought and criticism, it would seem that the task of being a self, that struggle rightly to integrate the bits and pieces of one's existence for oneself and with others, is believed to be either a rather easy thing or an unimportant thing. Easy, because being a self is supposedly no more than forming an identity through cultural resources with respect to one's preferences. Even the current interest in "spiritual practices" and disciplines of the self, made famous by Pierre Hadot and Michel Foucault, assumes a rather plastic idea of subjectivity; there is, apparently, nothing internal to the self that resists formation, no insurmountable limit to self-fashioning. Conversely, being a self is unimportant, we are told, because what really matters is social and cultural forces. Some thinkers who fear runaway moral relativism rooted in modern ideas of the self insist on social or ecclesial authority and the formation of the self in obedience to that authority in particular communities.[1] Finally, it is also obvious that we are living in a time in the West when the cultural resources of this civilization seem, for many people, powerless to address real challenges. These resources – peppered with criticisms over the last several centuries – seem to lack vitality and resonance. In most cases the "West" is the problem and does not have real resources for confronting the matters of life. This is especially true of classical ideas about the human self, ideas, as we all know, indebted to specific social, racial, ideological, and gendered conditions. From all sides, then, the question of how we can and ought to conceive of ourselves as selves falls upon deaf ears. Or so it would seem.

Is the human self really such a flimsy and unimportant thing? Is there no task – no arduous work – set before each of us in our fleeting days and nights? Are we really so malleable that what appears as a limit on self-fashioning is, finally, just an appearance, or, conversely, that obedience to authority and communal practices of forming the subject are sufficient? And is it the case that there are no resources – maybe even obvious ones – in our cultural heritages that can aid in thinking about the human adventure? The aim in this chapter is to explore certain classical – but now very foreign – conceptions of the human soul as a kind of *sacred space* that defines both the inviolable dignity of human beings but also the vulnerability, limits, and struggle of human existence. It is a space that can be violated and profaned by external forces but also by oneself.

My sense, then, is not that we have too exalted a sense of self or that we can just dispense with reflection on the meaning of being a self, but, rather, that the acids of criticism have left us conceptually poor, lacking complex images and metaphors with which to examine human life. The ancient and enduring injunction to "know thyself" is hard to meet when the very idea of the "self" seems vapid. In response to this situation I intend briefly to explore metaphoric schemes that dominated much classical Western thought and which, I think, need to be reengaged in our time. They are about the dignity but also the struggle, even warfare, of the soul with itself. This chapter reclaims and revises metaphors of the soul in order to help sort out viable resources for thinking about human existence in our time.

Two principles support the work of this chapter. One is widely held in the Christian and other religious traditions, although recently it too has fallen on hard times: *finitum capax infiniti*. The finite is capable of the infinite.[2] It is not at all clear, for instance, that the finite qua its own capacities reaches to the infinite; it might be that the "capability" for the infinite is something worked on, given to, infused within finite human life. Still, a theological humanist thinks that the finite products of finite human beings are nevertheless capable of the infinite, the divine. The hard work is sorting out what that means in a realistic, reasonable, and coherent way. My reflections are one stab at that work. I want to combat flimsy ideas of selfhood but also those who think we can dispense with such matters and turn merely to social forces and cultural practices.

This brings us to a second principle. Within critical intellectual labor there is a normative demand to meet sanely and responsibly the challenges of our time. Yet in order to advance a viable normative outlook theological and ethical reflection must engage and in fact endorse a moment of naturalistic explanation about human being and doing. One needs to chart the intersection between various accounts of the human in order to provide an adequate response to the challenge before us as well as a nuanced and differentiated portrayal of theological ethical thinking.[3] The normative aim of theological humanism will be clear by the end of the chapter.

Ideas of self or soul find their origin in a native sense of inwardness: the stream of desires, impressions, hopes, loves, lusts, confusions, and aspirations that flow in and through our lives. A chaotic bundle of energy, to be a self is nevertheless somehow to be capable of directing those energies towards some integration of one's being in relation to others and with respect to some norm or measure of goodness no matter how incomplete the project might finally be. The ancients called this the "soul." I will do the same. Further, as David Klemm has wisely noted, first-person experiences are in principle irreducible to natural facts. All purely naturalistic accounts that explain mind or self or soul in terms of neuronal mechanisms unavoidably leave out the felt experiences or "qualia" of thinking and perceiving and acting.[4] The metaphors of the soul I explore below are in good measure intense investigations of the felt "qualia" of being a self, a soul. Some of this felt sense of life was explored in the previous chapter on conscience and spiritual conviction. By engaging these schemes we take an indirect route towards articulating and understanding the soul, knowing that the "soul" remains opaque to direct immediate introspection. And this opacity of the soul is because the soul is only felt, only sensed, and not an object of cognition or empirical fact or symbolic designation.

Of course, there are good reasons to be suspicious of the idea of the soul. For some the idea is too private; others see it as disembodied; some thinkers contend that the self is the product of cultural formation – a surface over submerged social power; still others insist it is just a wisp of smoke, the airy stuff of idealistic rhetoric. Many of these criticisms are partially true and I am not interested in trying to contest them. Yet I am asking you to take another look. A renewed look at the "soul" cannot be undertaken by way of pure introspection; the self gazing at itself no longer seems a plausible or valid path to understanding even if we live with the felt qualia of inwardness. We need a detour of interpretation through religious and cultural resources in which we then try to catch indirectly something about the "soul." We need, in other words, a reflective and hermeneutical approach to the topic.[5] By adopting that pathway of thought, one might just redeem resources for our time. That is what I will briefly attempt.

2

Two paradigmatic metaphors for the inner-life used in the ancient world have had an extremely profound history of effects on modern Western outlooks even while they have analogies in the traditions of other civilizations. We might call these the legacies of Plato and Paul – thinkers who are presently – and happily – enjoying renewed interest.[6] I am seeking a third way beyond the divide between a paradigmatic Greek and typically biblical picture of the soul. This third way is the enterprise of theological humanism. Let me take a brief look at these metaphorical schemes, although they are extremely well known and maybe dead to many contemporary people because of their familiarity.

The Platonic image of the soul has exerted immense influence on the history of Western thought, reaching into modern Freudian psychotherapy and other forms of thought. Plato argues in the *Phaedo* and *Republic* X, in the famous myth of Er, that the soul is immortal. Yet his claim in the *Republic* IV is even more germane to our inquiry: the human soul, it is argued, is a bundle of erotic energy composed of three capacities or parts: reason, the spirited part (*thumos*) which has the "power to reflect about good and evil," and unreasoning appetite (439b–441c). There is justice in the soul when "reason" properly orders *thumos* and appetites. The struggle of the moral life is the proper, rational ordering of the soul. A struggle it is: the soul's nature and justice are conveyed by Socrates through the metaphor of a charioteer (reason) seeking to guide two unruly horses (spirit, appetite) all too ready and too able to buck their driver.

This metaphoric scheme of the soul pictures the inward struggle of the self as the quest for order, peace, and self-sufficiency. The tripartite conception of the soul has had enduring effect on the history of Western thought reaching into the Middle Ages and beyond. The peace of the self is defined by the soul's relation to itself in itself as an eternally existent substance. In other words, the justice of the soul for ancient Platonists and others was inseparable from a metaphysical claim about its immortality. In the course of Western history, this metaphysical claim has been rejected, even by recent advocates of "spiritual practices," a topic I cannot explore.[7] Importantly, this is where the Platonic picture becomes unhappily dualistic – an immortal soul controlling temporal passions. What is needed, it would seem, is an account of the soul as a dynamic of integrity within and not against the other powers and capacities of the self. Later we will speak about this in terms of conscience and its demand of the integrity of life.

In spite of these problems, it is not difficult to grasp how the Platonic account of the "soul" has intuitive plausibility; it resonates with a lot of common experience, the felt qualia of existence. The account supposes that human beings are creatures of desire, we want and value many things, and yet our desiring must be rightly ordered if there is to be some measure of tranquility in our lives. The crass hedonist or libertine disregards this demand of order usually to the destruction of life; greed and the lust for power also disorder social life. Additionally, the "Platonic" account insists that whatever order is to be attained must be reasonable or rational insofar as a genuine good of the self has to be knowable. And, finally, this account articulates a deep insight that was readily picked up by the ancient Stoics and by Christian thinkers throughout the ages, beginning with St Augustine. Insofar as "justice" is an attribute of the "inward man," as Socrates says, then in a profound sense only the self can do injustice to itself. The rectitude of the self cannot be taken from oneself against one's own will since it is a predicate of the self's own ordering. This is what the ancients meant, morally speaking, by self-sufficiency; it is a claim about the quest for moral invulnerability. Contemporary interest in personal "authenticity" and identity has some roots in this conception of the soul, shorn of Platonic and Christian overlays.[8]

This classic account, despite some recent retrievals of it, suffers from various problems beyond those already noted. Advances in psychology and biology challenge its *descriptive* adequacy. The position veers towards an invidious dualism of body/soul that cannot withstand the onslaught of scientific analysis and criticism. *Existentially* the position seems to lack the means to articulate the individuality of moral experience (the virtuous all start to look like Socrates!). Further, this account risks being circular in its *normative* dimension; it assumes what it is meant to demonstrate (i.e., the rationality of virtue). There is a *theological* problem, too. The soul is imagined as a kind of interior *sacred space* which is simultaneously immortal, and so divine, and yet seeking divinity, its unification with the good. The distinction between divinity and soul for Plato, Aristotle, and other Hellenistic thinkers is that although the soul is pre-existent and immortal, it is also changeable; to be God-like requires immortality *and* unchangeability, something attained through virtue.[9] Among Christians the soul is created and hence finite (it too is dust) and non-divine even if it aspires to union with God. In each case the self configures and yet effaces the theological difference, that is, it specifies the distinction between "God" and all other beings, and yet it also effaces that difference in its aspiration to be God-like. As Protestant theologians have noted, especially twentieth-century ones, this conceptual framework seems decidedly unbiblical and risks an apotheosis of the self that collapses the theological difference or reduces it to nothing more than the wooden opposition of creator/creature.[10]

These problems (descriptive; existential; normative; theological) illuminate why the "Platonic" picture of the human is alien to contemporary patterns of thought, and yet, oddly enough, how it retains some power of resonance with the experience of desire. It is not surprising that contemporary thinkers who seek a robust understanding of the self as backing for claims about human dignity have sought to retrieve some of these insights while overcoming enduring problems in the account.[11] I will explore some of these thinkers later, especially in the next chapter. Yet, I remain unconvinced by these proposals mainly because what they want to avoid is what I take to be the insight of the Platonic scheme, namely, that the self is an ongoing record of the struggle rightly to integrate its passionate and chaotic energies. As Nietzsche knew, and declared in *Twilight of the Idols*, it is a sign of weakness to seek to eradicate, even, as he puts it, castrate, desires and passions. "The church combats the passions by cutting them off in every sense; its technique, its 'cure'; is *castration*. ... But attacking the root of the passions means," Nietzsche continues, "attacking the root of life: the practices of the church are *hostile to life*."[12] The struggle of existence, seen in diminished form among ascetics, is an act of self-overcoming that increases vitality by ordering it toward more vitality. Many contemporary thinkers, it seems, want to eradicate the problem not by castrating the passions but by baptizing them, seeing passion as the path to the good and the holy.

More than most contemporary thinkers, Nietzsche was a paradigmatic Greek on this point; his heroic ideal is embedded in the enduring struggle of life. To be human is to exceed our all too human forms of life. An inner-problem in Western thought, as Nietzsche saw and represented it, is the extent to which the struggle of self-overcoming is a form of humanism or is itself anti-humanistic in outlook and aim.[13] Yet granting the saliency of worries about those who hope to relieve the tension within the Platonic picture by the eradication or baptism of the passions, they provoke reflection on a different metaphoric framework of our moral being.

3

The term conscience first appears in the Bible in Paul's Corinthian letters in his conflict with the Gnostics and is used at least twenty times in other contexts. The term continues the older Hebraic idea of the "heart" as designating the core of individual human being.[14] Heart and conscience, especially when later joined to certain Stoic ideas, span out to form a complex metaphoric scheme of the human self. In I Corinthians, the issue comes to focus on the "weak" whose conscience, that is, knowledge of right or wrong action, was offended by the idea of eating meat sacrificed to idols.

These individuals felt the "sting" or "pang" of conscience when engaged in what they believed to be immoral action. The Gnostics, contrariwise, saw conscience as the "spirit-self" which had to be educated in order to be saved, even when this education meant violating one's conventional beliefs about right and wrong. Paul grasps the fact that to violate conscience, even if it is empirically wrong in a specific judgment (Paul knows the theological insignificance of pagan practice), is to violate the integrity of the self. He counsels that the "strong" should respect the needs of the "weak" and thereby guard the tranquility of self and peace in the community.

From this conception of conscience flowed two ideas crucial to Western and Christian ethics: first, the inviolability of conscience, that is, the belief that conscience ought to be obeyed even if it could be mistaken, as Catholic moralists have long insisted; and, second, that moral integrity and sensibility are profoundly social even if they ought not be coerced. The question then becomes whether conscience is an autonomous *source* of moral norms or rather a *medium* for apprehending the moral law. To avoid the possibility of relativism when conscience is conceived to be the *source* of norms there developed traditions of casuistic reasoning but also various practices of educating conscience as a kind of *askesis*. *Descriptively* the idea of "conscience" is meant to articulate the experience of the integrity of the self with respect to judgments about right and wrong actions in relation to others. And *existentially* it enables one to clarify precisely human inwardness, our sense that who we are as persons is accentuated and not obliterated in right action, without thereby denying the fact that moral sensibilities are socially formed.

Freedom of conscience stems from this insight. Importantly, the right to that kind of freedom arose first in terms of freedom of religion; that is, faith cannot be coerced and remain faith. One can imagine that much contemporary "rights" talk (e.g. human rights) finds one of its origins in this idea. One could even say that the idea of "conscience" and its freedom specifies the most basic claim of human beings to proper moral considerability, that is, the right to have rights (to borrow a phrase from Hannah Arendt).[15] While conscience does not warrant political or social guarantees to specific rights, it does indicate that human beings have a right to dwell within a community that respects and enhances the integrity of life. When that right to have rights is violated, that is, if conscience is violated, human beings have a claim against their communities and also justified warrant to resist oppression in whatever form it takes, with the intent to win moral considerability.

However, the Pauline account of conscience, and other ones as well, address not only the most basic moral claim of persons but also specifically *normative* questions. In Romans 2:14–15 we read the following (cf. Romans 9:1):

> When the Gentiles, who do not possess the law, do instinctively what the law requires, these, though not having the law, are a law to themselves. They show that what the law requires is written on their hearts, to which their own conscience also bears witness.

Conscience bears witness to, or is a medium of, the moral law "written on the heart." This law has been variously conceived as the Noahide covenant among some Jewish thinkers, the so-called "Golden Rule," and Natural Law so basic to much Western theological and philosophical ethics. In these various forms, despite their obvious differences, self-knowledge is always a co-knowing, a *con-scientia* (*syn-eidesis*), of self with the moral law.[16] The expectation, then, is that human beings have a moral sensibility for the most primitive demands of justice. The moral law is not just a product of social convention, personal preference, or political utility; the moral law has a claim to reality, it has ontological depth, mediated through conscience.

Beyond descriptive, existential, and normative aspects of the metaphoric scheme of conscience, a scheme marked by ideas about the "call" of conscience, its "sting," weakness and strength, and freedom, there has always been a distinctly *theological* aspect. Especially in Protestant thought the image of the "voice of conscience" is often linked to a conception of the inner-self as a *sacred space* pictured like a courtroom in which the self stands before God. The terrified and free conscience, as Luther would put it, is defined by the futility of self-righteousness (terrified conscience) and the bounty of divine grace (free conscience). Paul Tillich, as we will explore later in Chapter 11, took this imagery to its ontological level and spoke of the divine as the "depth" of the conscience, thereby creating the reality of the trans-moral conscience. Others, like Martin Heidegger, thought about conscience as the call of *Dasein* to itself, to its ownmost authenticity.[17] The verbalization of conscience as a "voice" or "call," found also in some of the Pauline texts, is just one theological construal. Other thinkers, like the Stoics, spoke of the "spark" of conscience as manifestation in the human soul of the divine *logos*. In the Letter to the Hebrews and elsewhere there is the language of the "pure" and "defiled" conscience, often in relation to Baptism (cf. Heb. 9:14) in order to articulate its theological meaning. In each of these cases the idea is that the inner-self knows itself along with knowing the voice or spark or purity of God and God's law.

Of course, theological problems arise with the idea of conscience, analogous to those isolated before about the soul aspiring to unity with God. The difficulty is how to retain the distinction between God and conscience, and thereby to avoid, as St Paul already knew, the possibility of Gnosticism. There are grounds for worry about the Heideggerian formulation insofar as conscience is just the call of *Dasein* to itself. There is no human other who calls and convicts the self, and, further, the radical finitude of *Dasein* means that the only other ontologically conceivable is the other of my ownmost possibility, that is, my death. Little wonder, then, that many post-Heideggerian thinkers, ranging from Emmanuel Levinas and Jacques Derrida to Paul Ricoeur and Werner Marx, have, in very different ways, insisted on the claim of the human other. The struggle and sting of the self is thereby externalized, and, in its most ardent form, the question of the self is no longer salient or basic. This opens the theological question, existence before God, in and through the moral claim and ethical demand of the other. Reclaimed in this way, the discourse of "conscience" seems to resonate with common experience of human inviolability and rights.

4

I have attempted to explore the complexity of moral inwardness using cultural and religious resources that seem spent or impotent to many contemporary people. Importantly, around the metaphors of soul we have examined swirl related images and concepts: the bucking of horses and travail of the charioteer; the voice and also sting of conscience as an "inner-chamber." One needs to understand the self within the semantic density of these ideas and their interconnections. In one scheme human existence is pictured as endless striving for unchangeable perfection; in the other the "soul" is a co-knowing of self and the divine law. I have tried to indicate the legacy of these pictures in current thought in ways that relieve the tension within the self, and so make the problem of being a self an easy one, or in ways that collapse the difference of self and other into authenticity of the self, a move that has led some thinkers to reject the importance of the self in favor of the ethical claim of the other.

Theologically construed, these metaphors of "soul" picture the human self as a *sacred space*, but one within which the crucial difference between the divine and the self is too easily transgressed or is reduced to the abstractions creator/creature or inauthentic/authentic self. More profoundly, the "soul" can be a space of divinization and profanization. In either of those moves, humanism becomes theism or theism becomes nothing other than the consistent working out of a humanist intention. Those conclusions mean, I think, a dangerous apotheosis of human power and aspiration or the enfolding of human dignity and worth within hyper-theistic and authoritarian discourse (see Chapter 2). Each of the classic schemes, then, captures something intuitively right about human experience and a relation to the divine. Where positions differ is in how the relation between aspiration and law, unity with the good and purity of conscience, perfection and freedom, is conceived. They also differ on how to retain the theological difference, as I have called it. This "difference" is important in order to avoid the reduction of theism to humanism or circumscribing humanity within hyper-theistic discourse.

Where then does this leave us? Two insights seem worthy of note. First, we have isolated in the so-called "Platonic" account of the soul the deeper questions of how to avoid an invidious dualism while also retaining a robust sense of the vitality and passion of life against eradication or whole-sale baptism. The work to integrate the forces and capacities of life is just that, work. Additionally, the discourse of conscience can be used to articulate the right to have rights on behalf of human being as a bulwark against forces that efface moral recognition. Theological humanism is committed normatively to the "integrity of life" as the rule and measure of human existence. A picture of the soul as the labor of conscience integrating the dynamics of life while also designating the right to have rights seems aptly suited for picturing the self. It does so, one should note, with respect to felt "qualia" of experience, namely, the felt claim to inviolability and moral recognition in conscience and the erotic struggle rightly to integrate passional existence. Most importantly, it is crucial not to reduce one to the other, as if conscience is just a kind of passion or the passions can and ought to be self-integrating and the obvious ground of the right to have rights. Part of the trick, it seems, is to keep the semantic and hermeneutical density of alternate metaphoric schemes in play. It is to weave a third way through cultural resources, neither just Greek nor only biblical.

This conclusion brings with it a second insight. Interestingly, each account also turns on how the "soul," the integrity of self, can be lost, forsaken. In an age in which global media and market forces move unceas-ingly to forge our desires and perceptions, and so our inner-selves, and in which social and political forces compete for loyalty and thereby challenge claims to the dignity of human beings as such, might we not learn something about the vulnerability of the self to internal disorder and also the inviola-bility of human life manifest, as St Paul saw, in the string of conscience?[18] Insofar as these different schemes show the vulnerability of selves to the chaos of desire and the violation of the self in misplaced loyalty and author-ity, they provide hermeneutical tools to counter forces at work on the global scene. From within the criticism of inherited intellectual, cultural, and reli-gious legacies one reclaims resources to meet present-day problems. Is it not the case that the "soul" is now mightily endangered by manipulation of desire and tyrannous political and religious forces? In order to resist the denigration of human beings from within their ownmost vulnerability and to counter the violation of human dignity through forced conformity and domination, one needs a rich and robust idea of what makes human beings valuable creatures with the right to have rights. One important conception in that project is the "soul" as a *sacred space*, variously imagined, whose reclamation and reworking are part of the agenda of theological humanism.

Much current thought, it seems to me, tries to ignore the complex legacy of the interaction of the resources we have charted in these two paradigmatic schemes (Greek/biblical). Many thinkers really want to be Greeks, usually with Aristotle. Too many religious people, as we know from Chapter 1, want to retreat inside the moral confines of their communities and peer out at an alien and dangerous world. By exploring forms of thought emblematically associated with Plato and Paul, one can insist that if we are to overcome the loss of cultural resources we must think within tensions that have driven our heritage. This is a kind of third way thinking, neither Greek nor biblical but arising at their intersection. It is to think of the self within the drive of self-overcoming and in response to the solicitude of conscience and thereby to counter the forces of decadence and degeneration working in our cultures as well as to counter the authoritarianism too present in social and religious existence. I have sought to think together these paradigms precisely in terms of the theological difference. Neither humanistic nor anti-humanist this is the work of theological humanism. The remainder of this book is devoted to working out the implications of this kind of third way thinking.

Theological humanism articulates normative commitments. How could it be otherwise? Some of the most basic facts of our time are the endangerment to human and non-human life around this planet, the fanatic religious hatred of finite life and moral reasonableness, and also the endless profaning of life in all forms within overly "secular" societies. The terrifying possibility of human freedom is that the lust for more and more power will rid this world of life. The call of conscience must be heard anew – a call to respect and enhance the integrity of life and not just heroically endorse one's own authenticity. The tragic freedom of human love, the chaos that demands some order in our lives, motivates all too many religious people in various traditions to unflinching devotion and attachment to a God, which leads to the hatred of all that is ungodly. The claim of conscience must be brought against religious distortion with resolute gratitude for life. The cynical reduction of human life to its most profane level must be resisted by unfolding the aspiration of the soul and also the call of conscience that combats forces of profanation with a sense of the sacred. These real possibilities of the human domination of life, the religious hatred of finite imperfection, and the endless cultural spreading of the profane are betrayals of goodness. Against these horrible possibilities we need a kind of humanism that is open to a sense of the divine and the unconditioned but which endorses the transcendent reach and dignity of finite life in and through the inwardness of our own being. In these reflections I have merely tried to make a start at outlining a theological and yet humanistic vision of the soul.

Notes

1 For a recent discussion of this matter see *Universalism vs. Relativism: Making Moral Judgments in a Changing, Pluralistic, and Threatening World*, ed. Don Browning (New York: Rowman and Littlefield, 2006).

2 Of course, within the Christian tradition what makes the finite "capable" of the infinite is disputed even when there is an underlying consensus that the finite *qua* finite does not constitute that capability; somehow the infinite, the divine, is always involved in its own disclosure amid the finite. In Christian thought one finds this question debated in terms of how to understand the nature of Christ or the character of the Eucharist and also, as we will see, the conception of the self as conscience. It is not my intention in this chapter to wrestle my way through those debates.

3 On this see William Schweiker, "On the Future of Religious Ethics: Keeping Religious Ethics Religious and Ethical," *Journal of the American Academy of Religion* 74:1 (2006), 135–51; and James M. Gustafson, *Intersections: Science, Theology and Ethics* (Cleveland, OH: Pilgrim Press, 1996).

4 See, David E. Klemm, "Religious Naturalism or Theological Humanism? A Commentary on *Religion Is Not About God*, by Loyal Rue," *Zygon* 42:2 (2007), 357–67.

5 For a similar account of a reflective method of thinking see H. Richard Niebuhr, *Faith On Earth: An Inquiry into the Structure of Human Faith*, ed. Richard R. Niebuhr (New Haven, CT: Yale University Press, 1991), esp. ch. 2, "The Method of Reflection."

6 We are, in fact, in the midst of a renaissance of interest in Plato and Paul, usually pitted one against the other. For an example of the "new Paul" see Alain Badiou, *Saint Paul: The Foundation of Universalism*, trans. Ray Brassier (Stanford, CA: Stanford University Press, 2003). The most creative recent retrieval of Plato for ethics is the work of Iris Murdoch. See, for example, Iris Murdoch, *Metaphysics as a Guide to Morals* (New York: Allen Lane/Penguin, 1992); and *Iris Murdoch and the Search for Human Goodness*, ed. Maria Antonaccio and William Schweiker (Chicago: University of Chicago Press, 1996).

7 One sees this in thinkers like Pierre Hadot, *Philosophy as a Way of Life: Spiritual Exercises from Socrates to Foucault* (Oxford: Blackwell, 1995).

8 For an historical account, see Charles Taylor, *Sources of the Self: The Making of Modern Identity* (Cambridge, MA: Harvard University Press, 1989).

9 Even St Augustine, in *Civitas Dei*, continues this line of thought, noting that human beings are created good, but changeable, whereas God is eternal and unchanging.

10 On this see, for example, Michael Welker, *Creation and Reality*, trans. J. Hoffmeyer (Minneapolis: Fortress Press, 1999).

11 In various ways thinkers like Martha Nussbaum, Alasdair MacIntyre, Tzvetan Todorov, and Leon Kass have tried to redress these issues by developing a theory of capabilities (Nussbaum) or tradition-constituted rationality (MacIntyre) or claims about the finality of the other person (Todorov) or ideas

of human powers and vulnerabilities (Kass). It is not possible to address all these proposals here.

12 Friedrich Nietzsche, *Twilight of the Idols*, in *The Anti-Christ, Ecco Homo, Twilight of the Idols and Other Writings*, ed. A. Ridley and J. Norman (Cambridge: Cambridge University Press, 2005), p. 172.

13 On this see Jacques Maritain, *Integral Humanism: Temporal and Spiritual Problems of a New Christendom*, trans. J. W. Evans (Notre Dame, IN: University of Notre Dame Press, 1973).

14 The literature of "conscience" and its history is of course mountainous. For this chapter I have just drawn on standard reference works in biblical studies, like R. Jewett's article "conscience" in the *Interpreter's Dictionary of the Bible*, suppl. vol. (Nashville, TN: Abingdon Press, 1976), pp. 173–4, and W. Schrage's essay "Ethics in the N.T." in the same volume, pp. 281–9. One can also see standard works in the history of ethics, e.g., Kenneth Kirk, *Conscience and Its Problems: An Introduction to Casuistry* (Louisville, KY: Westminster John Knox Press, 1999); Albert R. Jonsen and Stephen Toulmin, *The Abuse of Casuistry: A History of Moral Reasoning* (Los Angeles: University of California Press, 1990); and John Mahoney, *The Making of Moral Theology* (Oxford: Clarendon Press, 1987). Also see William Schweiker, *Power, Value and Conviction: Theological Ethics in the Postmodern Age* (Cleveland, OH: Pilgrim Press, 1998).

15 On this see Hannah Arendt, *The Origins of Totalitarianism* (New York: Harcourt, Inc., 1968). Also see Richard Bernstein, "Can We Justify Universal Moral Norms?" in *Universalism vs. Relativism*, pp. 3–17. For an important restatement of justice in relation to rights language in a theological context see Nicholas Wolterstorff, *Justice* (Princeton, NJ: Princeton University Press, 2008).

16 These matters became even more complex with the introduction by St Jerome of a distinction between *synderesis* (a basic grasp of first moral principles not effaced by the sin of Adam, the "spark" of conscience) and *syneidesis* (the act of reasoning to a practical judgment), which has bedeviled the history of especially Catholic moral theology. I need not explore these matters in this chapter.

17 See Paul Tillich, *Morality and Beyond* (Louisville, KY: Westminster John Knox Press, 1995); and Martin Heidegger, *Being and Time* (New York: Harper and Row, 1962).

18 For an account of the threats and possibilities of the global age in relation to moral existence see William Schweiker, *Theological Ethics and Global Dynamics: In the Time of Many Worlds* (Oxford: Blackwell Publishing, 2004).

Chapter 5

Voices of Neohumanism

1

This chapter and the next explore a theme blowing around the world these days, namely, debates about humanism and human transcendence. The present chapter engages two contemporary thinkers who have been important in the revival of humanism in order to clarify the idea of human transcendence. As we will see below, neohumanists like Tzvetan Todorov and Emmanuel Levinas speak of "lateral transcendence." Theological humanism, I show, offers a related but different account of transcendence. Continuing the theme of transcendence, the next chapter will turn directly to the legacy of Christian humanism. The chapters build on the early discussions of conscience (Chapters 3–4) and also humanism and religion (Chapters 1–2) but add contemporary and historical elements to the theme of humanism. Later in Part II we will engage the work of some theologians and also philosophers. The task in those chapters will be to show why theological humanism drawn from Christian sources is needed in our global times. At this juncture it is enough to explore the contemporary debate about humanism as well as some of the history of humanism.

There can be little doubt that many questions face people in high-modern, reflexive and increasingly global societies. Yet if we step back we can see a world marred by legacies of violence, riddled with human divisions, and increasingly under the domination of technological power in which two questions are especially pressing. First, how, if at all, can we limit the relentless drive of technological power to enfold all life within its kingdom and thereby subdue any "outside" to the human project. Many people find this enfolding of life suffocating; they long for an "outside," for some transcendence. Some live with a sense of nausea about the violence, vulgarity, and wanton destructiveness of human powers. They long for some way to face intolerable facts of existence with a realistic and yet

Dust that Breathes, by William Schweiker © William Schweiker 2010.

vibrant gratitude for life. Along with Régis Debray, I will speak about this enfolding as the "overhumanization of the world."[1] This enfolding is at the root of many current protests against humanism.

A second question is equally pressing. How is this spiritual longing for some "outside" and transcendence of an overhumanized world related to our humanity? For some thinkers, transcendence leads beyond the human towards Gaia, the fate of Being, some idea of divine sovereignty, or auto-poetic social systems and cultural flows. For these positions, in order to limit the kingdom of human power and grasp an "outside," one must, in principle, negate any focus on human persons. Conversely, there are other thinkers who insist that transcendence is necessarily a human event and accordingly one's thinking must remain humanistic *in some form*. For these thinkers the dispute is over the "form" of such thinking and specifically about the reach of human transcendence.

The work of the present chapter is to examine representatives of this second option. One current form of humanism stands within but also revises the legacy of classical humanism in the West. This position is best seen in the recent work of Tzvetan Todorov. The other form of humanism I want to explore is associated with Emmanuel Levinas. He calls it a *humanism of the other* rooted in the demands of ethical responsibility. Here one finds what appears to be a radical departure from traditional humanistic thought. So, I focus on Todorov and Levinas insofar as they denote different agendas used to meet the threat of overhumanization and also to speak about transcendence.[2]

The larger aim in what follows is to clarify the contemporary moral landscape and to outline *theological humanism* as a normative stance in Christian faith. This is to suggest that a viable and vibrant theological ethics must undergo a fundamental revision, as noted in Chapter 2. Further, it must focus on the dynamics and challenge of "overhumanization" and yet develop its response to people's longings not against but through the dynamic of human transcendence. I hope to show, then, why one can and ought to adopt the stance of theological humanism in thinking about cultural dynamics and social processes. In good humanist style, this is not meant to be a coercive argument which the reader must necessarily accept on pain of some fatal contradiction. Rather than claiming victory in the arena of debate, I seek to articulate a specific option and stance in life and to show its importance and attractiveness.

The point of engaging Todorov and Levinas as representatives of broad intellectual trends is not a matter of convenience. They are fellow travelers, as it were. A viable form of theological thinking in our time should pass through the rigors of debate about the travail and exercise of human power within the vulnerabilities of life. A Christian theological humanist must grapple with the moral arguments of non-religious thinkers, such as

Todorov, and representatives of Jewish thought, like Levinas. Christians have engaged "Greek" and "Jew" throughout history and it is time once again to undertake the work of third way thinking, as I called it in the previous chapter. Of course, one must, eventually, engage other religious and moral traditions.[3] So the chapter serves both methodological and substantive concerns basic to theological humanism. Without a *theological* humanism one risks the reduction of value to human purposes, and, yet, without a theological *humanism* religious convictions are unconstrained by moral purpose. How this double focus differs from other forms of reflection and kinds of humanism will be clear in due course.

2

Theological humanism designates a religious attitude and a moral vision long present among many thinkers in virtually every tradition.[4] As an attitude, it conveys convictions shaped by a specific tradition, say, Christianity, but not confined to the dogmatic strictures and authorities of the religious community. A theological humanist insists on the historical and social embeddedness of thought and conviction. Given that admission, one cannot grasp some abstract thing called "religion" devoid of historical referent. It is more proper, then, to speak of a Christian or a Jewish or even a Buddhist theological humanist. Yet the theological humanist is weary of religious, ethnic, racial "adjectives" that qualify shared existence, especially when they imply exclusive right to moral insight and goodness. She or he joins the company of people who find the language and practices of traditional religious communities, say, the churches, not only forces of profound goodness but also too often obscure, sometimes dangerous and prideful, or simply irrelevant with respect to the pressing matters of life. As a humanist, one believes that moral insight abounds in other traditions and that the company of people of good will is not limited to one's own community and kin.

The attitude of a theological humanist is marked by reflective engagement with and yet distance from one's home tradition. One inhabits one's tradition in a specific way. Mindful of human fallibility, one is reticent to claim exclusive validity for one's own apprehension of religious truths. And if one insists that the human heart and mind, wrapped always in illusion, error, and sin, can nevertheless discern some truths, then no one tradition or community has all knowledge and wisdom. A Christian theological humanist believes that Christ is the savior of the world and that Christianity witnesses to an absolute truth, but as a human being, she or he cannot claim really to know what that absoluteness means for the whole world. For this very reason, a theological humanist insists on isolating the systemic distortions in his or her tradition that are the source of ethical and political lapses found in societies and lives shaped by that tradition. Rather than pinning the evils of the world solely on forces external to the tradition, forces like "modernity" or the "Enlightenment" or the "West," a theological humanist admits and addresses the profound ambiguity of his or her home tradition. Contrary to reactionary and fundamentalist outlooks, theological humanists take a genuinely "critical" attitude towards their tradition.[5]

While the theological humanist takes a genuinely critical stance towards her or his home tradition, it is, nevertheless, a faithful stance within that tradition. Against those critics who see every religious conviction as false consolation and the engine of oppression, or who glibly dismiss spiritual resources for thought, the theological humanist finds the materials of his or her tradition the most relatively adequate means to articulate and answer vexing human dilemmas about how rightly to orient life in the world. Stated otherwise, the theological humanist remains convinced that life is more complex, rich, ambiguous, painful, and wondrous than can be limited to the reach of intrahuman purposes and goods. And this is, of course, just what separates the theological humanist from anti-humanists but also from fellow travelers, namely, non-religious neohumanists. The enterprise of theological humanism represents another option. Neither confined to the walls of the church nor satisfied with overly general ideas about "transcendence," it seeks to articulate and assess human spiritual longings via a critical use of a specific tradition's discourse under the demand to respect and enhance the integrity of life.

These three things – analysis of spiritual longing, a hermeneutics of religious (here: Christian) discourse, and thinking under a specified demand of responsibility – structure the rest of the argument. Prefatory remarks in hand, let us turn to the argument. In order to do so, we need to return to the spiritual longings of the age mentioned before.

3

What is the spiritual longing of our time? In many respects, I will be reflecting on this question and also varying responses to it. Initially, we can say that a shift has occurred in the last decades which is reflected in art, cultural movements, and patterns of thought. In the late twentieth century, the challenge facing many thinkers was to confront and recall the intolerable horror of war and genocide, and then, reflectively speaking, to ask about *the meaning of being* in the light of systematic, rationalized destruction during World War II, the Holocaust, and afterwards? How was it, one asked, that destruction became rationalized in advanced nations to the end of effacing meaning, human life, and our sense of lived reality? It would seem that the task now is less about the meaning of being and much more about the worth of our humanity through encounters with others and our relation to the planet's environment. Matters have decidedly shifted in the direction of ethics. This is why the question of humanism has become so burning. The spiritual question now is about human responsibility for the integrity of life on this planet.

About humanism there is also a noticeable shift. Classical humanists sought to bring philosophy down to earth, that is, to turn reflection from non-human cosmic or divine powers to the struggle for human flourishing. People now find themselves in an age in which other forms of life are being increasingly enfolded into human powers. We are able to make ourselves, other species, and the environment conform to our wishes. This represents the triumph of the *chosen* over the *given*. Some call this apotheosis of human power the "end of nature," that is, the loss of any perception of what is other than the human project and so a contraction of the moral space of existence just to the reach of our power.[6] The complex interaction among realms of life on this planet is threatened through a reduction to purely human purposes. This global endangerment to life engulfs human existence no less than other creatures. We are witnessing the dawning of the posthuman from within the extension of all too human structures of power. The spiritual longing of the age, then, is not a quest for "meaning" but the desire for an "outside," a transcendence, to the human project that liberates from the horror of history. The question, once again, is whether or not and to what extent this "transcendence" is related or limited to intrahuman relations.

In the light of these developments, it is hardly surprising that one can detect a shift in sensibility at the level of cultural flows. From films like *The Matrix* and *Memento* to the eclecticism of postmodern architecture and developments in Internet Art, there are manifold attempts to articulate, understand, and assess the enfolding and encoding of existence within the reach of technological powers. Some artists and thinkers celebrate this fact and advocate forms of cyborg existence, as Donna Haraway has called it. Others, like Erazim Kohák and Hans Jonas as well as poets like Czeslaw Milosz, worry that the extension of human power blunts our sensibility to the ubiquity of value in the world and endangers future life.[7] At the level of cultural artifacts and the leading edge of contemporary thinking, the question of how to grasp and meet the challenge that overhumanization poses to the integrity of life is urgent for our time. This, once again, has made the question of humanism pressing.

Some distinctions are needed. Within the general notion of "overhumanization" we can also isolate distinct but related elements that must be addressed. The first element is admittedly ontological. It centers on the meaning and structure of human freedom or power, that is, the distinctive ability of human beings to shape, respond to, and create reality. The ethical challenge is to expose and limit any form of thought or action that seeks to enfold every form of life within distinctly human purposes. Relatedly, there is, second, an axiological element in the criticism of overhumanization. The claim is that most Western thought has been wantonly anthropocentric. Beginning with the thinking and acting "I" and its projects, others are valued only in relation to this "I." Overhumanization in this respect means the extension of the human kingdom wherein other life-forms, including the divine life, are valued as means to distinctly human ends. For most of human history, reality and human power were practically distinct; cultures could and did view reality from an anthropocentric perspective even though the reach of human power was rather limited. The signal fact of our age is the extension of human power so that it converges with the reach of our valuations. That convergence of reality and the value of power manifest in the concrete structuration of existence is what is meant by the idea of the overhumanization of the world.

The criticism of these axiological and ontological elements of overhumanization is found among most intellectual options in our time, including various anti-humanists, advocates of a "humanism of the other man," and also neohumanists. Briefly put, anti-humanist arguments shift reflection from the action of human beings to examine suprahuman realities, say, social systems or information flows or memes and genes. Anti-humanist positions answer the problem of "transcendence" in terms of these suprahuman forces and the experience of fatedness. The concern of the present chapter is not these arguments. The focus here is squarely on positions that remain humanistic and how these construe the problem of transcendence. Accordingly, I turn now to sort through the developments in neohumanism, presented paradigmatically by Todorov and Levinas. What these positions share and what makes their comparison possible is a concern for *lateral transcendence*, the claim that the "outside" to the kingdom of human power is found in the face of the other, in the "you." A Christian theological humanist must endorse but transform those accounts of transcendence.

4

The spiritual longing of many people in highly reflexive and differentiated societies is for some outside the kingdom of human power. The question is whether or not a person's own actions and relations are a prism for this event of transcendence. In response to this question one can examine two forms of humanism in current discourse. Each of these positions centers on lateral transcendence, that is, the focus on inner-worldly and intrahuman goods.

Neohumanists continue the humanistic project of self-cultivation noted earlier in this book and yet shift the question of the human good from the self to the finality of the "you," as Todorov argues. Concrete other persons and their well-being are the end, the good, or norm of self-cultivation. The most original constituting experience of existence is, then, a striving for wholeness with and for others. On the other hand, advocates of responsibility, like Levinas, begin with the other and not self-cultivation. The command of the other constitutes the self. The constitutive datum of life is boundedness to the other. The event of lateral transcendence, we can say, is from the other to the self rather than from the self to its finality in the you, as it is for Todorov. I will return later to these experiences of *striving* and *boundedness* to ask if they exhaust the root experiences that locate us morally in the world. But, first, what are the features of classical humanism that Todorov seeks to extend and revise and that come under sharp criticism in responsibility ethics and Levinas's humanism of the other man?

Humanism, we know from earlier chapters, is of course notoriously difficult to define. One can trace its lineage back to the Renaissance and the origins of the study of the "humanities" as well as chart the differences between secular, naturalistic, and religious humanists. Todorov has noted that humanists hold that "freedom exists and that it is precious, but at the same time they appreciate the benefit of shared values, life with others, and a self that is held responsible for its actions."[8] One can add to these ideals an awareness of human fallibility and, hence, the demand to test all truth claims by open debate and inquiry. Further, human beings are creatures of aspiration and desire. We are creatures in-between, as noted in Chapter 1. Human life is then always a restless act of self-surpassing aimed at wholeness never fully attainable in time.

The humanist agenda suggests that the point of life is self-cultivation aimed at *eudaimonia* (well-being). At times this agenda has been taken to an extreme. Some humanists have argued for an art of living rather than a morality; they understand philosophy as a way of life, as Pierre Hadot puts it, rather than as an ethics focused on the transcendence of personal interest.[9] Thinkers like Martin Heidegger insist that these extreme positions utterly define humanism and therefore any account of human striving undergirds the "overhumanization of the world." If the nature of human beings is to be a movement, a transcendence, a self-overcoming desire, can humanism ever treasure the given *per se* or must it always and unceasingly champion the chosen, the increase of human power aimed at fulfillment? When the point of life is 'self-cultivation,' what becomes of the radical demand of others upon us or a loving attention to the vulnerability of particular persons. A view of life aimed at self-fulfillment as defined by Aristotle and other classical moralists seems little concerned with the downtrodden, the weak, the vulnerable. As Seneca put it, a sage must make "the effort to rely as much as possible on himself and to derive all delight from himself."[10] Does self-cultivation narrowly and individually understood really define the humanist agenda?

Contemporary thinkers like Todorov are acutely aware of this problem in extreme forms of classical humanism. They insist that respect for the other, the finality of the "you," constrains the wanton extension of human power and so the dominance of the chosen over the given. Todorov is at pains to show that what he calls neohumanism entails more than an art of living; it necessarily entails a morality, the finality of the you, and this is bound to some notion of culture and moral formation. Humanism "marks out the space in which the agents of these [human] acts evolve: the space of all human beings, and of them alone."[11] As one might imagine, Todorov seeks to delimit the place of religious and theological claims within the neohumanist agenda. He admits that "religion remains a possible response to each person's inquiries into his place in the universe or the meaning of life."[12] Yet the force of his argument is to insist that claims about the divine too easily subvert the finality of the human "you" and hold that God is the only end in itself. Religious convictions, on his account, are a kind of anti-humanism because they specify a good other than the concrete "you" as the goal and end of action. Religion is necessarily other-worldly and thereby must be separated from the conduct of human affairs, relegated to the realm of private piety and questions of "meaning." The argument for lateral transcendence is precisely to make this point.

This is a curious argument. Todorov seemingly cannot understand that love of God and love of neighbor are not competing loves. What is more, his reading of "religion" is part and parcel of neohumanism's failure to articulate the source of value or worth. One is supposed to believe that the "you" is self-evidently an end in itself while remaining agnostic about the axiological status of the rest of reality. It is as if the human person is a flashpoint of goodness amid an otherwise value-empty universe. Like much contemporary thought, there is a loss in this argument of any sense of the moral depth of reality, how goodness ingresses in events and relations to infuse life with worth and purpose not reducible to human power.[13] Neohumanism remains inarticulate about the value or worth of the given in its assertion of lateral transcendence. It constrains overhumanization not by way of a perception of the goodness of life, but in terms of respect for the other person built on the idea of equality. That being the case, neohumanism unwittingly joins the project of overhumanization through a constriction of value to intrahuman relations. Why constrain human power if it serves the human as an end in itself?

The insistence on the finality of the "you" moves humanist thought in the direction of responsibility ethics and so towards a humanism of the other man. And yet there are differences. As H. Richard Niebuhr famously put it, the idea of responsibility articulates a vision of human life not in terms of striving for fulfillment or living under laws and duties but in relations of responsiveness and answerability.[14] Responsibility originates not with the self and its aspirations; it arises from the other who confronts one. Recently, Emmanuel Levinas has offered a version of responsibility ethics.[15] He argues that the other person is not met in patterns of mutual interaction and reciprocal answerability. The face of the other places the self in a position of infinite and unquestionable responsibility. As Levinas puts it in one essay, the "meeting with the other person consists in the fact that, despite the extent of my domination over him and his submission, I do not possess him. He does not enter entirely into the opening of being in which I already stand as in the field of my freedom."[16] Responsibility for the other instigates a vision of life different from forms of ethics focused on human flourishing or universalized maxims of action.

The discourse of responsibility suggests that in encountering an undeniable claim of the other, the self is constituted as a moral being. Levinas writes,

> the face is for an *I* – that the face is for me – at once the temptation to kill and the "Thou shalt not kill" which already accuses it, suspects me and forbids it, but already claims me and demands me. The proximity of my fellowman is the responsibility of the *I* for another.[17]

What takes priority is the other and yet within the dynamics of responsibility oneself and one's dignity are also disclosed. This is why, presumably, Levinas speaks about a "humanism of the other." Moral matters take precedence over epistemic and ontological concerns. Oddly enough, ethics as first philosophy can make no truth claim nor specify what constitutes human flourishing and well-being since truth and well-being require ontological specification.

Despite the rigor of Levinas's ethics, his humanism of the other is, unlike neohumanism, open to religious transcendence. God is a "trace" in the encounter with the face of the other. As he notes,

> I cannot describe the relation to God without speaking of my concern for the other. ... In my relation to the other, I hear the Word of God. It is not a metaphor; it is not only extremely important, it is literally true. I am not saying that the other is God, but that in his or her Face I hear the Word of God.[18]

The ethical encounter is the prism for the appearance of the divine. The ethical is not the condition for the postulates of God and immortality, as Immanuel Kant might put it. Rather, the ethical is the place for hearing the Word of God. Do we not have once again, although in more subtle form, constriction of moral space of life to the intrahuman? The event of the Word of God in Levinas's ethics does not transform or expand the moral universe to all forms of life; it merely confirms the primacy of the encounter with the human other. The ethics remains anthropocentric even as it escapes egocentrism. If we are to respond in an adequate way to the sensibility of the age and thus address the challenge of overhumanization to the integrity of life, surely more needs to be said about non-human life.[19]

5

On first blush it seems that "humanism" and "responsibility" designate in shorthand terms two fundamentally opposed outlooks on human life. Humanists are interested in the cultivation of freedom and natural capacities with the aim of fulfillment and flourishing accountable to the "you." Conversely, Levinas and other advocates of infinite responsibility focus on the unquestioned demand of the other on self; they begin with the "you" rather than the "I." This would seem a more radical claim about what constitutes our humanity than the insistence by other neohumanists on respect for the other, the finality of the you. However, it is precisely on this point about responsibility and the givenness of the other person that there opens an insight crucial for the project of theological humanism. This insight emerges once we isolate a weakness within these positions.

Neohumanists and advocates of radical responsibility despite their differences have both addressed what I called the ontological and axiological elements of overhumanization. Todorov and Levinas, if we take them as fair representatives of these movements, seek to limit the extension of human power, the domination of the given by the chosen, by revising or undercutting inherited beliefs about human beings as agents and also the value we place on human selfhood. Todorov rejects what he calls a prideful perversion of humanism in claims that nature must become subservient to human want. However, the limitation on human power arises not from within claims about the worth of finite life as such but from the finality of the other person, the you. Todorov shifts traditional humanistic argument, like Seneca's, from the moral priority of the "I" and self-cultivation to the "you." He understands the self in terms of a moral project. Yet this begs the question. Why should the "you" matter? Why does "lateral transcendence," the self-overcoming of personal interest in the recognition of the finality of the "you," bestow worth? Does the worth it bestows reach beyond the human kingdom? These questions are not addressed. Todorov would have us imagine that human worth, the finality of the you, is self-evident. Surely that claim is naïve and dangerous in an age of overhumanization.

For his part, Levinas labors mightily to provide a phenomenology of the good of the other, the good manifest in lateral transcendence. He challenges the entire legacy of "ontology" as simply a "philosophy of the same" driven by what he calls "totality." The discourse of responsibility as he deploys it is meant to provide a contrasting account of human existence. The face of the other, the manifestation of "infinity," breaks the totalizing drive of the thinking I with a good beyond being. Totality as an expression of overhumanization is undercut on both its ontological and axiological levels. In this respect, Levinas provides an account of the worth of the "you," its finality, merely assumed by Todorov.

Here too one can raise questions. Levinas reduces "ethics" to the unquestioned demand of the other on self. This demand, moreover, is void of cognitive content as well as direct reference to actual human needs and capacities that might provide content to what we mean by the "good." A full and robust account of the complexity of moral choice is missing or else it is relegated to the sphere of politics. There are no degrees of responsibility insofar as "responsibility" denotes a constitutive encounter rather than a moral project. That cannot be right. In fact, that idea of responsibility is dangerous in a world in which there are massive differences in access to and the use of structures of power. In this light the insights of neohumanists seem on the mark. We can and must make distinctions about degrees of responsibility. There must be some way to speak of the formation or cultivation of responsibility within a robust account of agency.

Under the pressure of overhumanization various humanists have revised their tradition in the direction of the finality of the "you" and thereby limited the *chosen* from within the *given*. Yet I have suggested that the finality of the "you" remains more an assertion than an argument insofar as the source of worth of the "you," its goodness, is hardly explored. That question is precisely where advocates of radical responsibility like Levinas begin. He explores a good manifest in the face of the other. In this way he too wants to undercut overhumanization or what he calls "totality." Beyond the pale of reflection is precisely what interests every humanist, namely, the formation of life, the way of education, with respect to a robust account of flourishing. As Todorov notes, "[m]en are not good but can become so: that is the most general meaning of this [educational] process, of which scholarly instruction is merely a small part."[20]

In the age of overhumanization one must relate responsibility and humanism in order to present a robust and satisfying vision of the moral and religious life. One needs to articulate the claim of moral worth on us, specify the non-reducibility of the goodness of the given other person to the power of the chosen, and also provide an account for moral formation. At the core of these concerns is the debate about transcendence. Is it possible to articulate a root experience that situates human beings in the world not just in terms of striving or obedience but within an event of the ingression of goodness that permeates and empowers human life? How is it, again, that one best speaks to the spiritual longing of the age? Having engaged other humanistic thinkers around that question, I now turn to the enterprise of theological humanism.

6

A contemporary response to overhumanization requires some claim about the finality of the you beyond classical humanism and eudaimonistic ethics with their limited focus on the good of self-cultivation. Further, an adequate ethics must explore the formation of our sense of responsibility and specify degrees of accountability. I have tried to clarify this double demand by reading Todorov and Levinas in and through each other's arguments. Were space allowed, it would be possible to outline an ethics of responsibility that includes a multidimensional account of human flourishing, the forma-tion of conscience, and yet also a stringent demand to respect and enhance the integrity of life, the finality of the you.[21] But for the sake of the present argument, I forgo those matters to focus instead on a point that neohuman-ists like Levinas and Todorov share. It is a point that relates and yet also differentiates theological humanism from those positions.

Despite their profound differences, advocates of Levinasian responsibil-ity ethics and various neohumanists – not only Todorov but others like Martha Nussbaum as well – insist that "lateral transcendence" is enough to answer the challenge of overhumanization. Yet given the neohumanist emphasis on lateral transcendence, it is unclear how and under what prin-ciple one would limit the extension of human power, especially if it serves the well-being of others. If the human other is a virtual replacement for God, why limit human power aimed at flourishing? To be sure, in Levinas's account of lateral transcendence the face of the other as the place of the Word of God radically curtails the extension of human power. Yet the appearance of the Word of God does not transform or expand the moral space of life beyond the encounter of self and human other. Insisting on "lateral transcendence" preserves the dignity and centrality of the concrete other person too easily lost in anti-humanist responses to the dynamics of overhumanization. Oddly enough, the arguments of neohumanists return anew, perhaps unwittingly, to the kingdom of human power. At the core of this paradox is the problem of transcendence, the self-overcoming of human freedom from within itself. How ought we to proceed in fashioning a way of thought and life to meet the challenges of the day?

The force of the arguments for lateral transcendence is to contend that something is awry if one aims at God through relations with other people.

Every humanist believes that human beings are ends in themselves and not means to some other end, even the end of God and God's glory. This is why neohumanists like Todorov relegate religion to private questions about life's meaning, and it is why, according to Levinas, God is a trace within the encounter with the face of the other. The point is well taken. It is, in fact, endorsed by theological humanism. It is why I have passed through the rigors of current versions of humanism. That passage will mean that theological ideas are transformed from within the practical challenges now facing people around the world.[22]

While insisting on the human good, there is a difference that marks theological humanism. This difference arises in terms of what is grasped as the most originary experience that situates us morally in the world. Neohumanists, I have argued, isolate that originary experience as *striving* for wholeness under the finality of the you. A Levinasian-like humanism of responsibility for the other focuses, contrariwise, on the *boundedness* of self before the command of the other. Each of these positions articulates those originary experiences in terms of their account of lateral transcendence. Theological humanism strikes out in another direction, to insist on a more complex account of transcendence, because it seeks to specify a different originary experience that locates us in the world as moral and spiritual creatures. This account centers on the ambiguity of human longing, our loves and search for integrity marked by the remembrance of death and the love of life. In order to grasp this point we must examine that ambiguity and how theologically to articulate its meanings.

The poet Czeslaw Milosz has put the matter pointedly in one essay: "If I believed that man can do good under his own powers, I would have no interest in Christianity. But he cannot, because he is enslaved to his own predatory, domineering instincts, which we may call *proprium*, or self-love, or the Specter."[23] One can easily imagine the resources of other religions making the same point; this insight about human weakness within power is not the treasure of Christianity alone. A realistic assessment of human existence must admit that neither self nor other, I nor you, can within human power answer the dilemma of power. The paradox of human existence is that we cannot from within ourselves answer the challenge of our existence. Nor can the other, the you, answer it for us. The Specter, the *proprium*, predatory instincts (call it what you will) lace every human life, including the life of the other man. There is a vulnerability within human power, the vulnerability to its own self-destruction as well as being the place for the ingression of worth not its own.[24] This is precisely why there is a longing for an outside to human power within the global expansion of overhumanization. This longing is indirectly manifest in the art, literature, and architecture now appearing within high-modern, reflexive cultures.

The event of lateral transcendence, the sensibility that the integrity of the other person is an end to be respected and enhanced, always exhausts itself if it does not empower one to do good in an act of self-overcoming. This exhaustion is just what we should expect from human beings, the fragments that we are. It is why an overhumanized world is increasingly less humane and more violent. Todorov, as far as I can see, avoids the ambiguity of human power. He actually believes, against evidence, that we can do good under our own power. That is the wager, as he calls it, of neohumanist thought. Levinas for his part circumvents the doubleness that arises in human existence by insisting that the command of the other is at the origin of the self. To hear the command is to have the ability to respond. Ought implies can, as Kant might put it. However, Kant was wise enough to confront the specter of radical evil that arises from within human freedom. The self-endangerment of human power is well known. It is what, realistically considered, requires that the ethical, responsibility with and for the other, remain basic in thought and life. It is also the reason one must chasten praise of later transcendence. As noted in a previous chapter, at the very origins of responsibility is the remembrance of death – the sense of human vulnerability to powers that limit our striving and our love of life. This seems to be Levinas's point about responsibility for the other who is vulnerable to our power and in whose face is uttered a claim to be respected and enhanced: do not murder me.

The travail of human evil is not the whole story about the ambiguity of human longing. It is not the only reason to challenge the reduction of human transcendence to lateral transcendence. One actually can and often does confront another arresting fact about the vulnerability of power. What are we to make of the fact that sometimes goodness appears in the world? Astonishingly enough, too little theology and too few ethics actually explore the surprising event of goodness in the world felt in our own love of life and the possibility of goodness within the fragility of life. When, in fact, an encounter with others empowers responsibility with and for others, then some power otherwise than human is manifestly present. Goodness appears in the world under its own capacity. This appearance is not configured as the goal of human striving, the *summum bonum*, nor manifest under the form of a command before the vulnerability of the face of the other. It appears in and through the transformation of existence and power to do good. The depth of humanity, for a theological humanist, is to dwell and act within those events and thereby imitate nothing less than the divine. And like the reality of *spiritual conviction*, explored in Chapter 3, so too this experience arises in our lives in and through the interweaving of the remembrance of death and the love of life that characterizes human existence, dust that breathes. A new symbolics of the good is needed that is just as subtle as the engagement with evil that marked so much twentieth-century thought. Acts of responsibility, actual moments of justice, are the real symbolism of the good; they are the *imitatio dei*.

Any grasp of the meaning of our lives is always through the interpretation of figurative expressions of existence. For many theologies of the last century, that "figurative expression" was emblematically seen in symbols and art and the biblical narrative around questions of meaning. Under the conditions of overhumanization, the figuration of the human dilemma is manifest in the vulnerability but also predatory impulses of human power. The theological humanist has a realistic grasp of propensities to evil and yet dares to examine appearances of goodness as a constitutive fact of human existence. This is the ethical transformation of theology required in our time.[25] Theological discourse remains necessary and resonant in order to avoid inarticulacy about the reach of transcendence and a reduction of thinking to a moralistic demand. Stated boldly, in the age of overhumanization, the appearance of the capacity to do good that overturns the celebration and limitless expansion of the human kingdom simply is the experience of God. The most originary experience of being in the world cannot be just about fulfillment or obligation or fatedness; it is and must be about the divine manifested in the power to do good, a primal yes-saying or gratitude for life.

The experience of *empowerment* is not aiming at God through other persons, despite what Todorov and Levinas might think. It is to grasp the working of the divine in and through the ambiguity of human power and the extent of moral relations. To grasp this fact is to situate a humanistic project within a theological circle. At the core of a viable theology for the present age is not the striving of self-cultivation under the finality of the you, nor is it boundedness to the unquestionable command of the other. At the core of theological humanism is the event of *gratitude* for and even *joy* over the power to respect and enhance the integrity of life manifest within the vulnerability of human power. It is the empowerment to act with and for others despite the ambiguity of human power. As ancient Christian writers put it, God does not save us without us. The appearance of the divine goodness is in and through the ambiguity of human freedom and the task of cultivating responsible existence.

In the end, a theological humanist must simply reject the terms of the debate about human transcendence that circulates among anti-humanists, neohumanists, and humanists of the other man. One does so out of a profound realism about the essential ambiguity of human power, instinct, and longing. A theological humanist also rejects the terms of the debate because they do not articulate appearances of the power to do good that can and do permeate our inner-worldly relations. It is the profound inarticulacy about the empowerment of goodness that leaves our spiritual longing unmet in an age of global cultural flows and overhumanization. Do we not want an originary experience of empowerment that transforms our lives beyond the weary despair and anomie about us? It is here that the theological humanist necessarily turns, in appreciation and critique, to the resources of a religious tradition in order to articulate the meaning and truth of these appearances of moral capacitation. For a Christian theological humanist, this would involve the complex relation of creation and redemption, incarnation and resurrection, a set of convictions, in other words, about the vulnerabilities of finite life but also the power to do good. These resources show that the originary structure of lived existence is missed if one focuses just on boundedness to the demands of the other or the striving for fulfillment under the finality of the you. Responsibility and flourishing arise out of and are empowered by gratitude for the infusing of finite life with the *power to do good*, the moral capacity for goodness. But as a maxim: ought implies thanks as the transcendent intentionality of can, of human capacity. Responsibility is rooted and made possible, for the Christian theological humanist, in gratitude, and this gratitude and responsibility intend, are appearances of, the divine presence among us.

Other traditions, I imagine, have equally complex modes of articulation. The point is that one can and must deploy theological resources to give an account of what suffuses but always escapes the reach of human power. There are sufficient warrants to adopt theological humanism as a compelling and satisfying outlook on and stance within life. This outlook and stance contend that without a complex *theological* humanism, one risks the reduction of value to intrahuman purposes. Yet it is equally true that without a theological *humanism*, religious convictions are unconstrained by moral purpose and fail to answer the longing of the age.

7

Developing a complete theology and ethics is obviously beyond the scope of this book. My effort in this chapter has been more modest. It has been to suggest and even show why theological thinking must engage cultural dynamics and social processes in order to understand and respond to this age. I have also argued for the perspective from which to engage in that task of thinking. The normative stance can and ought to be theological humanism. The possibility of this enterprise, the warrant for its adoption as a distinctive form of humanism, arises from the insight that an original experience of existence cannot be articulated in terms of fatedness before the agency of suprapersonal forces, striving in self-cultivation for wholeness, or even obedience to a heteronomous command of the other. For the theological humanist, an originary experience of existence is the appearance of the capacity to do good from within the ambiguity of human power which issues forth in gratitude for life.

Notes

1 See Régis Debray, *Transmitting Culture*, trans. Eric Rauth (New York: Columbia University Press, 2000).

2 Tzvetan Todorov, *Imperfect Garden: The Legacy of Humanism* (Princeton, NJ: Princeton University Press, 2002), p. 5. Also see R. William Franklin and Joseph M. Shaw, *The Case for Christian Humanism* (Grand Rapids, MI: Eerdmans, 1991); and Salvatore Puledda, *On Being Human: Interpretations of Humanism from the Renaissance to the Present*, trans. Andrew Hurley, with foreword by Mikhail Gorbachev (San Diego, CA: Latitude Press, 1997). Likewise, see Emmanuel Levinas, *Entre Nous: On Thinking-of-the-Other*, trans. Michael B. Smith and Barbara Harshaw (New York: Columbia University Press, 1998). Also see Paul Mendes-Flohr, "A Postmodern Humanism from the Sources of Judaism," *Criterion* 41:2 (2002), 18–23.

3 For a resource to begin to undertake that task see *A Companion to Religious Ethics*, ed. William Schweiker (Oxford: Blackwell Publishing, 2004).

4 While forms of intolerance, fundamentalism, and appeals to "orthodoxy" and traditional structures of power are widespread in the religions, there are nevertheless some in every tradition who adopt something like what I am calling "theological humanism." Think of so-called "Critical Buddhism" as well as progressive voices in Judaism, Hinduism, and Islam. Among Christians, the critical and yet devout conviction of Black, third world, and feminist thinkers has concerns analogous to those of theological humanism.

5 Current Christian theology is rife with thinkers and movements who seek to exempt Christian communities from the moral and political failures of the wider society. Obviously, a theological humanist adopts a decidedly different attitude towards the home tradition. For a summary discussion see Alister E. McGrath, *The Future of Christianity* (Oxford: Blackwell, 2002).

6 The term was made famous by Bill McKibben in his book *The End of Nature* (New York: Doubleday, 1989). For a recent attempt within postmetaphysical thinking to delimit the triumph of the chosen see Jürgen Habermas, *Die Zukunft der menschlichen Natur: Auf dem Weg zu einer liberalen Eugenik?* (Frankfurt: Suhrkamp, 2001), also published as *The Future of Human Nature* (Cambridge: Polity, 2003). Also see Francis Fukuyama, *Our Posthuman Future: Consequences of the Biotechnology Revolution* (New York: Picador, 2002).

7 See Donna J. Haraway, *Simians, Cyborgs, and Women: The Reinvention of Nature* (New York: Routledge, 1991); Erazim Kohák, *The Embers and the Stars: An Inquiry into the Moral Sense of Nature* (Chicago: University of Chicago Press, 1984); Hans Jonas, *The Imperative of Responsibility: In Search of an Ethics for the Technological Age* (Chicago: University of Chicago Press, 1984); and Czeslaw Milosz, *To Begin Where I Am: Selected Essays*, ed. with intro. by B. Carpenter and M. G. Levine (New York: Farrar, Straus & Giroux, 2001). Also see William Schweiker, *Power, Value and Conviction: Theological Ethics in the Postmodern Age* (Cleveland, OH: Pilgrim Press, 1998).

8 Todorov, *Imperfect Garden*, p. 5.

9   Pierre Hadot, *Philosophy as a Way of Life: Spiritual Exercises from Socrates to Foucault*, trans. Michael Chase, ed. and intro. Arnold I. Davidson (Oxford: Blackwell, 1995).

10   Seneca, "Consolation to Helvia," in *Seneca: Dialogues and Letters*, ed. and trans. C. D. N. Costa (New York: Penguin, 1997), p. 6.

11   Todorov, *Imperfect Garden*, p. 30.

12   Todorov, *Imperfect Garden*, p. 36.

13   For a profound phenomenological analysis of the ingression of goodness see Kohák, *The Embers and the Stars*. For a theological account of these matters see James M. Gustafson, *A Sense of the Divine: The Natural Environment from a Theocentric Perspective* (Cleveland, OH: Pilgrim Press, 1994).

14   H. Richard Niebuhr, *The Responsible Self: An Essay in Christian Moral Philosophy*, intro. James M. Gustafson and preface by William Schweiker, Library of Theological Ethics (Louisville, KY: Westminster John Knox Press, 1999).

15   I have tried elsewhere to chart the various forms of ethics linked to the idea of responsibility. See William Schweiker, "Disputes and Trajectories in Responsibility Ethics," *Religious Studies Review* 27:1 (2001), 18–24.

16   See Emmanuel Levinas, "Is Ontology Fundamental?" in *Entre Nous*, p. 9. Also see his *Otherwise than Being or Beyond Essence*, trans. Alphonso Lingis (Boston: Kluwer, 1991).

17   Levinas, "The Philosophical Determination of the Idea of Culture," in *Entre Nous*, p. 186.

18   Levinas, "Philosophy, Justice, and Love," in *Entre Nous*, p. 110.

19   For a fine discussion of this point that remains humanistic see Erazim Kohák, *The Green Halo: A Bird's-Eye View of Ecological Ethics* (LaSalle, IL: Open Court, 2000).

20   Todorov, *Imperfect Garden*, p. 233.

21   I have tried to develop such a position elsewhere. See William Schweiker, *Responsibility and Christian Ethics* (Cambridge: Cambridge University Press, 1995).

22   I might note that the practical revision of basic theological claims is not only deeply Christian, it is also typically Protestant in character. In this respect, my argument is a Protestant account of theological humanism. But I make this argument not out of an unquestioned fidelity to tradition. I tend to believe that every religion now living on the world scene must pass through a profound moral reformation in order to thwart ongoing religious violence. In this respect, *semper reformanda* is a demand facing everyone. The stance of that "reforming," I am claiming, must be both religious and humanistic, hence theological humanism.

23   Milosz, *To Begin Where I Am*, p. 327.

24   The nature of human fallibility has been extensively explored by Paul Ricoeur. See, for instance, his *Fallible Man*, revised translation by Walter Lowe (New York: Fordham University Press, 1986), and also *The Symbolism of Evil*, trans. E. Buchanan (New York: Harper and Row, 1967). For a recent engagement with Ricoeur's ethics see *Paul Ricoeur and Contemporary Moral Thought*, ed. J. Wall, W. Schweiker, and W. D. Hall (New York: Routledge, 2002).

25   Many of Paul Tillich's works could be noted, but one should especially see the famous "Über die Idee einer Theologie der Kultur," in *Religionsphilosophie der Kultur*, 2nd edn, ed. G. Radburch and P. Tillich (Darmstadt: Wissenschaftliche Buchgesellschaft, 1958), pp. 29–52. In this essay Tillich notes that what he calls "theology of culture" was originally named "theological ethics." I am, in effect, transforming the theology of culture through a retrieval and revision of its original ethical impulse. On this see William Schweiker, "Hermeneutics, Ethics, and the Theology of Culture: Concluding Reflections," in *Meanings in Texts and Actions: Questioning Paul Ricoeur*, ed. David E. Klemm and William Schweiker (Charlottesville: University Press of Virginia, 1993), pp. 292–313.

Chapter 6
The Christ of Christian Humanism*

1

In the long career of the Christian tradition there have always been individuals who have with care and deliberation sought to live at the intersections between biblical faith and non-biblical patterns of thought and life. Their lives were crisscrossed with multiple identities woven into an integral form of life. Sometimes called "apologists," like the great ancient Christian thinkers Justin Martyr and Clement of Alexandria, by the time of the Reformation and Renaissance they are called "humanists," partly because they sought to link the simplicity of the Gospel with the best of ancient learning. In our own time, the same aspiration has been called the reality of the "third man." Dominated neither by forms of Greek thought, to which the Christian message was proclaimed, nor by the circle of Hebraic life, from which the Gospel arose, this "third man," the philosopher Paul Ricoeur once noted, "this cultivated Christian, this believing Greek, is ourselves."[1] The reflections that follow stand squarely within this long, if now neglected, strand of Christian thought and life. As noted in the previous chapter, this will require a bit of digging into the history of Christian humanism. However, my overall purpose is more constructive than historical. I aim to clarify a form of life, an identity and way of being Christian, that is internally complex and yet integrated by devotion to what respects and enhances the integrity of life before the living God. This chapter focused on Christ thereby mirrors Chapters 1–2 on the question of Christian identity.

* This chapter was first published as "Flesh and Folly: The Christ of Christian Humanism," in *Who is Jesus Christ for Us Today?* Festschrift for Michael Welker, ed. A. Schuele and Günter Thomas (Louisville, KY: Westminster John Knox Press, 2009), pp. 85–102. Copyright William Schweiker.

Dust that Breathes, by William Schweiker © William Schweiker 2010.

Beginning in the fourteenth century in Italy, especially with certain forms of neo-Platonism, and then spreading to northern Europe, leading humanist thinkers helped to shape theology, education, rhetoric, and classical studies. The heart of the classical "humanist" agenda was the "humanities," which were organized around a vision of education coupled with the concern to reclaim classic texts – including the Bible – on the perfectibility of human life rooted in human potentialities.[2] It would be delightful to trace the work of various humanists (Petrarch, Erasmus, Pico, Melanchthon, Colet, More, Leonardo Bruni, and others) and their engagement with classical sources (Plato, Cicero, Lucian, etc.). It would also be important in a more extended inquiry to explore the immense impact of these thinkers on a wide array of literary forms and scholarly disciplines. That is not possible in this book.

These historical details are mentioned at the outset in order to note that I am trying to grasp basic ideas and develop leading concepts rather than provide a strictly historical account of Christian humanist thinking about Christ. I would like my argument to be judged on its theological and ethical merit rather than in terms of historical depth or accuracy. I am concerned to persuade you to adopt a specific outlook now possible and needed within the Christian community in order to avoid some of the problems now beset-ting religious people in our global times. I am also trying to show the energy and progressive force of ideas buried deep within the Christian tradition in a time when, it must be said, we suffer from cultural and religious exhaus-tion. So, I am using historical sources not to recover the past but, rather, to release potentials for the future orienting of life.

If truth be told, I am not too concerned in the pages that follow to advance Christological reflection in any technical sense of the word. Using an idea that I learned from Michael Welker, a theologian should never enter into the thicket of a specific doctrine or topic until he or she has some clarity about what might be said. To do otherwise is to risk falling unwittingly into false abstractions. Of course, work in Christology is without doubt important for Christian theology. Yet it is one task among many, usually the domain of the dogmatic theologian, and it does not necessarily specify the *point* of theological inquiry. My hope is to avoid the theologian's sin while also trying to further the legacy of Christian humanism in our troubled age. Insofar as a Christian humanist is a *Christian*, what can and must and may one say about Christ?

The non-dogmatic and practical tenor of this book enacts the stance of most Christian humanists. Our worry is that doctrinal considerations too easily degenerate into scholastic gamesmanship and thereby create invidious divisions among Christians. Likewise, the drive to doctrine is often moti-vated by a quest for certainty that denies humility about human capacities to know the truth, a kind of humility, even skepticism, which ought to characterize followers of Christ. The sin of a theologian from this perspective is not only to revel in false abstractions, but to formulate Christian convictions in ways that thwart the purpose and point of the Christian life. Put differently, Christian humanists see faith more as a way of life than a set of beliefs. The *point* of thinking is to aid in the lifelong task of conforming existence to Christ's love rather than to fashion new Christological formulations.

Theology is not an end in itself. It is a means. The aim, point, or purpose of thought is to understand and orient life. As a recent account of Christian humanism has put it, three themes have usually dominated this outlook on life and faith, themes that arise from the belief "that God in Christ has visited the habitation of the human race."[3] The themes include: first, the fact that in Christ the individual is saved from isolation and made the body of a living community; second, the awareness, basic to my argument below, that faith in the incarnation means that all finite existence – the earth, our bodies, daily objects of human use – can be the means for the work of the divine spirit among us; and, third, the idea, basic to this book, that true human freedom and perfection are found in faithful love towards Christ and the neighbor.[4] Taken together, these themes, and others as well, are why Christian humanists have always been drawn to politics and ethics and education or, as it is sometimes called, practical Christianity.

The specific task of this chapter is to reflect on the Christ of Christian humanism in and through interlocking levels of inquiry already anticipated. First, I set the problem of my reflection in terms of the reluctance of Christian humanists to engage in heavy dogmatic reflection given their practical conception of Christian faith. What then can be said about Christ by a Christian humanist? In order to answer that question, the second level of reflection isolates important depictions or images of Christ found in classical Christian humanist discourse. One image is the fully incarnate, fleshly, Christ. Because of the flesh of Christ, human bodiliness, comic or grotesque, falls within theological consideration. The Christ of Christian humanism is a response to mortality inscribed in human life, that we are dust that breathes. Yet, second, we also find Christ as fool who confounds the wisdom of the "world." Humility, we must say, is a profound good for Christian humanists. And this is because whatever we mean by "sin" it must entail a denial of our creaturehood, a denial of our dust, in ways that pit life against life, human beings against each other and against the living God. To reflect on flesh and folly as attributes of Christ is, therefore, to explore the bonds of death and sin that plague human existence. The wisdom that can and ought to guide life upends, disturbs, our usual standards of thought even as it exposes the limits of human insight and knowledge and heals the wound of existence – our bondage to sin and death – and so redeems the love of life.

In the third level of reflection I hope to reconstruct classical claims about Christ for the sake of a contemporary expression of Christian humanism. This account must make good sense of Christian faith, but it must also be practically viable within our world where life is endangered and conflict, often violent, rages among ideologies and religions. The cornerstone of reconstruction centers on how one understands the formation and importance of Christian *identity*. The force of Christian humanism is that one's identity as an incarnate but fallible creature exceeds any one description, and, further, must be oriented beyond itself towards life with and for others.[5] Christian humanism, and Christ as the Word in flesh that is folly, means that one cannot pit Christian identity against other block-like descriptions of human beings, like "pagan" or "Muslim" or "sinner." Any actual human existence is a complex relation among identities, some exceedingly broad (I am a human being who laughs, bleeds, and will die) and some more specific (I am a member of this congregation of the United Methodist Church in the USA, a father to my son, and so on). In our time, Christian humanism wants to show that Christians can and may and must decide in specific situations which identity ought to have priority in order thereby to respect and enhance the integrity of life. In some contexts, it is shared humanity that must take pride of place; in other situations more particular ecclesial, social, linguistic, gendered, racial identities can and ought to come to the fore.

St Paul grasped the insight, it seems to me.

> For though I am free with respect to all, I have made myself a slave to all so that I might win more of them. To the Jews I became as a Jew in order to win Jews. To those under the law I became as one under the law (though I myself am not under the law) that I might win those under the law. (I Cor. 9:19–20)

Paul goes on to insist that he became outside of the law for those outside the law, became weak for the weak, and so "became all things to all people" that some might be saved. If the aim or point of Christian existence is the labor of love for others in conformity to Christ, then, Paul suggests, it is possible to stress or emphasize some of one's identity (Jew, Gentile, weak, free – Paul was all of these) in specific situations. Christian existence is not mono-dimensional, defined by just one description – even the description "Christian" – because it is oriented beyond self. And that is just the point of Christian humanism. We will see this means seeing *Christ as the conscience of God*. The labor of human conscience, the call to faithful labor on our moral identities for orienting life, is thus the focal point for the Christian humanist because of who Christ is and what he does.

2

The connection between Christ and humanity in Christian faith is of course neither new nor surprising. It is not surprising since Christians have always confessed Christ to be savior, and, accordingly, that he must be truly human. "What he has not assumed," Athanasius, the so-called Father of Orthodoxy, insisted, "he cannot save." That is also why the connection between Christ and humanity is not new in Christian theology. It is, in some way, at the very origin and core of the Christian witness.

Of course, how Christians *ought* to think about Christ's relation to our fallible and fault-ridden humanity is constantly debated. For some the incarnation of the eternal Word is the focus of attention; others center on the crucified and risen Christ. One can explore the presence of Christ in the Eucharist or concentrate theological inquiry on the eschatological, coming Christ. For theologians, especially classical Protestants, interested in moral and political questions, the various titles for Christ – prophet, priest, king – have been used to understand Christian existence. Others have linked Christ to the development of the so-called theological virtues, among Catholic thinkers, or, more recently, to liberation from various forms of oppression. It is hardly surprising, then, that the renowned Church historian, Jaroslov Pelikan, could write a book titled *Jesus Through the Centuries* in which he traces the many different ways Christ has been understood and imagined: Rabbi, King of Kings, Cosmic Christ, Bridegroom of the soul, Prince of peace, and so on.[6] There appears to be no end to the reflection, especially as Christian communities around the world seek to understand and inhabit their faith in new and distinctive ways outside the dominance of European modes of thought. We witness an endless proliferation of Christological thinking. Christ as the one who is believed, the object of deepest trust and loyalty, is also the one whose identity and work constantly spark thought and imagination about the divine and the meaning of existence.

The relation of Christ to humanity, that Christ is "true man" as well as "true God" (to use the creedal formulation), is important for any form of properly *Christian* humanism. For a long time there have also been within Eastern and Western Christianity ways to speak of the "humanity of God." This language arises within the Christian tradition when the incarnation of God in Christ, the event of God becoming human, is taken as central to Christian thought and life. As Thomas Merton once wrote, "True Christian humanism is the full flowering of the theology of the Incarnation." Even Karl Barth, late in his career, spoke of the "humanity of God," the decision of God to be God for us in Christ. In the revival of Orthodox theology in the twentieth century, especially among Russians, *bogochelovechestvo*, or

Godmanhood, was central. It was a way to rethink and reclaim the Orthodox idea of *theosis.*[7] Similar ideas are found elsewhere. Classic Greek religion sought to humanize the gods, often portraying the deities in all too human ways but with the message that human excellence is the point of life. In Buddhism, Hinduism, and other "religions" there have always been personifications of deities and their relations to human beings.

Without entering comparative theology, it must be admitted that there is a difference between (say) Barth's formulation of "the humanity of God" and Merton's kind of "Christian humanism." For Barth and many Orthodox theologians what matters is that God *became* human in Christ; a theological, and not humanistic, point is at stake, even if it carries profound human import. The Christian humanist, it seems to me, hardly denies the theological claim but wants to attend to the human import. As an outlook and orientation in life, Christian humanism uses the distinctive claims and speculative resources of a tradition in order to articulate a specific way of human life. Yet a Christian humanist also hopes to find points of contact with other people who share similar aspirations and convictions. So while one draws from the Christian tradition, one does not write only for Christians. Of course, some Christians find this a betrayal of what is uniquely Christian and many humanists will hardly see the relevance of theological claims for human existence. Part of the argument of this book is to stave off charges of betrayal and irrelevance while holding fast to the main concern to present the Christ of Christian humanism.

Here then is the first question any Christian humanist must answer. Why the reluctance to insist on doctrinal uniformity about what is obviously the core of Christian faith? Why insist on the un-ending task of interpreting Christian claims about Christ rather than seeking to achieve creedal clarity? The question is longstanding. In one of the most famous disputes over Christian humanism, Luther attacked Erasmus for seeming unwilling to make "assertions." In his *The Bondage of the Will,* Luther muses that it is Erasmus's charitable bent of mind and love of peace that keeps him from making assertions. But, Luther continues,

> To take no pleasure in assertions is not the mark of a Christian heart; indeed one must delight in assertions to be a Christian at all. ... Away, now, with Sceptics and Academics from the company of us Christians; let us have men who will assert, men twice as inflexible as very Stoics![8]

Luther's charge is that Erasmus is finally a skeptic who fails to see that Christian faith requires clarity of conviction and confession. One must draw a boundary around Christian existence in and through the confession of the Gospel. Of course, the core of Luther's treatise is the question of the freedom or bondage of the will, the point (no doubt) of greatest dispute between him and Erasmus. We will return to the question of freedom later. At this juncture what emerges is precisely the reason for suspicion of "assertions" among Christian humanists.

The clue to an answer lies in Luther's grasp of a specific bent of mind and also the good of peace for a Christian humanist. If one understands the Christian confession of Christ, that is, God's identification with the human lot, then precisely because of that confession and because of the human condition it is neither proper nor possible to circumscribe Christian identity within one description. What prohibits a Christian in the full freedom of her or his faith from learning along with the Academics (Thomas Aquinas did)? Why not find common ground between Stoic insights and Christian faith (many of the Church Fathers did)? If God is flexible with us, why not be flexible with others? In other words, the Christian humanist's reticence to use the clarity of "assertions" to draw unbridgeable boundaries between human beings arises from the belief that in those cases "assertions" are contrary to Christ's way and word. The astonishing claim of Christian faith is that the God of all reality is related to, identified with, human flesh and folly, and, therefore, things human and things divine must be included in the embrace of Christian faith. It is the scope of the divine embrace and the bond of shared humanity that are the *point* of Christian assertions rather than those assertions defining the boundary marker that sets Christians over-against others.

One way to understand Christian humanism's reluctance to insist on doctrinal uniformity is to see that the point of faith is charity and not clarity; the tenets of faith find their perfection in the life of love. Nestled in that idea, I am suggesting, are also some claims about the nature of Christian identity deeply rooted in beliefs about God's action in Christ, and also of human existence itself. If we are to understand the "Christ" of Christian humanism, we must then turn from debates within dogmatic theology to the actual picture of Christ developed among Christian humanists. I focus next on ideas or images or metaphors (variously used by different thinkers) among classical Christian humanists, namely, those of "flesh" and "folly."

3

The use of the ideas of flesh and folly in order to think about who Christ is and what he does is drawn from a wide array of Christian humanist discourses. These ideas are by no means the only terms used to speak of Christ. Yet they do capture something basic to the Christian humanist mindset. Because of Christ's incarnation, human mortal existence, our being dust that breathes, can bear the infinite. The matter of our being as living flesh is endorsed by and oriented towards the divine. Of course, each of these ideas (embodied spirit oriented towards the divine; finite existence can bear the infinite) needs careful elucidation. But the main idea is clear enough. Unlike some religions where enlightenment or redemption entails an escape from or transcendence of finite, bodily existence, for the Christian humanist incarnate existence is treasured in its finitude as a place for a relation to the divine. This does not mean a wholesale materialism, where matter and matter alone provides an adequate framework for understanding human existence. That God was incarnate in Christ means that one must conceive of matter and spirit in their union but without confusion.[9] This is why Christian humanists insist on the distinctive drive, the aspiration and energy, of human life: to be human is to seek the over-coming, the transcendence, of our given condition towards the divine. However, self-overcoming is not against or beyond but rather in and through the "flesh."

Now it is the aspiring drive of human life that calls forth the other idea used to speak of Christ, and precisely in its connection to flesh. To say that Christ is *folly* is to signal that most of the time most of us aspire to what is deemed wise or powerful or prestigious or honorable not in relation to the love of God and one's neighbor, but in reference to ourselves and the gaze of others. We treasure the appearance of our own identities, the "dear self" (as Immanuel Kant called it). We prefer, as the Gospels have it, to pray in public where others see us, rather than in secret where God alone searches the heart; we prefer to give our wealth in public places rather than conceal our generosity in order to give glory to God. Instead of living temporal existence as a medium of love for God and others, it is seen as end-in-itself. Here is the root of human folly, namely, the human-all-too-human denial of humanity in the aspiration to deify temporal existence. Folly arises within our fleshliness and then turns against itself. It indeed wishes to connect flesh and divinity, but in such a way that our finitude is our god. As some modern thinkers, like Martin Heidegger, might put it, our ownmost possibility for authentic being is found only through an encounter with ourown being-towards-death such that our mortality, and not the needs of others or the living God, is the pathway to truth.[10] For the Christian humanist, the folly in this thought is the presumption that the self answers its ownmost question, and, accordingly, denies its finitude, its flesh or dust. The folly of Christ, or, better, Christ as folly, is one who pours out life with and for others in love of God and appears inauthentic, fallen and abject, but redeems flesh in its finitude.

It is the co-implication of flesh and folly that we must briefly explore, or so I believe. We can do so via a detour through two instances of these ideas in the writing of classical Christian humanists. While often associated with Catholic rather than Protestant thought, Rabelais and Erasmus explore the connection of flesh and folly. Engaging their texts is meant to stress that one can give priority to a shared *Christian* identity rather than to focus on confessional differences that have divided the Church. At the far end of this detour we will reach the constructive claims I think Christian humanists must make about Christ in our time.

Erasmus supposedly wrote *Praise of Folly* during one week in 1509 and dedicated it to Thomas More – whose name is the foil, a *double entendre* in the title (*Moriae Encomion*). Further, the text draws inspiration from the satire of Lucian of Samasota, a Syrian Roman author, whose works are often called "serio-comic," treating serious topics comically. More and Erasmus had been translating Lucian, and *Praise of Folly* as well as More's *Utopia* are in this tradition. Technically speaking, the work is an "enco-mium." That is, rhetorically, it is high-sounding or formal praise and derives its name from the Greek "komos," for revelry. In this case, Folly praises herself as the source of human happiness. The text was fabulously successful and also condemned from the first but ran many editions in many languages. While Erasmus hardly thought it his best work – his work in translation being that – it is a good introduction to the man's mind. And, like Rabelais, it is clear that three basic constants of human existence (birth, sex, death) are the forces of our highest aspirations and also our deepest folly.

The text seems to move in and through four movements in which Folly takes on different voices. Chapters 1–30 are straightforward and gleeful comedy in which Folly tries to show that she is the source of all good that comes to human beings. In chapters 31–47 there is a shift to parody in which Folly exposes the vices of virtually the entire range of the social order and people in various groups and professions. By chapters 48–61 we arrive at what is, for some scholars, the heart of the work. In pure satire there is an attack on the presumption and stupidity of many, especially theologians and even Erasmus himself. There is, in chapters 62–68, a final reversal and disclosure. Christ himself is Folly – the one who, although foolishness to the world, brings human felicity.

Erasmus as a Christian humanist found himself at odds with two other forces in Christianity. First, there were the scholastics with a rigid ortho-doxy that held that what was needed for salvation was acceptance of norms of belief and practices of the sacraments. They gave little attention to the human mind's need to understand its experience or individual moral aspira-tion. Then, second, there was Luther and the reformers for whom the very idea of moral perfectibility and aspiration was dangerous. The Evangelical reformers joined Erasmus in the criticism of scholastic forms and also the humanist bent to reclaim the original Christian texts, to get good versions and translations of the Bible. Against these options, Erasmus, as Terence Martin has written, outlines "an ethics of discourse crafted from both classical and scriptural resources, centered on irenic dialogue, and modeled on the love of God in Christ."[11] The Christian life opposes coercion with persuasion, force with love, and unbending belief with reasoned conviction. Erasmus and other Christian humanists, including (importantly) John Calvin, called this outlook the "philosophy of Christ." Wherever truth is found, wherever insight into just and virtuous life is gleaned, it can and ought to be interwoven with the Christian message. In this respect, it is not too easy or too glib to repeat the ancient maxim that nothing human is foreign to one.

But of course it is no small thing to decide what counts as human. Erasmus probed the folly of human beings and in the *Praise of Folly* insisted on skepticism *vis-à-vis* human knowledge while lampooning presumption to truth. This is serious laughter. Rabelais agrees. In his "advice to readers" he begins *Gargantua* thus: "When I see grief consume and rot / You, mirth's my theme and tears are not / For laughter is man's proper lot."[12] Of course, Rabelais has been interpreted in various ways: a teller of bawdy tales, a hermetic even cabalistic writer, an atheist and proto-Marxist critic of medieval society, and also some kind of Christian, liberal but orthodox in some way.[13] As Florence Weinberg has noted, "Rabelais's entire approach, his *serio ludere*, the grotesque mask, is deeply justified by his conviction that true wisdom often disguises itself as foolishness (the converse is not always true, not all fools are wise)."[14] Indeed, the book, from its opening to its end, claims to be a tale with no deep meaning at all. It seeks to disguise the wisdom it hopes to convey. Many a reader has failed to grasp the indirection in Rabelais's communication of the Gospel. Only those with ears to hear and eyes to see will learn the true in the hidden.

While Erasmus, at least in *Praise of Folly*, made this point by exposing the prideful foolishness of those who believe themselves to be wise, Rabelais focuses on flesh. Tracing the birth and education of the giant Gargantua, he explores the presence of divine spirit under the bawdiness of boozing, sex, flatulence, and the carnival. About his conception, Rabelais writes that Gargantua's father and his mother, "a fine, good-looking piece," often "play the two-backed beast, joyfully rubbing their bacon together, to such effect that she became pregnant of a fine boy and carried him into the eleventh month." Musing on the length of the pregnancy and the ways in which women try to avoid that consequence, he concludes "if the deuce doesn't want their bellies to swell, he must twist the spigot and close the hole."[15] With similar honesty, Rabelais traces the boy's education and his many adventures.

In celebration of his hero and praise of fellow boozers, Rabelais conceals within a Dionysian festival a drunken wisdom, the wisdom of the Christ. Here the scope of salvation is extended to everyone. Weinberg continues, "We end as we began, with the knowledge that all things are revealed to the true seeker. All mankind … can be saved in the end."[16] The bonds and desires of the flesh can lead to death, of course. Some will be drunk with their own wisdom; some will not see that earthly desires need to be purified. This is not to deny "flesh" in order to escape folly. Salvation is not a denial or negation of human existence in all of its bawdy and broken ways. The human adventure, portrayed through Gargantua in its most gigantic and outlandish form, can reveal divine grace. God has not scorned our lot.

A good deal of modern Christian theology is less skeptical than Erasmus and certainly more prudish than Rabelais's celebration with his fellow Pantagruelists. That is, I imagine, just what Rabelais and Erasmus would expect from theologians. In our time, there is obsession over God's identi- fication with human existence without, apparently, much reflection on what that could actually mean in human terms, how one would communicate such an outlandish message, or the ludic character of the confession itself. We read about God's solidarity with the outcast, God and erotic power, and the suffering of God, but these claims remain mainly at the level of abstractions. While Erasmus and Rabelais could practice the ancient art of "serious play," *serio ludere*, as well as use the classic tactic of serious comedy (*serio comic*) found in Lucian and others, contemporary theolo- gians – for all their delight in postmodern "play" – are rarely found laugh- ing over human foibles or divine wisdom.[17] Maybe the legacy of Dante's *Divine Comedy* and Milton's *Paradise Lost* clinches the reach and depth of Christian laughter despite the writings of Erasmus, Rabelais, and others. Of course there are many kinds of laughter and some of them destructive as well as violent. Still, if Christianity is the "philosophy of Christ," then, in M. A. Screech's words, it "teaches men and women how to spiritualize their souls and to 'animate' their bodies."[18] This philosophy enables one to confront death and life mindful of folly and flesh but also of the difference between the laughter of the "world" and the Folly of God – the Christ.

The question that provoked the inquiry of this chapter now returns: what is the "Christ" of Christian humanism for our day? This is especially press- ing in a culture where little is now seen as bawdy, where the domain of the profane expands daily to choke off the human spirit, and so nothing much shocks about the fate of human existence. How might this grand legacy of thought about the human condition in the light of the philosophy of Christ be revised and carried forward in a world of global dynamics? Without doubt, we need to train our gaze on our most treasured possession – our carefully wrought and dearly bought *identities*. For where your treasure is, there too will be your heart.

4

I began this chapter by noting that the *point* of theological reflection for the Christian humanist is the Christian life. It is, to use classic terms, to

articulate the philosophy of Christ for the right orientation of human existence. And I also noted that in our time people's identities are too often
circumscribed within one description, and, we can now say, are sipped as
holy wine, a treasure of heaven. Within the whirl of global dynamics there
are powerful forces at work seeking carefully to demarcate people's identities in order to provide solid boundaries between communities and so to
enshrine it as the Holy of Holies. There are also forces working to persuade
us of our sovereign power to shape at will and whim who we are and what
we will become. The highest good, apparently, is the freedom to fashion
and morph one's identity. These strategies of identity-formation usually fail
precisely because of the reflexive interaction among peoples on the global
field. We explored that fact in Chapter 1. No community is free from interactions with others that shape the context of life; no one is sovereign over
all of the forces, natural and social, that shape existence. Yet the failures
to control the formation of identity lead to harsher and even more violent
means to retain the boundaries or to reassert the right of self-formation.[19]
What is needed, I believe, is a vision of the internal complexity of identities
and the various ways one can and ought to live with them in oneself, one's
community, and the world. The sovereignty a human being actually has
over self is more limited, more deliberate, and yet more important than
often thought. The sovereignty we ought to see is to orient the "dear self"
beyond itself for a life of love of responsibility with and for others. These
facts show one promise, for Christians, of Christian humanism in our time.

In our current situation we need to articulate the complexity of any
person's or community's identity in order to find non-coercive points of
contact among people without loss of distinctiveness. And we must admit
that much of who we are, much of what we cannot escape, has been given
us, like it or not. The worry, to say it again, is that once an identity is
defined through just one description anyone who has a different identity
will be seen in opposition. Identity then becomes, to recall Amartya Sen's
apt terms, an "illusion of destiny," something which cannot or will not be
escaped or changed, that pits people against each other. With that horrific
possibility in mind, I explored briefly in the second step of this chapter some
central ideas about Christ found among the great Christian humanists of
the Renaissance and Reformation period. They explored the meaning
of Christ in relation to what would seem to be features of any human life,
namely, fleshliness and also foolishness. Yet it is not at all clear what their
claims, much less their skepticism and even hermeticism, could mean in our
global context. Revisions are again needed in how Christian humanists
think about Christ and the Christian life.

Actually, I have already hinted at what I believe needs critical revision
in the legacy of Christian humanism in order to carry that legacy forward
into our own day. It is a subtle but important shift from the priority of

confession to the problem of *identity*. Insofar as early Christian humanists could assume the stability of a wider Christian culture, their challenge was how to navigate between the clashes of *confessions* that plunged Europe into thirty years of war.[20] Even more recent Christian thinkers, ones we have not been able to explore here, confronted the modern challenge to the plausibility of religious faith in terms of a conflict of confessions, a scientific versus religious outlook.[21] That debate usually assumed a good measure of social stability and coherence. In the global age, the question of the conflict of cognitive claims, the clash of confessions, is more deeply situated in the social and cultural proliferation of identities and the claim to sovereignty of those identities. The connection between these two concerns is obvious, of course. An identity without confession is empty. A confession without an identity is formless. The connection between confession and identity enables one to remain a Christian humanist and yet also requires revisions in that orientation to faith and life. How so?

If conflict among peoples is to be lessened and managed, then it must become possible to decide in specific situations which of several identities provides contact with others and directions for cooperative action. And that means – shockingly – that one's identities can and ought to serve a good beyond itself. This is not a facile optimism or naïve idealism. Genuine realism about possibilities for action acknowledges that in a particular situation human differences might not be overcome and conflict then ensues. Yet even then violence can be blunted, if not escaped, if some bond of commonality places a limit on the use of force. But, again, this means that none of my specific identities, including my Christian identity, can trump my whole existence and claim exclusive right to orient action. In some contexts I need to see myself as a human being who faces death, who loves his family, who is prey to folly and fully enfleshed, and who bleeds *just like, in principle, every other human being.* In this case, my more distinct identities (say, United Methodist Protestant Christian or friend of Michael and Ulrike Welker) are set in the background and seen as supportive of shared humanity. That commonality can and must delimit the scope and extent of violence, because, as we know, unending conflict requires the *dehumanization* of the other. Of course, there will be other situations where I must stress more particular identities, say, in the midst of theological debate with fellow Christians or among theists of various kinds or talking and laughing with friends. Yet even in those cases, something shared is the condition for cooperation and persuasion and also limit to forms of coercive interaction.

Notice two things about the argument which build on the claim about religious identity made before in Chapters 1–2. The argument now entails a practical rule and, more importantly, a specific stance towards oneself, one's community, and the identities of others. Together, these are important features of a viable form of contemporary Christian humanism. First, at each point of encounter with others the task is to find the relevant *commonality* that is the condition for cooperation or the limit on coercive interaction. This is, I will call it, a humanistic procedural rule for decisions about what priority to give to one's various identities in specific situations. It requires that no specific identity be deified as the singular description of one's existence because, as St Paul knew, one's life can and ought to be dedicated towards right relations with and for others. Thus, second, this rule implies and enacts a more basic stance possible in our time. The various "confessions" (the cognitive, linguistic, traditional, and practical contents) that shape one's identities are subsumed under a more general project of fashioning a life dedicated to what respects and enhances the integrity of life with and for others before God.[22] This stance, I suppose, arises out of the deep humanistic longing for peace within self, among others, and with God. Whatever its origin, it is important to see that the rule for decision-making implies the deeper moral and religious stance. Someone who accepts the stance ought also to abide by this rule. Anyone who can grasp the intelligibility of the practical rule thereby endorses, at least implicitly, the co-ordinate stance in life. Both the rule and the stance would seem to apply not only to individuals but also to communities insofar as the idea of "identity" is analogically applied to persons and communities.

This strategy for orienting life is deeply embedded in the very idea of Christian humanism insofar as it signals the complexity of a life: one is a Christian (of some sort) and a humanist (of some sort) and has other local identities, too. Yet the conditions of that outlook are also found at the crossing point of the predicates applied to Christ. Human beings are bound together in their mortality, their fleshliness, and also their presumption to wisdom, their folly. Because of our penchant to folly, one ought to be properly skeptical about one's grasp of the truth; because of one's mortality, the plight of other human beings, even given their folly, can be recognized. These facts warrant both the rule and the stance just noted. And Christ, as we have seen, inhabits this human realm to heal and redeem it. The Christian humanist thereby undertakes the labor of life for both human and Christian reasons. There is no justification for the charge made by current Christian particularists that if a situation demands priority of one's humanity (or one's Christian identity) that is somehow a betrayal of the Christian confession (or humanistic convictions). Confessions, like identities, find their *point* in a way of life. One can and must treasure a life dedicated to love and responsibility rather than the particularities of our identities and the convictions we embody.

Now, the affirmation of the right and responsibility of people to make decisions of priority about their identities actually reclaims another aspect of Christian humanism mentioned before but hardly explained. It is a distinctive form of *freedom*. This was a point that divided Protestants and

Catholics, it put Luther against Erasmus, and even today can raise the hackles of Christian particularists who wish to see Christian identity constituted through conformity to churchly authority. For those theologians, identity can and ought and must become one's destiny. Freedom is little more than license and so the sad and troubled legacy of modern possessive individualism.[23] That is not the idea of freedom presented here. Rather, freedom is the capacity to labor responsibly for the integrity of life in oneself and in others. It is the ability to give priority to and reasons for orienting life in specific situations. It means that one's identity is neither an undeniable destiny nor, in more theological terms, a foreordained election. Whatever our ultimate end, in this life and at this time human beings can and may and must responsibly orient life in ways that foster life and limit destruction. In Christian terms, freedom is made perfect in love rooted in Christ's flesh and divine folly.

How then is one to speak of freedom as intrinsically linked to the joys and demands of responsibility? That is, how is one to avoid the idea that freedom is just license and thereby unconstrained by Christian or humane purposes? Can one avoid the rush to authority and the seductive destiny of identity? How is freedom linked to the aspiration to the integrity of life? This is not the time or the place to enter into an extended discussion of freedom and responsibility. Ideas of freedom are legion and so too conceptions of responsibility. Yet to my mind, the best way to think about this is to conceive of "conscience" as the claim of responsibility on freedom. More precisely, the claim of responsibility is that in our actions and relations we are to respect and enhance the integrity of life before God.

"Conscience" is a term for the most basic mode of our being in which the capacity for action (our freedom) is infused with a sense of responsibility. It names the distinctive human ability to make decisions and choices about how to orient and conduct one's life. Conscience is that power to make decisions and choices about the relative priority one can and ought to give to identities in relation to others. It is the call to orient the self beyond its several identities towards actions and relations that respect and enhance the integrity of life. For precisely this reason, a basic right of human beings is freedom of conscience. No human being can rightfully be coerced to conform their identities and life to any power – no matter how seemingly legitimate or how divinely authorized – that denies the capacity of conscience as the labor of one's life. This right, Christian humanists claim, is rooted in God's way with us in Christ. Indeed, we might say that for a Christian humanist, *Christ is the conscience of God*. That is, Christians confess that in Christ is manifest the freedom of God oriented towards what respects and enhances the integrity of finite life made manifest in flesh and folly. We are neither coerced nor elected in faith, but bidden by Christ to a life of fidelity, responsibility, love, and joy.

The Christian humanist is less anxious about being a Christian over-against the "world" than many other contemporary theologians counted among the ranks of Christian particularists. The high-priests of much current theology seem so certain that the Christian story offers peace to a fallen world that they hardly notice the good will of their "pagan" neighbors. A Christian humanist is also less worried about the supposed unique-ness of the Gospel than most traditional Confessions would insist. Christ said that only God was good and yet so many Christian denominations log the one and true path to the divine within the lines of their prayer books. To be sure, the Christian life is a distinctive way of living the human adventure, but it is still a way of being human. The anxiety of the Christian humanist in our time is different. It is the fear that religious, cultural, and social forces will stunt conscience and demand unity rather than integrity of identity. More profoundly, the anxiety is about human freedom, the failure of conscience, or a weakness of will (to put it in different ways) so that our commitments and responsibilities with and to others become constricted by our petty identities. The law of sin and death, the abyss of existence, continually enslaves our lives and shackles the conscience to pit us against ourselves, people against people, and the human heart against the love of God all in the name of our dear selves. Our folly ever remains with us inscribed in the mortality and pain of flesh. The laughter we can muster at folly is always and necessarily and sadly serious.

When the will fails and conscience is stunted, the Christian humanist with simple faith in the power of God must wield the only weapons she or he has consistent with that faith, the weapons of education, irony, satire, and forms of resistance to human fault and wretchedness that are at once comic and serious. What can be more foolish and more dangerous than to believe that Christian convictions should stunt the scope of love in the name of Christian truth? Truth so sure and certain and proclaimed and lived without love is its own folly. But it is not the folly of God that finds habitation in love with our mortal lot. It is not the folly of faith that finds hidden in the flesh and folly of Christ the power to revoke the law of sin and death.

There is, perhaps, nothing deep or profound in that thought. It discloses nothing new or radical about our plight or the Christian convictions. Christian humanism is only a practical thing, after all. It leaves to others the mysteries of faith, those who toil among the doctrines. It is the outlook of the "third man," the believing outsider, the one whose life is crisscrossed with multiple convictions about how to orient life humanely and faithfully. A Christian humanist does not know that much about God and God's ways. She or he just wants to find a way to orient life freed from the grip of the law, the destiny, which makes convictions and identities the motor of death among peoples. That way is the philosophy of Christ.

5

I suppose by now you have surmised that I have no intention or even desire to deliver to you neatly packaged in crisp doctrine the Christ of Christian humanism. I have neither been able to ascend to the godhead in order to glimpse the Logos made incarnate, nor to descend to the depths of his suffering that breaks the law of sin and death. And I certainly have not been able to revel in the presence of his spirit made real under the fragility of human language, the turmoil of community, or the baser elements of life, bread and wine. All that I have been able to do, quite frankly, is to meditate on existence in the light of the flesh and folly of Christ. That is the meaning, I suppose, of the Christ of Christian theological humanism – that life in its terror and joy, its ignorance and aspiration, its sorrow and laughter, flesh and folly, nevertheless evokes gratitude before God and empowers a life of love and responsibility.

Notes

1 Paul Ricoeur, "Faith and Culture," in *Political and Social Essays*, ed. David Stewart and Joseph Bein (Athens, OH: Ohio University Press, 1974), p. 126. Also see Lewis S. Mudge, *The Gift of Responsibility: The Promise of Dialogue Among Christians, Jews, and Muslims* (New York: Continuum, 2008); and John W. de Gruchy, *Confessions of a Christian Humanist* (Minneapolis: Fortress Press, 2006).
2 On this see *Humanist Educational Treatises*, trans. and ed. Craig W. Kallendorf (Cambridge, MA: Harvard University Press, 2002).
3 R. William Franklin and Joseph M. Shaw, *The Case for Christian Humanism* (Grand Rapids, MI: Eerdmans, 1991), p. 11.
4 For a profound meditation on the material mediation of the divine, see David E. Klemm, "Material Grace: The Paradox of Property and Possession," in *Having: Property and Possession in Social and Religious Life*, ed. W. Schweiker and C. Matthewes (Grand Rapids, MI: Eerdmans, 2004), pp. 222–48.
5 Importantly, similar arguments have been made by prominent intellectuals in various traditions. See the Palestinian-American literary critic Edward W. Said, *Humanism and Democratic Criticism* (New York: Columbia University Press, 2004); the Indian-American economist Amartya Sen, *Identity and Violence: The Illusion of Destiny* (New York: Norton, 2006); and the Chief Rabbi of the United Hebrew Congregations of the British Commonwealth, Jonathan Sachs, *The Dignity of Difference: How to Avoid the Clash of Civilizations* (New York: Continuum, 2002); and also de Gruchy, *Confessions of a Christian Humanist*. Also see *Humanity Before God: Contemporary Faces of Jewish, Christian and Islamic Ethics*, ed. W. Schweiker, M. Johnson, and K. Jung (Minneapolis: Fortress Press, 2006). I have developed some of these ideas in

previous and current writing. See William Schweiker, *Theological Ethics and Global Dynamics: In the Time of Many Worlds* (Oxford: Blackwell, 2004); and David E. Klemm and William Schweiker, *Religion and the Human Future: An Essay on Theological Humanism* (Oxford: Wiley-Blackwell, 2008).

6   Jaroslav Pelikan, *Jesus Through the Centuries: His Place in the History of Culture* (New Haven, CT: Yale University Press, 1985). For a fine discussion of the issues in ethics see James M. Gustafson, *Christ and the Moral Life* (Chicago: University of Chicago Press, 1979).

7   Thomas Merton, "Virginity and Humanism in the Western Fathers," in *Mystics and Zen Masters* (New York: Farrar, Straus & Giroux, 1967), p. 114. For a statement of this outlook in Protestant theology see Karl Barth, *The Humanity of God*, trans. John Newton Thomas and Thomas Wieser (Richmond, VA: John Knox Press, 1960), and in Russian theology see Paul Valliere, *Modern Russian Theology: Bukharev, Soloviev, Bulgakov: Orthodox Theology in a New Key* (Grand Rapids, MI: Eerdmans, 2000).

8   Martin Luther, "The Bondage of the Will," in *Martin Luther: Selections from his Writings*, ed. John Dillenberger (Garden City, NY: Anchor Books, 1961), pp. 167–8.

9   Within the current science and theology discussion this is often conceived through ideas about "dual aspect monism" or emergence. I cannot enter those conceptual discussions in this chapter, but, clearly, my own argument finds resonance with those arguments.

10   This is the argument famously made by Martin Heidegger in his work *Being and Time*. It is crucial that some prominent post-Heideggerian thinkers have looked to the encounter with the other, and not only the fact of death, to understand human existence. On this see, for instance, Emmanuel Levinas, *Humanism of the Other*, trans. N. Poller and intro. R. A. Cohen (Urbana: University of Illinois Press, 2003); and Paul Ricoeur, *The Just*, trans. D. Pellauer (Chicago: University of Chicago Press, 2003).

11   On this see Terence J. Martin, *Living Words: Studies in Dialogues about Religion* (Atlanta, GA: Scholars Press, 1998), p. 251.

12   Francois Rabelais, *Gargantua and Pantagruel*, trans. J. M. Cohen (New York: Penguin, 1974).

13   For a helpful discussion see Florence M. Weinberg, *The Wine and the Will: Rabelais's Bacchic Christianity* (Detroit: Wayne State University Press, 1972). Also see Mikhail M. Bakhtin, *Rabelais and His World*, trans. Helene Iswolsky (Bloomington: Indiana University Press, 1984).

14   Weinberg, *The Wine and the Will*, p. 149.

15   Rabelais, *Gargantua and Pantagruel*, pp. 46–7.

16   Weinberg, *The Wine and the Will*, p. 151.

17   For an excellent study see M. A. Screech, *Laughter at the Foot of the Cross* (Boulder, CO: Westview Press, 1999). On the use of inhumane, cruel laughter see Jonathan Glover, *Humanity: A Moral History of the Twentieth Century* (New Haven, CT: Yale University Press, 1991). Also see William Schweiker, *Theological Ethics and Global Dynamics: In the Time of Many Worlds* (Oxford: Blackwell, 2004), esp. pp. 153–71.

18   Screech, *Laughter at the Foot of the Cross*, p. 255.
19   For postcolonial and feminist perspectives on these issues see Arjun Appadurai, *Modernity at Large: Cultural Dimensions of Globalization* (Minneapolis: University of Minnesota Press, 1996); and Saskia Sassen, *Globalization and its Discontents* (New York: New Press, 1998).
20   For a fine discussion see Stephen Toulmin, *Cosmopolis: The Hidden Agenda of Modernity* (New York: Free Press, 1999).
21   I am thinking here of theologians ranging from F. Schleiermacher and E. Troeltsch to twentieth-century thinkers like Karl Rahner, Paul Tillich, Robert Scharlemann, Wolfhart Pannenberg, James Gustafson, David Tracy, and others.
22   On the elaboration of this imperative of responsibility see William Schweiker, *Responsibility and Christian Ethics* (Cambridge: Cambridge University Press, 1995).
23   This argument is usually associated with a wide range of thinkers, such as Stanley Hauerwas, Paul Griffiths, Sam Wells, Stephen Long, George Lindbeck, Jean Bethke Elshtain, John Milbank, and others, who differ among themselves in striking and profound ways.

Part II
Thinkers

Chapter 7

Human Only Human?

1

Part I of this book examined topics important for clarifying the task and purpose of theological humanism drawn from Christian sources. Part II undertakes an examination of important thinkers whose work, I believe, helps one develop and also to test theological humanism as an outlook and stance in life. As noted in the Introduction, this chapter and the next one engage two philosophers decidedly interested in religious questions and humanism. The root issue in these chapters is how best to think about human existence, our lives as dust that breathes, and so different variations on the question of the meaning and purpose of human life. I aim to show how theological humanism can engage, learn from, and yet move beyond these prominent voices in current thought about the dynamics of human existence. The next chapter explores the thought of Iris Murdoch, the renowned British novelist and moral philosopher. In this chapter I want to engage the work of the French philosopher Paul Ricoeur. His far-ranging corpus of writings is marked by sustained attention to the meaning and task of being human. His position can be formulated by the epigram in the title of this chapter. We are human *only* human. Later I will contrast this with the lead formula of theological humanism: human *truly* human. This chapter thereby also continues the reflections on Christ and Christian humanism outlined in the previous one.

Throughout his career, Ricoeur examined human fallibility and also capability. He understood human beings as incomplete creatures who strive for some kind of wholeness in their lives by means of cultural products and

---

* This chapter was first published in a different form as "Paul Ricoeur and the Prospect of a Hew Humanism," in *Reading Ricoeur*, ed. David M. Kaplan (Albany, NY: SUNY Press, 2008), pp. 89–108. Copyright William Schweiker.

Dust that Breathes, by William Schweiker © William Schweiker 2010.

practices that endow life with meaning. It is hardly surprising, then, that Ricoeur examined questions of meaning in studies dedicated to metaphor, symbol, and narrative. Those studies are best seen as detours (so Ricoeur called them) on the way to the more basic concern for "capable man." Further, attention to human capability and fallibility, and thus the priority of action to consciousness, required a significant shift in thinking about being itself. "Should we not say," Ricoeur wrote in one essay, "to exist is to act? Does not being, in the first instance, signify an act?" "Being," he continued, "is act before it is essence, because it is effort before it is representation or idea."[1] The domain of representation and idea, the whole realm of human meanings, thereby reveals and also conceals the effort to be. The interpreter who wants to understand the human effort to exist must engage forms of representation in order to clarify the meaning of that struggle. Ricoeur thereby offers a reflexive, hermeneutical philosophy of human beings as acting creatures who express their effort to exist in labor, cultural artifacts, and language. He engaged in a grand and intricate interpretation of things human in order not only to clarify the significance of theories, symbols, and works of art, but to catch a glimpse of humanity *in via*, including the problem of evil that haunts the human adventure.[2]

In what follows, I examine in some detail the connection in Ricoeur's work between the "effort to be" and his commitment to a form of humanism. Individually, these aspects of his work have received considerable attention. The humanistic cast of his thought has long been evident. It reaches from his earliest writings for the journal *Esprit*, influenced by the personalism of its founder Emmanuel Mounier, to the last lectures and texts.[3] Many of the tributes to Ricoeur following his death similarly noted the humanistic cast of his life and work. There have also been fine studies about the importance of the effort to be, attestation, capability, and the "will" in his corpus. That focus on his work was natural insofar as Ricoeur undertook early in his career to write a "Philosophy of the Will" and ended his active life still speaking of human capability. All of these ways to enter into Ricoeur's sprawling and complex corpus of work are well known and obviously important. They have contributed to the assessment and appreciation of his thought.

What has not been sufficiently explored is the precise way in which Ricoeur's humanism reflects his basic philosophical orientation toward human capability and fallibility, that is, the effort to be. The converse is also true. It has not been shown how his attention to human capabilities determines the basic outlines of the form of humanism he judged viable and even required for the present age. The purpose of my inquiry, then, is to gain some clarity about the connection between humanism and Ricoeur's account of the human effort to be, including some of his religious convictions. The other intention of this chapter is to advance contemporary humanistic thought, especially at the meeting point of philosophical, religious, and theological concerns. I will do so through sustained attention to a question that strikes to the core of the affirmation of our capacity or power to act: what is the measure – the norm – of the human effort to be? How is it related to the dignity of human life, one's own and that of others? Is there a theological dimension to the measure of human power?

In order to answer these questions adequately, I need to show that an account of the measure of the effort to be is not grounded only in some account of human existence and power, but also, and in its own way, opens up theological reflection within humanistic inquiry.

2

What does one mean by "the effort to be" or a "measure" and their relation? And why are these important ideas for contemporary humanists? To be sure, asking about the "measure" for the "effort to be" seems a rather abstract way of putting a question that is actually woven into the texture of every human life. The raw struggle for life, the pitch of human wants and desires for fulfillment against the onslaught of age, death, and suffering, and likewise the pangs of love that long to embrace the beloved beyond the sorrow of loss all testify to a *Wille zur Leben*, a will to life, in human existence. To be or not to be is the question, Hamlet thought, but, in fact, the desire to be, the sense that it is good to be, is the primitive datum of human existence linked to the struggle to live. We have a primitive, a basic, love of life. The decision to end life, the act of suicide, is then always an intentional act that must overcome the more primitive desire to live. Albert Camus thought that "[t]here is but one truly serious philosophical problem, and that is suicide. Judging whether life is or is not worth living amounts to answering the fundamental questions of philosophy."[4] But that problem is formulated in the order of critical judgment and philosophical reflection. More directly, more immediately, life makes a claim on us. While pessimism has been a seduction for some Western thinkers and always stalks the human psyche, most people most of the time love rather than hate life.

On the plane of actual existence arguably the more basic question than whether to be or not to be is rather about the good or norm for our effort to exist. Is the mere preservation of one's own life or the life of those dear to one the good to seek? What claim, if any, do others make upon my capacities, my power to act in the world? Which others matter? Is the measure of human capability just the increase of strength, the celebration of power and independence marked, say in Greek thought, by ideas of honor and glory and happiness (*eudaimonia*) rooted in the natural vitalities of existence? Is the norm for human action a command to care for the poor, the widow, and the stranger, a commandment of the God of the Bible, or is that command uttered simply and solely in the face of another suffering human being? How do these norms, whatever their content or origin, relate to the tenacity of the will to live that saturates our existence? Must one quiet the rage of the will to life in order to reverence other forms of life?

These are hardly abstract matters even if they can be formulated in abstract terms. The question of the relation between the effort to be, the will to life, and its proper norm or measure presses on daily existence insofar as to be human, as Ricoeur insists, is to be with others and to live in shared institutions. Further, this question is at the center of current debates about humanism and Ricoeur's own response to competing philosophical positions. Put as a formula, Ricoeur's type of humanism arises from an attestation to being in the self and yet also insists that we are "human, *only* human." Acknowledgement of the limits on human thought and action, limits rooted in our finitude and the reality of others, is necessary to a proper grasp of our existence. Only when human beings repent of idolatry about their own power and knowledge is the dignity of human life manifest. In this respect, Ricoeur contends that theological discourse and religious convictions use limit concepts to denote limit experiences. They specify the finite condition of human existence while also indirectly configuring an attestation to being.

As explored below, Ricoeur outlines this position in contrast to the Nietzschean formulation of "human, *all too* human" and also Emmanuel Levinas's humanism of the other, what I designate by the formula "human, *otherwise than* human."[5] Recall that Nietzsche mused that "the world is beautiful, but has a disease called man." He sought to announce the coming man, the *Übermensch*, as a new form of existence. The daybreak of the *Übermensch* is the finality of human, all too human history. As shown in a previous chapter, according to Levinas the face of the other disrupts the drive to totality that is also the legacy of Western thought and life, especially under the dominance of Greek philosophy. The question of the limit and value of human power is thereby variously construed in these formulae. For Nietzsche, the will-to-power finds its limit only in the coming *Übermensch* and so after the time of "man." With Levinas, the power of the self is decisively limited by the advent of the other, the command "Thou shall not Murder" uttered by the face of the other as if from Mt Sinai. According to Ricoeur, the limit to and value of human power are rooted in the attestation of *oneself as another* and the acknowledgement that we are human, *only* human.

These formulae constitute a typology of important expressions of contemporary humanism which I will elaborate in more detail later. Their full force for understanding current options in thought will thereby become clear as this chapter proceeds.[6] They are also the opening to my specific

constructive intentions that mark the far end, the horizon, of these reflections. Against Nietzsche's paradigmatically "Greek" affirmation of human
power where the vitalities of Will are to be ever increased, and Levinas's
insistence on the finality of the other rooted in his sensibilities about Jewish
law, my argument enacts in thinking the reality of the "third man."
Dominated neither by forms of Greek thought, to which the Christian
message was proclaimed, nor by the circle of Hebraic life, from which the
Gospel arose, this "'third man,'" Ricoeur notes, "this cultivated Christian,
this believing Greek, is ourselves."[7] This is not to say that Greek or Hebraic
forms of humanism are impossible or even invalid. Quite the contrary is
the case. That is a reason to examine the positions of Nietzsche and Levinas.
The point, rather, is that a Christian theological humanism, born from the
tumultuous and yet exciting encounter of Greek and biblical modes of life,
signifies yet another distinctive way of being in the world. It is the reality
of the "third man," as Ricoeur calls it, as a human possibility. Yet while
drawing on Ricoeur's thought precisely at this point, I also want to press
beyond his argument towards theological humanism. This too will be a
form of thought arising within the reality of the "third man," but now
articulated in ways that transform Ricoeur's project and other contemporary expressions of Christian humanism.[8] The reasons for undertaking this
turn of thought, as well as some judgment about Ricoeur's assessment of
that turn, will also become clear in due course.

So, in what follows I want not only to listen to but also to deploy the
resources of the Christian tradition in the service of understanding and
orienting human life. At the conclusion of these reflections I will designate
a type of theological humanism developed from Christian sources.[9] The
formula is "human, *truly* human." The hermeneutical move that must be
made, I judge, is from understanding the human "in the mirror of scripture," as Ricoeur emblematically puts it, to understanding existence "in
Christ."[10] I hope, then, to bring to articulation a form of humanism distinctive in its features but conversant with other positions which, like Ricoeur,
attend to the effort to be.

I turn now to the current debate about humanism within strands of
postmodern thought. This will enable us to develop in a further step of the
inquiry the typology of positions announced above and thereby to specify
the humanistic intent of Ricoeur's philosophical project.

3

A survey of intellectual trends in early and late twentieth-century thought
reveals that many of the convictions and values of traditional humanism
fell to criticism. By the term "traditional humanism" I do not mean a

specific set of thinkers or texts or even a particular period in Western intellectual history. While certain thinkers, notably Erasmus, Pico, More or, later, Vico and Kant, and certain periods, especially the Renaissance and the Enlightenment, are often taken to define "humanism," I am much more concerned with a set of ideals or convictions that characterize a humanistic outlook. Tzvetan Todorov, as noted in other chapters of this book, formulates this outlook in terms of what he calls the autonomy of the I, the finality of the you, and the universality of the they.[11] Put otherwise, freedom of the self, the moral claim of others, and an inclusive moral community are basic humanistic values. Humanists also insist on human fallibility, and so humility in our appreciation of truth. And, finally, humanists believe, in Edward Said's words, that "human history as made by human action and understood accordingly is the very ground of the humanities."[12] Put most simply, for a humanist the purpose of thought and action is human flourishing, achieved by means of the distinctive human power to act and so to create history, whatever other non-human purposes might obtain. These humanistic ideals reached a cultural height and prestige in the West during the eighteenth and nineteenth centuries.

Given these beliefs, it is not surprising that we are now amid a widespread debate about the viability of humanism. In an age of global dynamics, there is the possibility for expanded cosmopolitan or worldwide commitments, say to human rights, which challenge the tribalism of local loyalties and powers. Yet many now worry that humanistic ideals are the imposition of Western beliefs on other peoples and cultures. Further, the various forms of technology that characterize the global age are driven by anthropocentric values which endanger not only the natural environment but also myriad forms of non-human life. For many people, humanism cannot be reconciled with ecological sensibilities and concern for "animal rights."[13] Additionally, as Ricoeur foresaw, there are new threats to the dignity and worth of the individual person. Individuals are being subsumed into the working of massive and complex political, economic, ideological, and technological systems. Yet those systems, it would seem, can hardly be understood, let alone analyzed, if one clings to the traditional humanistic conviction that human beings and human beings alone "make" history. If we are to have a realistic grasp of the forces shaping the world, surely we must attend to the matrices of social power and the dynamics of complex systems freed from the humanistic bias for human agents.[14] All of these developments characterize the "postmodern" or global age. They put unique pressure on humanistic thinkers to defend their ethical commitments as well as to demonstrate the explanatory power of conceptions of history and society bound to human capacities for action.

Amid these challenges to humanistic ideals, one problem seems properly basic for this chapter. The explosion of technological power in our age has rightly challenged the unchecked celebration of human freedom and power among earlier humanists. It is not surprising, then, that the various kinds of "neo-humanism" that dot the intellectual and cultural landscape insist that classical ideals about freedom, individual dignity, and the historical efficacy of human action must be grounded in and limited by the worth of the other. In order to preserve human dignity and expand moral sensibility, thinkers around the world and in various cultures have sought to revise basic humanistic ideals more attentive to the moral claim of others and an inclusive moral community.

In this light, Ricoeur's work can helpfully be seen as part of the debate about the viability of humanism. In contrast to those who reject humanism, Ricoeur held, like other contemporary neo-humanists explored throughout this book, that all works of culture and society give expression, often indirectly, to the freedom of the human self. The dignity and freedom of the human self, or the autonomy of the "I," is perhaps the dearest of all ideas to humanists. It is a conviction that Ricoeur tenaciously defended. As he noted,

> I look at my work as an attempt to provide a survey of the capabilities, so to say, of the very *I can*. … It can be read in terms of four verbs which the "I can" modifies: *I can speak, I can do things, I can tell a story,* and *I can be imputed*, an action can be imputed to me as its author.[15]

In each case, the capacity of speech, action, historical understanding, and responsibility is predicated in complex ways on the "I" even as this "I" is only understandable in terms of these capabilities and their expressions. The effort to be, the *I can*, is basic, then, to all representations of the self in speech, action, narration, and the imputation of responsibility. What about the limit on human capability? In his Gifford lectures, *Oneself as Another*, Ricoeur's trajectory of thought about the limit on the "I can" comes to its highest expression when he explores the various forms of capability with respect to "aiming at the good life with and for others in just institutions." This maxim from the "little ethics" of that text summarizes, in terms parallel to Todorov, the neo-humanistic contours of Ricoeur's thought.[16] The maxim places Ricoeur's work within the larger agenda of those thinkers dedicated to reformulating humanistic ideas in ways appropriate to an age of the global spread of technological power and with it global endangerments to life.

It is beyond the purpose of the present inquiry to clarify in greater detail Ricoeur's place within the myriad forms of neo-humanism. Insofar as my concern is the connection between the effort to be and humanism, it is much more important to examine Ricoeur's engagement with thinkers who, like himself, hold that will or desire or power is basic in human existence. In order to do so, I must develop further the typology of positions noted above, and this will likewise enable me to isolate the distinctive shape of Ricoeur's project. The typology likewise serves the further aim of these reflections to think with and beyond his work about the form of life of the "third man."

4

Ricoeur asserted his own humanistic outlook in an early essay, "What Does Humanism Mean?" I have cited the passage earlier in this book, but it bears repeating. Ricoeur wrote:

> Man is man when he knows that he is *only* man. The ancients called man a "mortal." This "remembrance of death" indicated in the very *name* of man introduces the reference to a limit at the very heart of the affirmation of man himself. When faced with the pretense of absolute knowledge, humanism is therefore the indication of an "only:" we are *only* men. No longer "human, all too human:" this formula still shares in the intoxication of absolute knowledge; but "only human."[17]

Careful attention to this passage enables us to isolate the contours of Ricoeur's humanism in contrast to the Nietzschean formula "human, *all too* human," Levinas's humanism of the other and its summary formula "human, *otherwise than* human," and, finally, theological humanism: human *truly* human.

In Ricoeur's early essays, and also much later in *Oneself as Another*, he explicitly sets his thought against Nietzsche. In his Gifford lectures Ricoeur identifies Nietzsche with the diminution of the self. Interestingly, in the early essay noted above the Nietzschean formula of "human, all too human" is associated with an excessive confidence in absolute knowledge. Against that excess, Ricoeur insisted on the limits to human knowledge, while in *Oneself as Another* he opposes Nietzsche's seeming reduction of the self to non-human causal forces. How can we explain the contradictory judgments about Nietzsche's thought and their significance for reading Ricoeur?

Ricoeur's point, on my understanding, is that humanism is inseparable from a perception of human beings as mortal, as death-bound. It is important to remember, as Tony Davies notes, the semantic density of the word "humanity." "The root-word is, quite literally, humble (*humilis*), from the Latin *humus*, earth or ground; hence *homo*, earth-being, and *humanus*, earthly, human."[18] To be earth-bound is, on Ricoeur's accounting, to be death-bound – dust that breathes. There is a limit at the heart of the human project. Nietzsche's announcement of the coming of the *Übermensch* after a history dominated by the nihilism of human, all too human values aspires to a level of knowledge not possible for mortals. In other words, for Ricoeur humanism necessarily expresses itself in a philosophy of limits and the Nietzschean project strives to exceed that mortal limit. "Man" cannot be overcome or transcended. We are human, *only* human, Ricoeur insists, and thereby we must forgo any pretense to know or to achieve a form of existence beyond "man."

This initial response to the Nietzschean agenda only partially captures Ricoeur's thought as seen from the beginning to the end of his corpus. He always argued that at the heart of human being is not simply the limit of mortality, but, much more, an attestation, a fundamental desire to be. Mortality, as the quote above stresses, is a limit but it is one *within* the affirmation of man himself. The desire to be, attestation to the goodness of being, and not the *Wille zur Macht* is what defines the human being.[19] The limit on that affirmation of self arising from within one's self is mortality, our awareness of death. While enduring the fact of mortality, there is nevertheless an attestation to the goodness of being "at the very heart of the affirmation of man himself." According to Ricoeur, this affirmation opens another horizon to human time other than the fate of death. Through the power of the imagination the desire to be reaches beyond mortality towards eternity in affirming its existence while also enacting its own limit. Nietzsche's attempt to reduce the human to the "will to power," no less than his hope in the coming *Übermensch*, must be brought to criticism. If the formula "human, all too human" betrays an aspiration to absolute knowledge of the coming "man" not possible for finite creatures, the reduction of human existence to the "will to power" fails to grasp the desire to be in its depth or scope. In the end, Nietzsche suffers inconsistency, exuding epistemic confidence bound to ontological reductionism.[20] And that fact is, apparently, the reason for Ricoeur's seeming contradictory judgments about Nietzsche's agenda.

What then is the "limit" on the human effort to be? How, if at all, is it related to the ethical turn in contemporary neo-humanism emblematically stated, in Todorov's words, as the finality of the "you" and the universality of the "they"? It is around this point that the ongoing encounter between Levinas and Ricoeur revolved, an encounter spanning many, many years. Levinas's claim, most boldly stated, is that the face of the other is the absolute limit on the drive to totality, that is, the drive of the self to subsume all being into the self.[21] The other utters a command as if from the height of Mt Sinai, the mountain of God: "Thou Shall Not Murder." For Levinas, the self is a servant, a hostage, of the other, and so infinitely responsible for the life of the other. The limit on the self, the assertion of the ethical intentionality of humanism, is the face of the other and not in the heart of self-affirmation. "I" am because the other commands me to be responsible.

In this respect, it is the death of the other, and not my own death, that discloses the unique singularity of human existence and designates the limit on human power. As Ricoeur notes in *Oneself as Another*,

> the face of the other raises itself before me, above me, it is not an appearance that I can include within the sphere of my representations. To be sure, the other appears, his face makes him appear, but the face is not a spectacle; it is a voice. The voice tells us, "Thou shall not kill." Each face is a Sinai that prohibits murder.[22]

To be sure, Levinas always acknowledged the significance of pleasure in human life and also the origin of language and representations in the face-to-face encounter. He likewise argued that in the domain of politics, reciprocal obligations of justice mean that I can make a valid claim on others.[23] Nevertheless, responsibility is an affirmation of the life of the other otherwise than the drive to totality arising from within the effort of the self. This is a humanism of the other, as noted in Chapter 5.

It is at this juncture that Ricoeur sought to think through consistently the attestation to being. As he notes in the quote cited above, mortality introduces a "limit at the very heart of the affirmation *of man himself.*" What I find within myself is that through all the mediations of the desire to be, through labor, culture, and speech, I am also and always *as another*. There is an "otherness" at the core of the human self which, reciprocally construed, enables co-jointly an affirmation of self and other. Ricoeur specified this otherness in a number of ways: the fact of embodied freedom; the relation of *bios* and *logos* in symbols; the dual horizon of human time and eternity configured in narratives; the mutual co-inherence in subjectivity between *ipsem* and *idem* identity; and the moral injunction to love others *as* oneself. The explanation of the fine details of those arguments spanning Ricoeur's corpus is beyond the scope of this inquiry.[24]

How then does Ricoeur's argument differ from Levinas's position? The argument, if I understand him rightly, is that we are "only men," and that means, in distinction from Levinas, that human beings never escape, and, in fact, will never escape, the tenacity of the effort to exist. An encounter between beings who are "only men" always risks the reduction of other to self or the servitude of self to other. The asymmetrical relation of actor and patient in all human relations is the condition in which violence all too easily breaks forth. But the proper *aim* is a good life by means of responsibility for and with others within just institutions. In order rightly to appreciate Ricoeur's point here, one needs to see a subtle shift in his consideration of "the affirmation of man himself," a shift I bracketed when considering Ricoeur's humanism in response to the Nietzschean project.

Ricoeur does not seek to establish the otherness of the other in terms of the *origin* of self-consciousness and thus the birthplace of the "I" and its representations. Levinas for his part does seek to isolate the origin of self-consciousness either in the totalistic drive of the ego or in the encounter with the face of the other. Ricoeur, having forsaken the search for a pristine origin of consciousness, specifies the trajectory or aim of responsible selfhood. If the defining fact of human being is not *cogito* (the thinking "I" as the origin of representations), but, more simply, the desire to be, then human beings in affirming themselves at one and the same time affirm the being of others, even while there is the possibility of fault and violence rooted in the power to act. The responsible life is the enactment of mutual respect with the aim of existence with and for others. This is why Ricoeur, following the Golden Rule and also Immanuel Kant's formulation of the Categorical Imperative, insisted on reciprocal regard in formulating the moral law: treat humanity in oneself or another always as an end and not merely as a means to some other end. The categorical imperative is the screen through which the search for the good life must necessarily move in light of the ever present possibility of violence. Any end that I seek, any conception of the good life, can only count as such if it meets the test of justice. To recall Todorov's phrase, Ricoeur insists on the finality of the "you," the moral claims of others.[25] Yet this moral demand does not escape, cannot escape, the human, only human character of the effort to be and the lurking threat of untold violence.

It is important that the moral demand which limits any pursuit of the good life is found, according to Ricoeur, "at the very heart of the affirmation of man himself." Contrary to Levinas, the limit that constrains the wanton use of power in seeking the self's good is not heteronomous to the self, it is not from the demand of the other, but, rather, arises within self-affirmation, the attestation to the desire to be in myself and all others. Yet in a way decidedly different from Kant, on whom Ricoeur so heavily relies, the law-giving power of (practical) reason is not the heart of autonomy, of freedom. Mindful of the danger of violence, Ricoeur reformulates the meaning of freedom. "Ethical freedom," he writes, "is not a claim which proceeds from me and is opposed to any control; it is, rather, a demand which is addressed to me and which proceeds from the other: allow me to exist in front of you, as your equal."[26] In short, the limit is annunciated by the other to me, as Levinas rightly saw, but with respect to *equal dignity*, as Kant insisted. The moral demand is the prism through which any aim in life must pass if it is to be justified. Yet the source of human dignity and its aim is neither the other as other (Levinas) nor the law-giving power of reason (Kant) but in the desire to be, the attestation to being, in self and other.

Ricoeur's humanism articulates the measure of human power not as the increase of strength in order to overcome all-too-human existence and thereby incarnate the *Übermensch*. The limit on power is not to be found in the ultimate perfection of power. Likewise, the measure of the effort to be is not a law announced in the face of the other that places the self on trial and instigates infinite responsibility for the other. From Ricoeur's perspective, these forms of humanism share an unsustainable premise, namely, that by the increase of power or within the encounter with the other, the human as mortal and yet self-affirming will be transcended. According to Ricoeur, we are "only men"; our form of life cannot and will not be overcome either in the future or in the face of the other.

The full complexity of the desire to be and its limit must then be grasped if we are to understand Ricoeur's brand of humanism and also isolate the point of departure for thinking beyond him. The desire to be, we can now say, bears within itself an irresolvable tension and perplexity, an *aporia*. To desire being is at once to affirm being and yet to do so from within the lack of being; to desire is to affirm, to seek, within lack, and so marked with finitude. The limit on this desire arises from within mortality. It is why, as seen above, Ricoeur's humanism heralds "the remembrance of death." However, were that claim alone adequate for his brand of humanism, then privation, nothingness, sheer finitude would define the most basic contours of thought, and, further, being towards death, my own or that of the other, would be the necessary and sufficient condition of thinking. Death is indeed necessary for valid reflection on human existence, but it is not sufficient. In facing death, as a finite end, there is also an attestation, an affirmation of life.

How might this *aporia* be represented so that through interpretation we can understand the full texture of the human project? In Ricoeur's judgment, death, as one temporal horizon of human existence, has its meaning in its other, that is, in the human capacity to imagine "eternity" as a horizon of meaning which exceeds finite limits.[27] Eternity, likewise, has its meaning, for human beings, in its other: the orientation towards death that is the limit in the heart of self-affirmation. The fact that *I can tell a story* represents, configures, within the order of discourse both the limit (death) and the affirmation (eternity) that are at the heart of self-affirmation. Narratives render productive the *aporia* of human existence in time.[28] The dual temporal structure of human being rendered productive in the capacity to narrate an account of one's life is, one must admit, an intuition, a grasp of (or being grasped by) a self-evident value, as Todorov noted.

The *aporia* of the desire to be, Ricoeur seems to be saying, imposes itself with the force of self-evidence and, when considered consistently, leads to a humanism of limits, the insight that "we are *only* men." This is where, as they say, the spade is turned. Ricoeur's account of the "third man" and with it the insight that we are human, only human, claims for itself the same level of plausibility, an equal force of self-evidence, as the *Wille zur Macht* for Nietzscheans and the face of the other on Levinas's account. That being the case, one cannot assume, I believe, that a definitive refutation of other forms of thought is possible or that a necessary vindication of one is likely to arise. That is why, we can now see, I could arrange these positions in a typology of forms of humanism focused on the effort to be. A genuine typology would not be conceptually useful if one could, in principle, establish the validity of just one position. So, what confronts us after having briefly surveyed Ricoeur's type of humanism in contrast to others is not the certainty of having validated one position. What confronts us, surprisingly, is a space of freedom, the possibility, that is, to choose among accounts of human existence. Yet if that is the case, has the argument simply regressed yet again to a celebration of human power without measure, without norm? Are we left just to choose without any norm or measure to define a good and true choice? With these questions we reach the far end of this inquiry and also the opening to *theological humanism* which attests to the truth of human existence as the power to be responsible with and for others, chastened by the depths of fallibility, and yet, in its religious impulse, thankful for the gift of life.

5

Ricoeur's humanism of limits insists that human existence is always open both to the ever present possibility of death and yet in imagination, and so in hope, to a horizon of meaning that exceeds finitude and death. Cultural forms, works of art, and religious symbols provide configurations of human temporal existence through which one can grasp via careful interpretation the outlines of basic structures and dynamics of human being. And those same works open a vision of reality in which human beings can find their ownmost possibilities for life. Incomplete creatures we are, but we are also beings who create meanings in order to discover the truth of our lives and thereby endow existence with significance. There are no shortcuts to understanding human existence. Symbols, especially religious symbols, articulate the intersection of primal vitalities of life, of *bios*, with the rigors of thought, *logos*, and thus display an intelligibility of existence even in its brokenness. Narratives, as noted, configure the dual horizon of human time, death and eternity. Metaphors disclose the dynamic of meaning creation through the clash of literal and fictive claims rooted in human sensibility and imagination. A humanism of limits, we can say, simply articulates these *aporias* of human being in the world. The *meaning* of existence is attained through the interpretation of the manifold representations of the human effort to be. Not surprisingly, Ricoeur's philosophical project had to be undertaken through "detours" of interpretation in order thereby to articulate and to understand the meaning of being human.

At this point in our reflections, a further question naturally arises. Are the types of humanism surveyed above exhaustive? Is there any other account that can make some claim to the force of self-evidence about the limit and value of the effort to be? The types, as we have seen, claim, at one extreme, that the limit on human power is with respect to its destiny of self-overcoming, the emergence of a new form of human life after our *human, all too human* existence. At the other end of the typology is the claim, appealing to the evidential power of the face of the other, that the limit on human power does not and cannot arise within the self's effort to be and thereby is, in this respect, *human, otherwise than human*. And, finally, Ricoeur, as we have seen, enunciates a type of humanism which, we might say, mediates these extremes. It is a strictly philosophical account of the reality of the "third man" made possible in Christian faith. He locates a limit to the effort to be "at the very heart of the affirmation of man himself" and in the realization that we are *human, only human* specifies the norm of human power in terms of the demand to aim at the good life with and for others in just institutions. Are these the only options available to a humanist who seeks to unfold with the force of self-evidence the limit on the effort to be? More pointedly, if one lifts the brackets Ricoeur places on theological thinking within his philosophy, is there another possibility for considering the reality of the "third man"? And what might that form of thinking contribute to the current debate about the task of humanism in our age?

Another option is in fact possible. I want to outline this possibility and how it indicates the stance of "Christian theological humanism." This too will be a vision of life for the "third man," but it departs from Ricoeur, and so too Levinas and Nietzsche, insofar as the limit on human power is not my own mortality, the death of the other, or the end of human, all too human history. The limit on human power, the measure of our effort to be, is the love of life, the depth of which is the love of God. The possibility of this measure, and so another form of humanism, arises from greater attention to a point noted previously in these reflections and yet quickly suspended in order to engage Ricoeur's argument. The point, recall, was that the hatred of life, articulated in a systematic pessimism or the challenge of suicide, is not coequal, it does not bear the same evidential weight, as a primitive love of life.[29] What if one attends to this love and its self-evident force in human existence?

To be sure, Ricoeur seemed to have grasped this point and that is why he insisted on the "affirmation of man himself." Yet as we have seen, because he specifies this "affirmation" within the "effort to be," rather than with reference to the *love of life*, the limit of human power must be found in what is other than the attestation to power, namely, in death as the end of power and thus the end of the capacity for violence. This *aporia*, that is, that the affirmation of life bears its limit in mortality, means that we are human, *only* human. Ricoeur's humanism, we might say, demarcates philosophically the space in which human existence can unfold within its own finite limits. He insists on this point, as we have seen, because the celebration of self-overcoming is finally beyond our capacities even as the command of the face of the other can never quell our self-affirmation. The question remains, however, if the "other" to the love of life which forms the limit to human power is in fact mortality.

It is at this juncture that the narrative and symbolic resources of the biblical traditions enunciate another possibility on the plane of representations, which, I wager, can be redeemed in terms of their self-evidential power. Death may indeed form a limit to my power, so too the command not to kill the other or even the emergence of a new form of humanity. In other chapters of this book I have shown how the limit of death demarcates the origins of responsibility, the demand that human power respect and enhance the integrity of life and not just the unending maximizing of human power. Yet none of the limits on power rooted in mortality, (say) the death of the other or the "end of man," limit the love of life by what exceeds human existence. They specify humanism not with reference to a love other than what is human, but in terms of another human being. The transcendence that marks the limit to human power is circumscribed by intra-human relations. That is why, most simply, these are various kinds of neo-humanism. Yet does it not also confront me with the force of self-evidence that the love of life is just that, a love of life that both exceeds and yet embraces human being, including the human will to life? How then to articulate this intuition? What representations that present the human effort to be can be used to articulate this love and its meaning for the limits on human power? Will this require a new type of humanism?

The biblical religions present in symbolic and narrative form the insight that the love of life finds its limit in the longing for the divine and thus intensifies the scope of human transcendence. In the love of God is disclosed a limit to the idolatry of any finite love, any elevation of self, other, or specific attachment to divine status. In the love of God, in other words, is represented the insight, the intuition, that we are human, *truly* human, only when our love for life embraces finite existence, our own and others', within a love of, and attestation to, what exceeds the finite and yet endows mortal existence with distinctive dignity. We are, as Ricoeur rightly saw, human, *only* human; the love of life is the animating impulse of the effort to be. Yet when this love is embraced by a love of divine life, then, the biblical texts suggest, we are human, *truly* human. In fact, we might say, using

Christian categories, that the "fall" into sin is precisely the regress from the *truly* human to being *only* human, to live limited by death rather than by the love of God. And in fact within the myth of the "fall," the account in Genesis, the connection is drawn between death and turning from God.

It is not surprising, then, that the biblical texts formulate the law of life, the proper limit on human power, in terms of the complex relation between the command to love God with one's whole heart, strength, and mind and the command to love one's neighbor as one's self.[30] The great double love command, I suggest, specifies as a maxim of action the limit that the love of life in fact places on human capacity. The self-evident force of this maxim is found not in our mortality and violence (Ricoeur) or power (Nietzsche) or the vulnerability of the other (Levinas). It is found in that the love of finite life is also and always a longing for the divine. St Augustine and many others rightly captured this biblical insight by noting that in every love what is co-loved is the divine, the living God. This insight must then be formulated not only as a type of humanism but also as a kind of piety, a religious longing. One can specify it as *theological* humanism whose basic formula is *human, truly human.*

That is not enough, however. Insofar as theological humanism is developed from Christian sources and with reference to the "third man" more needs to be said. One ought not to efface the "humanism" and the celebration of human vitalities through attention to the love of God.[31] The claim of the Christian message is that the "God" who is co-loved in the love for life is the power of life itself and yet this God has been manifested in human time in the human Christ, a power made perfect in the loving service of others. That insight enables the Christian imagination to intensify the law of freedom initially inscribed in biblical discourse in terms of the double love command. As St Paul puts it in Galatians 5:13,

> For you were called to freedom, brothers and sisters; only do not use your freedom as an opportunity for self-indulgence, but through love become slaves one to another. For the whole law is summed up in a single commandment, "You shall love your neighbor as yourself."

Once life is seen "in Christ," then the double love command is intensified in the direction of love for the human other as the limit on human and even divine power. The contrast is no longer intra-human versus extra-human transcendence; there is an ingression of the love of God into mutual love of neighbors. This requires that Christian theological humanism articulate itself through predicates borrowed from Christological formulae: one is called to be human, *truly* human in the freedom of love just as Christ is "true God and true man." Yet this formula of Christian theological humanism, I suggest, is not without the force of self-evidence; it is not mere dogmatic assertion. As shown, the love of life, our own self-affirmation, the reciprocal claim of self and other, and a longing for the divine become articulate in the idea, the representation, of the Gospel of love. This is why the Gospel can resonate, can make sense, to "Greek" and "Jew"; it is the possibility of the "third man" who is neither slave nor free, Greek nor Jew, male nor female existing in a freedom other than the vitalities of nature or the giving of the law (Gal. 3:28).[32]

At the outset of this chapter I noted that it is not at all clear that Ricoeur would reject this new formulation of a humanism of the "third man." However, it is obvious that he did not articulate his position in this way, owing, I suppose, to the strict division he drew through most of his career between philosophical and theological reflection. My point is that within the reality of the "third man," that form of life marked as the believing Gentile, a type of humanism is possible wherein the limit on the effort to be is not simply the sting of mortality but much more the longing for the divine. Once this longing, itself an attestation and a struggle, finds representation in the biblical witness, the limit on human power is the transformation of freedom in service and love to the other as oneself. Here is enacted, in a way contrary to Nietzsche, the overcoming, the perfection, of human existence. And this limit, manifest in the Christ, is also the claim of the Christian conscience whose force of self-evidence is no less than Sinai.

6

The destination of these reflections has been to enunciate the possibility of *theological humanism* drawn from Christian sources rooted in the love of life reformulated through the freedom of the Gospel. Yet in concluding, it might be asked why this revision in the humanistic agenda is needed for Christians, for the "third man," in our age. In my judgment, the development of theological humanism around the formula *human, truly human*, is required in order to accomplish a task that Ricoeur himself saw in the dawning of the global age and yet did not fully address. "The time in which we live," he wrote, "is one of planetary consciousness." And in this situation "[w]hat the theologian should rediscover here is that true Christian universalism which is a universalism of 'intention' completely distinct from the universalistic 'pretension' of the Christianity of the Constantinian Age."[33] Only when the humanism of the "third man" is formulated in order to respect and enhance the integrity of life rooted in the love of life and disciplined by the free service of others manifested in Christ can it hope to speak to the needs and longings of an age riddled with endangerments to human and non-human life. By isolating a new formula for humanism, I have sought to outline some features of that form of life.

Notes

1　Paul Ricoeur, "Nature and Freedom," in *Political and Social Essays*, ed. David Stewart and Joseph Bein (Athens, OH: Ohio University Press, 1974), pp. 31–2.

2　For an excellent account of Ricoeur's life and thought, see Charles E. Reagan, *Paul Ricoeur: His Life and His Work* (Chicago: University of Chicago Press, 1996). Also see *Meanings in Texts and Actions: Questioning Paul Ricoeur*, ed. David E. Klemm and William Schweiker (Charlottesville: University Press of Virginia, 1993); and *Paul Ricoeur and Contemporary Moral Thought*, ed. John Wall, William Schweiker, and W. David Hall (New York: Routledge, 2002). These volumes include important bibliographies of Ricoeur's work and scholarship on his corpus.

3　For one of his last statements that underscores Ricoeur's humanistic concern, see his "Ethics and Human Capability: A Response," in *Paul Ricoeur and Contemporary Moral Thought*, pp. 279–90.

4　Albert Camus, "The Myth of Sisyphus," in *The Myth of Sisyphus and Other Essays*, trans. Justin O'Brien (New York: Vintage Books, 1991), p. 3. On this point also see John Lach, *In Love with Life: Reflections on the Joy of Living and Why We Hate to Die* (Nashville, TN: Vanderbilt University Press, 1998). It is instructive in this light also to consider again Leo Tolstoy's *A Confession*, trans. A. Maude (Mineola, NY: Dover Publications, 2005).

5　The Nietzsche texts are well known, and Ricoeur begins *Oneself as Another* with the contrast between Nietzsche and Descartes. Also see Emmanuel Levinas, *Humanism of the Other*, trans. Nidra Poller, intro. Richard A. Cohen (Chicago: University of Illinois Press, 2003).

6　Of course, any typology is fraught with dangers because it seeks to isolate the most basic contours of positions rather than to offer sustained analysis of any one position. And, likewise, a typology can appear to isolate merely logical rather than living options. Problems granted, it is still helpful to have some means to organize the contemporary intellectual scene and a typology is one way to do so.

7　Paul Ricoeur, "Faith and Culture," in *Political and Social Essays*, p. 126. Actually there is another problem here longstanding in Western thought, which I cannot pause to explore, namely, the relation of "law" and "nature" in the guiding of human life.

8　In terms of Protestant Christian thought, the most powerful expression was given by Paul Tillich when he spoke of "ecstatic humanism." See his *Morality and Beyond*, foreword by William Schweiker (Louisville, KY: Westminster John Knox Press, 1995). For a brief examination of Tillich's project in our contemporary context see Max L. Stackhouse, "Humanism After Tillich," *First Things* 72 (April 1997), 24–8. For a discussion of Protestant and Catholic humanism see R. William Franklin and Joseph M. Shaw, *The Case for Christian Humanism* (Grand Rapids, MI: Eerdmans, 1991).

9　On this see William Schweiker, *Theological Ethics and Global Dynamics: In the Time of Many Worlds* (Oxford: Blackwell, 2004). Also see the essays on theological humanism in *Literature and Theology* 18:3 (2004).

10 On this see William Schweiker, "The Reason for Following: Moral Integrity and the Christological Summons," *Faith and Philosophy* 22:2 (2005), 173–98. Also see Robert P. Scharlemann, *The Reason of Following: Christology and the Ecstatic I* (Chicago: University of Chicago Press, 1991).

11 Tzvetan Todorov, *Imperfect Garden: The Legacy of Humanism*, trans. Carol Cosman (Princeton, NJ: Princeton University Press, 2002).

12 Edward W. Said, *Humanism and Democratic Criticism* (New York: Columbia University Press, 2004), p. 10.

13 For the most ardent expression of this point see Peter Singer, *Unsanctifying Human Life: Essays on Ethics* (Oxford: Blackwell, 2002).

14 One finds this argument made, on the one hand, by so-called systems theorists, and, on the other, by theorists who explore patterns and circulation of power in societies. See, for example, Nikklas Luhmann, *Theories of Distinction: Redescribing the Description of Modernity*, ed. W. Rasch (Stanford, CA: Stanford University Press, 2002); and Thomas E. Wartenberg, *The Forms of Power: From Domination to Transformation* (Philadelphia: Temple University Press, 1990).

15 Paul Ricoeur, "Ethics and Human Capability: A Response," in *Paul Ricoeur and Contemporary Moral Thought*, p. 280.

16 See Paul Ricoeur, *Oneself as Another*, trans. Kathleen Blamey (Chicago: University of Chicago Press, 1992).

17 Paul Ricoeur, "What Does Humanism Mean?" in *Political and Social Essays*, pp. 86–87.

18 Tony Davies, *Humanism* (New York: Routledge, 1997), p. 125.

19 While it is beyond the scope of this chapter, this is the decisive reason why Ricoeur can endorse both Spinoza's idea of the *conatus* and also Aristotelian teleological claims while rejecting the metaphysics of the will found in the pessimism of Schopenhauer or the vitalism of Nietzsche. See, for instance, his essay "Nature and Freedom," in *Political and Social Essays*, pp. 23–45, as well as the collection *History and Truth*, trans. Charles A. Kelbley (Evanston, IL: Northwestern University Press, 1965).

20 One can sense this contradiction build through the progression of essays in the famous *Genealogy of Morals*. See Friedrich Nietzsche, *The Birth of Tragedy and the Genealogy of Morals*, trans. Francis Golffing (New York: Anchor Books, 1956).

21 See Emmanuel Levinas, *Totality and Infinity: An Essay on Exteriority*, trans. A. Lingis (Pittsburgh, PA: Duquesne University Press, 1969).

22 Ricoeur, *Oneself as Another*, p. 336. I think the equation of killing and murder in this passage from Ricoeur is confusing. I do not see in Levinas's work a general, even universal, prohibition of "killing" but more precisely the categorical prohibition of murder. In *Totality and Infinity* Levinas wrote about ontology as a "philosophy of war," but it is not clear even there that overcoming "ontology" would mean the end of a conception of justified killing.

23 See Emmanuel Levinas, *Totality and Infinity*, and also *Alterity and Transcendence*, trans. Michael B. Smith (New York: Columbia University Press, 1999).

24   So too I cannot pause to assess the adequacy of arguments by those who contend that his conception of selves "runs the risk of reducing otherness to selfhood" and thereby falls to Levinas's criticism. See Richard Kearney, "Narrative Imagination: Between Ethics and Politics," in *Paul Ricoeur: The Hermeneutics of Action*, ed. R. Kearney (London: Sage, 1996), p. 186. On this also see John Wall, *Moral Creativity: Paul Ricoeur and the Poetics of Possibility* (Oxford: Oxford University Press, 2005).

25   There is of course considerable scholarship on the forms of Kant's categorical imperative and also its meaning. On this see Christine M. Korsegaard, *The Sources of Normativity*, ed. Onora O'Neill (Cambridge: Cambridge University Press, 1996). Also see William Schweiker, *Responsibility and Christian Ethics* (Cambridge: Cambridge University Press, 1995).

26   Paul Ricoeur, "A Critique of B. F. Skinner's *Beyond Freedom and Dignity*," in *Political and Social Essays*, p. 63.

27   One might note here that Ricoeur has retained and yet revised Martin Heidegger's understanding of time as the "meaning of being." For Ricoeur, "time" is indeed that "upon which" we project our ownmost possibilities, but those possibilities, rooted in the effort to be, exceed being towards death.

28   This is of course the force of Ricoeur's theory of narrative. See his *Time and Narrative*, 3 vols, trans. Kathleen McLaughlin and David Pellauer (Chicago: University of Chicago Press, 1984–8).

29   The question here is not the moral permissibility of suicide in extreme cases, but, rather, a question of principle. For a subtle discussion of these matters see James M. Gustafson, *Ethics from a Theocentric Perspective*, 2 vols (Chicago: University of Chicago Press, 1984, 1988).

30   On this see William Schweiker, *Power, Value and Conviction: Theological Ethics in the Postmodern Age* (Cleveland, OH: Pilgrim Press, 1998). For Ricoeur's reading of the command see his "Ethics and Theological Consideration on the Golden Rule," in *Figuring the Sacred: Religion, Narrative, and Imagination*, ed. Mark I. Wallace (Minneapolis: Fortress Press, 1995), pp. 293–302.

31   A common criticism by some neo-humanists, like Todorov, is that religious discourse, and especially Christian faith, is self-mutilating. That is, religious faith displaces proper concern for specifically human goods with a demand to love God in such a way as to demean human care. It should be obvious that my own formulation and Ricoeur's as well are not open to this charge.

32   There is of course considerable interest now in St Paul, but this interest, as far as I can see, has not, sadly, been linked to any form of Christian humanism. See, for instance, Alain Badiou, *Saint Paul: The Foundation of Universalism*, trans. Ray Brassier (Stanford, CA: Stanford University Press, 2003).

33   Paul Ricoeur, "From Nation to Humanity: Task of Christians," in *Political and Social Essays*, pp. 134, 151.

Chapter 8

Goodness and Fictive Persons*

1

In the last chapter I explored the work of Paul Ricoeur, a thinker steeped in the Christian tradition who tried to formulate a version of humanism mindful of the limits on human power and capability. The argument from the perspective of theological humanism turned on how one understands the relations among the remembrance of death, our dust or mortality, and the love of life, the breath of spirit. Christian theological humanism, we saw, insists that in Christ, there is the possibility both to acknowledge human limits but also to embrace a love of life, even new life. In this chapter I want to engage another important contemporary figure, Iris Murdoch. She was a friend of religion, especially some version of Buddhism, and she also insisted on the importance of consciousness, the interiority of existence, against those who see the moral life mainly in terms of rules, duties, social institutions, and stories. On both of these points, it is important for a theological humanist to engage her work. However, when considering the work of Iris Murdoch it is crucial somehow to connect her moral philosophy to her life as one of the twentieth century's most prolific novelists. How to do so?

This chapter examines a theme that, I believe, is found not only in her ethics but also in Murdoch's novels, at least some of them. Probing the connection between morality and art, at least good art, is actually a way to explore what it means to be a human being and the dilemma of our existence. Murdoch intimates that we are straddled between two necessities:

* This chapter was first published in a shorter version as "The Moral Fate of Fictive Persons: On Iris Murdoch's Humanism," in *Iris Murdoch and Morality*, ed. Anne Rowe and Avril Horner (London: Palgrave Macmillan, 2010), pp. 180–93. Copyright William Schweiker.

one can be called the necessity of virtue – the claim of the Good on our lives – and the second, the necessity of death, of mortality. As we know from other chapters of this book, Christian theological reflection has something at stake in the connection between death and the love of life. Human beings, Christianly understood, are dust that breathes. In this chapter I will speak about the tension between these necessities that Murdoch explores as the background to the moral fate of fictive persons, as the chapter's title puts it.

I start, then, with the connection between art and morals. Once the first claim is clear, I will turn, in a second and more controversial move, to show that Murdoch anticipated many concerns found in the current renewal of humanism. I am not suggesting that she had anything at stake in the history of humanism or what often flies under the banner of humanism, which she once called "a flimsy creed." Things turn on definition, of course. I strive to define rightly the kind of humanistic outlook discerned in Murdoch's work. The chapter is a journey through layers of reflection beginning with the connection between art and morals, moving through the current debate about humanism, to, finally, Murdoch's humanism open to religious reflection. At this third step of reflection I will probe the connection between morality and death in order to clarify some of her deepest claims. The final level of non-dogmatic religious reflection, reflection on what is ultimately important, is the inner-aim and purpose of this chapter. "To do philosophy," Murdoch once wrote, "is to explore one's own temperament, and yet at the same time to attempt to discover the truth."[1] Think of the chapter – this entire book – as a stab at that way of thinking; basic temperaments are explored and hopefully some truth will be discovered.

2

In one essay, Murdoch forcefully delineated the relation between art and morality. In "The Sublime and the Good," she wrote,

> Art and morals are … one. Their essence is the same. The essence of both of them is love. Love is the perception of individuals. Love is the extremely difficult realization that something other than oneself is real. Love, and so art and morals, is the discovery of reality. What stuns us into a realization of our supersensible destiny is not, as Kant argued, the formlessness of nature, but rather its unutterable particularity; and most particular and individual of all natural things is the mind of man.[2]

This passage deserves sustained reflection; it is rich but also perplexing.

Murdoch's most basic claim is that love – as a perception and discovery of the reality of individuals distinct from the self – is the essence, the defining feature, of art and morality. The enemies of art and moral goodness, she tells us, are convention and neurosis, both of which block right perception and responses to other people. All of this, it seems to me, is well known in Murdoch's thought.[3] And it meant that she worried about the "fate," the destiny, of actual persons, characters, both in the artistic realm of "fiction" and also in the way in which the human ego denies the reality of others, makes them "fictions" in its picture of itself. "The tragic freedom implied in love," she wrote, "is this: that we all have an indefinitely extended capacity to imagine the being of others."[4] This is tragic because imagination and love collide: what we love can be concealed by what we imagine; the human imagination creates fictive objects of love. To worry about the moral fate of fictive persons is then to worry about the tragic freedom of love at work in both art and the moral life. Often in the novels – for example, in *The Black Prince* – sexual love in particular wrestles characters out of their egos and enables a search for some good in the world and real other people. But the dangers of the ego are also scrutinized, say in *The Sacred and Profane Love Machine*. That is why the passage above from "The Sublime and the Good" is so important to examine in detail.

The challenge in getting at the tragic freedom of love centers, I believe, on making sense of Murdoch's rather surprising claim that what stuns us about "our supersensible destiny" is particular other people. What does this mean? To get the gist of that claim, her reference to Immanuel Kant is important.

Kant, in *The Critique of Judgment*, says that we experience nature as "dynamically sublime" when we consider it as "a power that has no dominion over us" (§28).[5] This feeling of the sublime is about a conflict between imagination and reason. Reason demands a grasp of the whole; the imagination cannot meet that rational demand. The "irresistibility of [nature's] power," Kant writes,

> certainly makes us, considered as natural beings, recognize our physical powerlessness, but at the same time it reveals a capacity for judging ourselves as independent of nature and a superiority over nature ... whereby the humanity in our person remains undemeaned even though the human being must submit to that dominion. (§28)

As Murdoch notes, "on the one hand we experience distress at the failure of the imagination to compass what is before us, and on the other hand we feel exhilaration in our consciousness of the absolute nature of reason's requirement and the way in which it goes beyond what mere sensible imagination can achieve."[6] Importantly, Kant drew a connection between this experience and respect for the moral law, the *Achtung*. While Murdoch thinks that Kant's theory of aesthetic judgment, both the beautiful and the sublime, is wrong, his grasp of the connection between the sublime and the demand of morality "must," she says, "be pregnant with something marvellous."[7] What is this "marvellous" insight? Two things must be noted.

First, for Kant the sublime and the respect for the moral law disclose that human beings are not inscribed within or reducible to the totality of the nature system. The starry heavens above and the moral law within, as he notoriously put it, disclose that the demand of reason arises from a supersensible realm beyond history, beyond nature. This is why they can never be fully rendered or expressed in human artifacts. Morality evokes a sense of the holy, according to Kant. The holy is what we find inviolable in ourselves and in others, namely, the law-giving power of reason with its demand for intelligibility and moral freedom. The moral law discloses humanity in me that exceeds my particular, odd, fault-ridden, broken, embodied, and finite existence. Human beings, then, particularize in their personhood this supersensible power of reason, the inviolability of humanity. In respect for the moral law, as Murdoch notes, "we feel pain at the thwarting of our sensuous nature by a moral requirement, and elation in the consciousness of our rational nature; that is, our freedom to conform to the absolute requirement of reason."[8]

An analogous dynamic is found in the experience of the sublime and the clash between imagination and reason. "The freedom of sublimity," Murdoch explains about Kant, "does not symbolise, but *is* moral freedom, only moral freedom not practically active but only, as it were, intuiting itself in an exultant manner."[9] The marvelousness of this insight must be grasped because it is one, as far as I can see, that Murdoch accepts. Aesthetic and moral experience disclose the transcendent reach of human existence into a supersensible destiny while also posing the problem of human existence as a conflict arising in the heart of every human life.[10]

Of course, how this supersensible destiny and moral conflict are rightly to be conceived is precisely the point where Murdoch departs from Kant. That is the second thing to note about his "marvellous" insight. On Murdoch's reading, Kant's aesthetics and ethics fail because the demand of reason extracts one from history and the messiness of actual life. His ethics thereby has no place for the tragic. She quips: "We are supposed to live by exceedingly simple and general rules: suppression of history, suspicion of eccentricity."[11] On reaching that conclusion Murdoch then states her own position in the words I quoted before from "The Sublime and the Good." To summarize: love as the essence of art and morals is the perception of individuals; it is a discovery of reality – the reality of the other person. Yet in this discovery we are stunned with the realization of a "supersensible destiny" by a particularity, specifically, the particularity of the *mind of man*. That supersensible destiny is not like Kant in rational freedom, or humanity incarnate in individuals, but within eccentric forms of personal consciousness.

The shock is that in the core of our inmost being, in consciousness, is found the locus of the tragic freedom implied in love, namely, the perception of others in collision with the dynamics of the imagination of self-picturing. Whereas for Kant our supersensible nature is the power of reason to legislate maxims of action with the categorical power to command obedience, for Murdoch what discloses our supersensible destiny is the work and peril of the imagination marked by love and its tragic freedom. Freedom thereby poses the challenge of the moral fate of fictive persons: how to write novels that attend to the particular and eccentric forms of consciousness in characters and, further, how in our moral lives to perceive the reality of others who exceed the ways we picture ourselves and them. It is this problem, I suggest, that is probed in novels like *The Black Prince* and others; it is probably why *Metaphysics as the Guide to Morals* culminates in "void." Others always exceed our ability to picture them and yet there is a relentless drive to picture ourselves and our world. This instigates the struggle of the moral life.

What then of the difference between art and morality? For Murdoch this turns on the idea of *form* and also the possibility of genuine tragedy. "What makes tragic art so disturbing," she claims, "is that self-contained form is combined with something, the individual being and destiny of human persons, which defies form. A great tragedy leaves us in eternal doubt. It is the form of art where the exercise of love is most like its exercise in morals."[12] Art, insofar as it is pleasing and entertaining, is a crafted object. But great art, and especially great literature, at least for Murdoch, is about that reality that defies form, the human being. Great art tries to render or express through its medium and style, its form, what cannot be presented. And it wrestles with this problem. It enacts in *form* the struggle of the moral life.

Persons defy form in at least two ways, it seems to me. Any actual human being cannot be reduced to artistic form, or to some social totality, or to a political agenda, because, as we have seen before in this book, to be a human being is to have a supersensible destiny that exceeds all sensible form. This is why art is not life; it is why art, as Murdoch insists, consoles and delights. She even says, in "The Sovereignty of Good Over Other Concepts," that the "pointlessness of art is not the pointlessness of a game; it is the pointlessness of human life itself, and form in art is properly the simulation of the self-contained aimlessness of the universe."[13] The fact that human beings defy form is why the moral life cannot be represented in Kantian-like duties and laws that we are to obey, but must, rather, be a sustained and never-ending adventure of attention and love under the idea of a perfect Good. Not surprisingly, characters in Murdoch's novels shatter each other's perceptions of them; not surprisingly, her account of the moral life is messy and yet also austere in its demand.

Human beings defy form in another way. We fail to see that consciousness is always producing form, always at work making pictures of ourselves and others. We defy the real for the imaginary. We are all artists. That is the problem. One of Murdoch's most famous claims is about the seam between art and self-understanding and form. She declared: "Man is a creature who makes a picture of himself, and then comes to resemble the picture. This is the process which moral philosophy must attempt to describe and analyze."[14] Her famous and ambiguous claims about the demand to "unself" turn precisely on this point. It is also the reason Murdoch worried so much about the demand on the artist and the moral distortions and false consolations of human consciousness. The claim that human beings defy form not only demarcates the difference between art and morals, it also articulates the distinctly human struggle of the tragic freedom of love.

Before taking another step of inquiry a further point needs to be made. For both Kant and Murdoch the moral demand is endless and unconditioned because human life is sensible and free, for Kant, and enmeshed in the tragic freedom of love, for Murdoch. This mixed-character of our being (sensible/supersensible) is disclosed in the experience of the sublime and respect, for Kant, or the workings of love in consciousness, for Murdoch. We are creatures "in-between," as it were. A human being is a movement, a self-overcoming, a struggle between sensible and supersensible natures. Not just the dignity and moral vocation of human beings arise from this fact of our mixed being. Evil and despair also transpire here. Kant defined moral evil as the subversion of maxims of action when an immoral maxim rooted in sensibility triumphs over reason's demands. "Evil be thou my good," as Satan cries in *Paradise Lost*, is, per definition, radical evil. Moral transformation is always required. In order to succeed at that arduous task and so to make oneself virtuous and worthy of happiness, Kant thought he had to postulate the ideas of a perfect judge (i.e., God) and also immortality – an endless time of moral striving. The Good, we might say, puts a certain necessity on human beings to fulfill the demands of morality and thus to be worthy to be happy. This necessity, the demand of freedom, warrants postulates of God and immortality.

Murdoch too, as we know, believed that the moral life centered on change, the transformation of consciousness. While she grasped the unconditional nature of morality and also the evil and despair that haunt human life because of the tragic freedom found in love, morals would have to proceed without God or any idea of immortality. A different temperament is at work; a different response to the necessity that morality puts on us. We dwell within the "self-contained aimlessness of the universe," she says, which reaches out beyond our powers of knowledge and imagination. Ideas about God and immortality are too easily false consolations because they claim to grasp the whole of reality. I will return to that matter of God and death later in this chapter. For now we can leave it "pregnant with some-thing marvellous."

3

I have been trying to probe the link between Murdoch's ethics and her understanding or theory of art. Love and its tragic freedom are the essence of art and morals. Murdoch's celebrated demand of unselfing through rigor-ous attention to the reality of others means that one task, maybe the central task, of the moral life is to get the self out of the way, to escape forces, internal and external, that intertwine the self in itself. One needs to shatter form, break the images, for a vision of what is real on its own terms. Tragedy as a form of art is one that tries this shattering while also rendering lived reality through form. The author and the moralist must protect and promote the reality of persons against forces both within art and within existence that too easily and too readily efface persons through the triumph of form.

The novels and the philosophy are different but conjoint strategies that aim to show the moral plight of persons, fictive and real. Murdoch's argu-ment about the tragic freedom of love connecting art and morals entails, I have suggested, a stunning insight about our "supersensible destiny." Or to put it another way, the tragic freedom of love that connects art and morals is also a key, a clue, to what it means to be a human being and the moral demand at the core of our being. If that is so, then Murdoch's art and her philosophy are profoundly humanistic in orientation and intent. That possibility brings us to the second step of this inquiry.[15]

Currently there is a revival of interest in humanism among some leading philosophers, critics, social commentators, and religious thinkers as well.[16] The concern is to counter the dehumanizing forces of intolerance, fanati-cism, and ignorance well known on the global scene. Neohumanism, as I explored in previous chapters, makes a shift from the priority of the self found in classical humanism to an ethical concern for the other. That is why it is *neo*humanism. The freedom of the self, the moral claim of others, and an inclusive moral community are basic humanistic values. As Tzvetan Todorov writes,

> Humanism is neither a "naturalism" nor an "artificialism;" it defends its values neither because they are embodied in the natural order, nor because the will of the most powerful has decreed it … . [For the humanist it is] because these values of freedom, respect for others, and the equal dignity of all impose themselves on him with the force of self-evidence, and seem to him more suitable to the human species than others.[17]

Correlate to these self-evident values, neohumanists also insist on human fallibility, and so humility in our appreciation of truth. And, finally, humanists believe, to recall Edward Said's words, that "human history as made by human action and understood accordingly is the very ground of the humanities."[18] Put simply, the purpose of thought and action is human flourishing achieved by means of the distinctive power to act and so to create history, whatever other non-human purposes might obtain.

Beyond these ideas and ideals are two other attributes of neohumanism important to grasp. One is a claim about human transcendence, that is, our capacity to reach out beyond ourselves, to overcome our given condition under the pressure of what is better, more just, more perfect. Most neohumanists, as noted in Chapter 5, like to talk about "lateral transcendence" as opposed to some kind of other-worldly religious transcendence. They worry that talk about religious transcendence will invariably efface concern for other human beings. By the term "lateral transcendence" is meant, then, that human freedom and love find their term, their aim, in other human beings. What has finality and universality, as Todorov noted, is other human beings and them alone. This means, additionally, that there is no aim or telos to human existence beyond the realm of historical, social existence. On these points, Murdoch seems to agree. The point of the moral life is to escape the tenacious grasp of the ego. We are simply here, she says. "And if there is any kind of sense or unity in human life, and the dream of this does not cease to haunt us, it is of some other kind and must be sought within a human experience which has nothing outside it."[19]

Along with "lateral transcendence," another attribute of neohumanism is important to note. Recall that for Todorov key values like freedom, respect for others, and equal dignity of persons "impose themselves" "with the force of self-evidence, and seem ... more suitable to the human species than others." What we can say about the source or ground of basic values, of the Good, is not its metaphysical status so much as how it appears or imposes itself with a kind of self-evidence. In Murdoch's terms, what stuns us into an awareness of our supersensible destiny and also the reality of the Good is discovery of the reality of other persons. Their being imposes itself upon our attention with the force of reality; it stuns us. And this is why, for her, "value" or the "Good" are not products of will.[20] Of course, the tragic dynamics of freedom, we now know, is that the omnivorous ego seeks to reduce others into fictions of its own imagination. Murdoch concludes that "nothing in life is of any value except the attempt to be virtuous."[21]

Murdoch agrees with some of the main features of so-called neohumanism and, importantly, anticipated by decades those arguments with her insistence on the reality of the other person, the messiness and incompleteness of human life, and also her conception of transcendence, our supersensible destiny. This is why George Steiner is basically right when he says that Murdoch's novels enact the "contradictory ideal of immanent transcendence, of down-to-earth 'rapture' or illumination," and, further, that this ideal is found in her "morality of love, of individualized reciprocity, whose foundations can, ought to be, those of rational humanism."[22] Yet if that is the case, does Murdoch contribute anything distinctive to neohumanism, or, to put it differently, what is the nature of Iris Murdoch's humanism?

If we are to get Murdoch's humanism right, then we need to probe further the idea of lateral transcendence and connect it with the shock at our supersensible destiny in the tragic freedom of love. What many neohumanists apparently do not grasp, but Murdoch does, is the danger inherent in saying that the value of others merely asserts itself with self-evidence. That simply is not enough, metaphysically speaking. Right perception might be missing and if that is so, if one simply does not feel the weight of another person's moral dignity, what then? Does their value somehow vanish because it is not perceived? Clearly a stronger argument about the *reality of value* is needed in order to make sense of what I have called the necessity of virtue. Interestingly, Murdoch's position on this metaphysical point is a place of criticism of her work by neohumanists like Martha Nussbaum and criticisms of Kant, Plato, and Christian ethics by others, including Todorov. What is the criticism and does Murdoch have an answer to it?

The criticism goes like this. The Christian command to love the neighbor, even the enemy, and Kant's insistence that what we respect is "humanity" in persons, and Plato's claim, say in the *Phaedrus*, to love the divine good in a person, and Murdoch's more austere claims about the Good and unselfing, mean that concrete individuals are loved, respected, not for what they actually are but as instances of a more general idea. Christians, supposedly, see human beings as interchangeable "neighbors," loved without discrimination or attachment. Plato apparently is awkward with particularity and entranced with the Idea of the Good. For Kant one cannot even love oneself but must reverence "humanity." In each case, individuals become images or symbols or forms of the Good that have to be seen through, decoded, broken open in order to grasp the real Good. The failing shows up, the criticism goes, in treatments of the body and the priority given to reason or consciousness or soul over the body and sexual love.

Of course, critics of Murdoch admit that her novels do in fact get at sexual love and eccentric selves. Martha Nussbaum concludes, "Murdoch's art can depict more about the human particular than her characters can see, insofar as they are Platonic lovers."[23] Murdoch's art redeems her philosophy of love. Stated otherwise, neohumanists are suspicious of the account of transcendence found among Christians, Platonists, Kantians, and, at least in her philosophy, Murdoch as well. They worry because it is not limited to lateral transcendence. The critics would hardly be surprised that in *Metaphysics as a Guide to Morals* Murdoch wanted a Godless theology – but still a theology – and that she found something truly marvelous in Kant's connection of the experience of the sublime and respect for the moral law.[24] I do not think the critics are right about Murdoch, never mind their interpretations of Christian love or Plato or Kant. Yet in order to get things clearer we need to return to that passage from "The Sublime and the Good" with which we started and introduce a crucial clarification. I am trying to think with Murdoch and yet I must also follow out the logical trajectory of her argument to its further implications.[25]

Recall that love is a perception of individuals; it is the discovery of reality. But what stuns is the "unutterable particularity" of "the mind of man." The argument seems to be that the abstract, the real, the Good is only experienced in the breaking down of the power of consciousness by what defies form, the real individual. That event simply *is* the reality of the Good. While metaphysically real and basic, the Good is only rendered or expressed or seen in particular persons who break open, defy, the form-making power of consciousness. Yet the Good is not limited to any particular individual. We can, in acts of love, "see" the Good in anyone – that power to break open self-enclosed consciousness. Whatever one wants to say about Plato or Kant and their care for actual persons, Murdoch, on my reading, is not saying that the Good is real or manifest anywhere else than in loving attention to particular persons. That is the only place it is known even if the reality of the Good is not equivalent to discrete individuals. And because of this metaphysical claim, the criticism of Murdoch is wide of the mark. A different temperament is at work.

Murdoch's critics are not captivated by what she found marvelous in Kant, namely, that the connection between art and morals has its own *unique mode of appearance*, the demand of reason arising within its own failure, as Kant had it, or the discovery of the other persons, as Murdoch says, entangled in the tragic freedom of love that thereby limits art and invigorates morals. The necessity of virtue, we can say, remains despite our failure of perception; the reality of the Good or the moral law exerts force within consciousness and often against consciousness. Where Murdoch and Kant differ is in terms of how best to describe that *mode of appearance*: a demand of reason or that of love and vision. Yet they share the conviction that "lateral transcendence" is what the mind cannot capture in its own terms, namely, the unconditional claim of morality that has its analogy in aesthetic experience. Human beings are mixed creatures in whom the supersensible appears within the struggle of the sensible. Only this insight, Murdoch seems to suggest, enables one to have a clear grasp of what art or morality is all about. If one does not see what kind of creatures we are revealed or manifest in the sublime and in morality, then art and love and morality do not make much sense. They lack rational grounds;

they vaporize into the fog of feeling or a burst of will. If one does grasp this point, then there is a return to matters of ultimate concern and our sense of what is holy, but within a humanism of the tragic freedom of love. Murdoch is a chastened neohumanist. Other people are the term and reach of transcendence, but this means the death of the self and awareness of the reality of Good that appears with the necessity of virtue.

4

I have explored how Murdoch connects art and morals, and my account is probably uncontroversial and maybe obvious. Yet I have also shown how her thought on this topic commits her to some form of neohumanism even if it also distinguishes her from those thinkers who reject an account of human beings as mixed creatures at the innermost core of our being. I suppose that is my most controversial claim. I hope this argument has convinced you that there is something marvelous in these ideas. It just rings true, I believe, that within aesthetic and moral experience is disclosed something about the depth and complexity of our own being and the existence of others not reducible to bodiliness; lived reality exceeds mere physical, sensible existence and destiny. It still makes sense to speak of a supersensible destiny.

Even more profoundly, Kant's and Murdoch's arguments show that freedom and consciousness are constituted in some complex way through what has reality other than ourselves but which appears within ourselves and others, that is, the magnetism of the good or the claim of the moral law. Our inner-life is open to self-transcendence in and through encounters, perceptions, and relations with others. And this imposes a kind of *necessity* on us from within freedom: the necessity of virtue. For both Murdoch and Kant there is then a double otherness in human beings and this makes us distinctly precious creatures, but also beings vulnerable to fault and evil. The drive of self-consciousness is, for Kant, the tension between sensible desires and respect for the moral law while, for Murdoch, it is the tragic freedom of love, that is, the one-making activity of consciousness that too easily conceals realities distinct from the self. Self-consciousness is riddled with the conflict and struggle between the necessity of virtue and the freedom to abide by or deny that claim of morality. Moral goodness is victory in this battle of our lives, lasting or fleeting. It is a self-transcendence through consciousness of the Good (Murdoch) or the Moral Law (Kant) that transforms or unselves us. Moral goodness is a self-overcoming, a transcendence of ourselves and so a supersensible destiny. The texture of moral experience is the pathway to the holy, the sense of the sacred. This is why Murdoch's humanism of love's tragic freedom is open to religion in a way that most neohumanists are not.[26] Murdoch is a chastened *religious* neohumanist.

If Murdoch is right, then, we are creatures who in moral and aesthetic experiences confront the unconditioned. The question then becomes: has the sense of the sacred, the unconditioned, which defies form been adequately conceptualized? And, in fact, I have been exploring two different outlooks. Kant conceived the unconditioned, its necessity and evidence, through the idea of categorical duty. Murdoch does so in terms of the magnetism of the Good and love and attention and consciousness. Is there any way to decide which of these conceptions is most adequate for articulating the claim of the unconditioned on human existence, a claim that appears in art and morality? What standard could possibly apply? Fate, that is, the inescapability of death, now comes to the fore. And here I have to push the logic of Murdoch's position in ways she really did not.

The previous steps of these reflections have uncovered a certain kind of necessity at the root of freedom, namely, the necessity of virtue; awareness of this necessity reveals our supersensible destiny. But insofar as we are mixed creatures, there is another necessity in human life. Questions of the unconditioned and the holy are deeply bound to our experience of time, our mortality. Murdoch is clear that the novel and the tragic and morality spin on these matters as well. Does our experience of the unconditioned in art and morals disclose anything about the temporal reach and complexity of human existence and reality? What is the metaphysical significance of the unconditioned?

Kant thought we need the idea of immortality and also God in order to stave off despair and to bolster moral effort. Somehow, he reasoned, happiness and virtue have to go together. Each imposes a necessity upon us, as it were. As an embodied, mortal creature I cannot escape the desire for happiness; as a free rational being, my freedom is bound to the necessary, universal moral law. My existence is straddled between these necessities. The union of virtue and happiness is what Kant called the "highest good" and it is an idea without which human beings cannot make moral sense of their existence. If we thought that evil would always triumph, the wicked would always flourish, and the good or innocent always suffer, then, Kant held, we could not render our lives morally intelligible. Respect for the moral law and our desire for happiness, the unconditional claim and the inescapable desire of our being, must be reconciled, or, he believed, morality would appear a sham. Ought implies can: because reason requires intelligibility we are warranted, we are permitted, to think beyond empirical conditions for an answer. We need some notion of infinite time to make ourselves virtuous and so worthy of happiness in order to reconcile virtue and happiness. Under reason's own demand, we are thereby allowed rationally to postulate the idea of immortality and also the idea of God as the judge of virtue who bestows happiness.

For Murdoch things are different. The moral life is pointless. The universe is aimless, or so it seems. Value is discovered when we are realistic and perceive justly. And as she says, "Good is a transcendent reality means that virtue is the attempt to pierce the veil of selfish consciousness and join the world as it really is. It is an empirical fact about human nature that this attempt cannot be entirely successful."[27] If we ask how the world really is, we are often told, in her philosophy and in some of the novels, that it is suffering and death. Late in *The Black Prince*, Francis tells Bradley that Priscilla is dead. Bradley responds:

> Love ought to triumph over time, but can it? Not time's fool he said and he knew about love if anybody did, he was bloody crucified if anybody was. Of course one's got to suffer. Perhaps in the end the suffering is all, it's all contained in the suffering. The final atoms of it all are simply pain.[28]

Of course, a character is not the mouthpiece for Murdoch's thought, especially Bradley Pearson. Yet something abiding and true of Murdoch's thought is reflected in Bradley's temperament.

According to Murdoch moral goodness is incompletely realized in a human life and, further, it shatters the turmoil of egoism and suffering. It also reveals something. What? Does it reveal the rational permission to hold an idea of God and of immortality? No. That love is the sign that we are spiritual creatures, she says in *The Sovereignty of Good*. What else? "Goodness," she writes, "is connected with the acceptance of real death and real chance and real transience and only against the background of this acceptance ... can we understand the full extent of what virtue is like."[29] Virtue is bound up with *acceptance* of the necessity of real death, with our radical mortality. The acceptance of mortality, not its overcoming, is the deepest truth against which virtue makes sense.[30]

This stark and hard claim is also deeply humanistic: human; made from dust; born to die. Humility, awareness that one just is dust, marks a good person. Virtue is the death of self-preoccupation and so true objectivity. Philosophy, as Plato famously taught, is learning to die. Murdoch insists that tragedy is the highest art. The fate of the moral life is an unsuccessful one but, importantly, there are moments when the reality of the Good pierces the human world from within the human world. This is immanent and lateral but also religious transcendence in the acceptance of death as the background of virtue. Human beings are not creatures thrown into a meaningless void who have to create value through acts of will. Murdoch rejected existentialism. Yet we must ask: is the logical conclusion of her thought the idea that mortals exist in an aimless universe and grasp the supreme reality of the good only in acceptance of real death? Is the inner-meaning of the good life the acceptance of the necessity of virtue against the backdrop of the necessity of death? Is that the inner-meaning of genuine love?

I cannot hope to answer those questions in this chapter. Yet Kant and, further behind him, the Christian theological tradition have different, if no less realistic, temperaments. The metaphysical ground of morality for Kant is moral freedom. Respect for rational freedom, awe over the holy, is the background of virtue. The most basic reality for Christians is divine life and not death, and, further, new life in redemption through Christ. We are creatures. We do not have our bodies, consciousness, or life from ourselves. Awareness that we are creatures combats pride and evokes gratitude for being.[31] A life enjoined by divine life is also marked by humility, also knows suffering, will die. Love is the hallmark and principle of the moral life. Perfect love, love of God and neighbor, discloses that through the broken-ness of life, through the tenacious prideful grip of the self, through sorrows of death, something nevertheless shines – the living power of goodness called, in theological terms, the being of God. The meaning of our super-sensible destiny has changed. Not learning to die, but learning to live: that is the motto of a humanistic ethics drawn from the biblical traditions. To state this otherwise, while Murdoch likes Simon Weil's claim that selfishness dies when the soul is exposed to God, there is another strand of Christian thought: the true self is found in the living God, the life of one's life, as Augustine put it.[32] The enemies of goodness are pride and ingratitude; the background of virtue is resolute gratitude for life, a kind of real joy.[33]

Now the point is not to launch into a defense of Christian morals. It is also not to suggest that in a single chapter, book, or lifetime one could give a definitive proof of a Murdochian or Kantian or Christian outlook. We are probing temperaments but also seeking the truth. I am claiming that Murdoch's kind of humanism exceeds the reach of contemporary neohumanism in its insistence on a supersensible destiny and the transcendence of the Good. Yet it is a humanism which in its temperament is a step away or before or aside or behind one drawn from biblical sources. Why? Because for those sources and the temperaments they express and shape the background of virtue is not the acceptance of death but a conviction about the gift of life. Some will be pleased with Murdoch's stand. Others will chide Murdoch for being too "spiritual" or for not being religious or Christian enough.

My conclusion is neither pleasure nor chiding. It is, rather, to isolate those points where her work helps us fight forces of the inhuman. Murdoch's thought on art and morals is an important bulwark against illusion, fanaticism, and fantasy found in all cultures, religions, and selves. What is more, her account of the tragic freedom of love opens anew the most basic of all religious questions in ways that, surprisingly, theological humanism might answer. Theological humanism intimates that a sense of the holy is somehow bound up with the gift and dignity of life despite the realities of suffering and the sting of death. The moral fate of persons, what is disclosed in our mortality and timeliness, is not just suffering and death and the reality of the Good along with the unsuccessful struggle for virtue whose background is acceptance of death. Through all of the real pain and moral struggle something else hits with the force of self-evidence. Finite life reaches out to deeper life and it is against the background of a conviction, a resolute gratitude, that love of others and self gains power and sense. Murdoch might find this false consolation. One can only respond to her: look again.

5

What does my argument, and even the way I have presented it, mean for thinking about the connection between art and morality? Murdoch thought that Western philosophy could be seen as a debate between Plato and Kant, and this chapter has covered some of that history. But I think that if one asks about art and morality within our civilization something else really comes to the fore. This civilization is driven most basically, if not exclusively, by the creative interaction and conflict between its Greek, Roman, and biblical sources – as we saw in other chapters.[34] Surprisingly, within strands of these traditions there are points of agreement, especially about the unconditioned claim on human beings as mixed creatures. That is why Kant and Murdoch can reach similar marvelous insights. But there are also points of profound disagreement which I have unfolded not just in terms of the difference between will and love in defining freedom, but, more profoundly, in terms of the metaphysical significance of life and death. At a deep level, Western thought is the tracking of different assessments of what is disclosed in human mortality and the gift of life.

Much current thought, it seems to me, tries to ignore this complex legacy. Many neohumanists want to be Greeks. Too many religious people, as we know, want to retreat inside the confines of their communities and peer out at an alien and dangerous world. What I have attempted to do by isolating Murdoch's humanism and the opening to theological humanism is to insist that we must think within tensions that drive our heritage. Ethics and aesthetics in the West are a long and ongoing dialogue about the relation of death and life in disclosing the meaning and value of the structures and dynamics of reality. Is the good real but reality aimless? Can the depth and reach of life be disclosed in the folly, travail, and suffering of fictive and real human beings? Why love life? Do answers to these questions matter for how we can and ought to live? Yes.

The most basic facts of our time are the endangerment to human and non-human life around this planet, the fanatic religious hatred of finite life and moral reasonableness, and the endless profaning of existence in late-modern cultures. The terrifying possibility of human freedom is that the lust for more power will rid this world of life. The tragic freedom of love in the unflinching devotion and attachment to one's God can lead to the hatred of all that is ungodly. Unbending skepticism about the aspirations of the human spirit leads to a gritty profaning of every domain of life. These real possibilities are the final betrayal of goodness.[35] Against these horrible possibilities we need a humanism open to a sense of the holy and the unconditioned and yet which also endorses the transcendent reach and dignity of finite life.

Notes

1 Iris Murdoch, "On 'God' and 'Good'," in *The Sovereignty of Good* (London: Routledge & Kegan Paul, 1970), p. 46.

2 Iris Murdoch, "The Sublime and the Good," in *Existentialists and Mystics: Writings on Philosophy and Literature* (London: Allen Lane, 1998), p. 215.

3 Not only did she constantly challenge the "fat and relentless ego," but Murdoch also believed the artist must enable characters to have their own life, their individuality. It is also true that in her moral philosophy attention to the concrete other individual, the labor of love, is basic. The famous example of D and M from *Sovereignty of Good* explores the transformation of consciousness through sustained attention to the concrete other. Against those types of thought in art or philosophy that celebrate will and individual choice and thus reduce the moral act to the moment of decision, kinds of thought she associated emblematically with existentialism, Murdoch's focus is on attention, vision, and love for the individual that exceeds the self and limits its choices.

4 Murdoch, "The Sublime and the Good," p. 216.

5 Immanuel Kant, *The Critique of the Power of Judgment*, trans. Paul Guyer and Eric Matthews, ed. Paul Guyer (Cambridge: Cambridge University Press, 2000). I have merely given the reference to the section.

6 Murdoch, "The Sublime and the Good," p. 208.

7 Murdoch, "The Sublime and the Good," p. 213.

8 Murdoch, "The Sublime and the Good," p. 208.

9 Murdoch, "The Sublime and the Good," p. 209.

10 Little wonder, then, that later thinkers, existentialists and others, probed the dynamics of freedom in order to articulate the meaning of being human, and in very different ways. Jean-Paul Sartre celebrated existential choice. Martin Heidegger found in the call of conscience, the call of *Dasein* to itself, authentic being. Paul Tillich and other theologians found in the freedom of *Agape* the being of God.

11   Murdoch, "The Sublime and the Good," p. 215.

12   Murdoch, "The Sublime and the Good," p. 219.

13   Murdoch, "The Sovereignty of Good Over Other Concepts," in *The Sovereignty of Good*," p. 86.

14   Iris Murdoch, "Metaphysics and Ethics," in *Iris Murdoch and the Search for Human Goodness*, ed. Maria Antonaccio and William Schweiker (Chicago: University of Chicago Press, 1996), p. 252. On this see contributions to *Iris Murdoch and the Search for Human Goodness*, as well as Maria Antonaccio, *Picturing the Human: The Moral Thought of Iris Murdoch* (Oxford: Oxford University Press, 2000).

15   A survey of intellectual trends in early and late twentieth-century thought reveals that many of the convictions and values of humanism were in dispute. Self-styled humanists tended to focus on science, the criticism of religion, and, most importantly, freedom, say in Sartre's famous essay "Existentialism is Humanism" which provoked Heidegger's "Letter on Humanism." Obviously, Murdoch rejects the existentialist picture of human life. Is that the end of the story? By the term "humanism" I do not mean a specific set of thinkers or texts or even a particular period in Western intellectual history. I am much more concerned with a set of ideals or convictions that characterize a humanistic outlook.

16   I will note some of these thinkers below, but for a recent discussion among religionists see *Humanity Before God: Contemporary Faces of Jewish, Christian, and Islamic Ethics*, ed. William Schweiker, Michael Johnson, and Kevin Jung (Minneapolis: Fortress Press, 2006).

17   Tzvetan Todorov, *Imperfect Garden: The Legacy of Humanism*, trans. Carol Cosman (Princeton, NJ: Princeton University Press, 2002), p. 42.

18   Edward W. Said, *Humanism and Democratic Criticism* (New York: Columbia University Press, 2004), p. 10.

19   Murdoch, "The Sovereignty of Good Over Other Concepts," p. 79.

20   This is a point on which Murdoch's debt to G. E. Moore is most obvious. The good is a real but non-natural property that supervenes on natural realities.

21   Murdoch, "The Sovereignty of Good Over Other Concepts," p. 87.

22   George Steiner, "Foreword," in *Existentialists and Mystics*, pp. xiv, xvi.

23   Martha C. Nussbaum, "Love and Vision: Iris Murdoch on Eros and the Individual," in *Iris Murdoch and the Search for Human Goodness*, p. 48. Of course, the question of how to understand Christian love is massive. For one account see William Schweiker, "Distinctive Loves: Gratitude for Life and Theological Humanism," in *Humanity Before God*, pp. 91–117.

24   See Iris Murdoch, *Metaphysics as a Guide to Morals* (London: Allen Lane, 1992), pp. 511–12. The best study on Murdoch's moral philosophy is Maria Antonaccio, *Picturing the Human: The Moral Thought of Iris Murdoch* (Oxford: Oxford University Press, 2000).

25   For a trenchant response to the criticism I offer, see the writings of Maria Antonaccio, especially her forthcoming book, *A Philosophy to Live By: Engaging Iris Murdoch*.

26   Of course, a massive question arises at just this point, one too complex for this chapter to address even if I were fully competent to do so. Murdoch holds two

claims: that we are in the midst of an "aimless" and thoroughly material universe and yet within this condition human consciousness has come to be. How are we to explain the origin of consciousness in such a universe, especially if one must avoid, which I think we must, some kind of metaphysical dualism where mind and body are two separate and distinct things? The trouble with forms of dualism is well known scientifically and philosophically. Murdoch, as far as I know, never bothered to address the issue, nor will I try to do so. Of course, Plato had an answer, and it is one that Murdoch seems to reject. But I register all of this just to note a massive problem on the horizon of Murdoch's thought.

27   Murdoch, "The Sovereignty of Good Over Other Concepts," p. 93.
28   Iris Murdoch, *The Black Prince* (New York: Viking, 1973), p. 359.
29   Murdoch, "The Sovereignty of Good Over Other Concepts," p. 103.
30   It would be important on this point to explore Murdoch's complex engagement with Heidegger's thought, something I cannot attempt in this chapter.
31   On this see, for example, Martin Luther, "Sermons on the Catechism," in *Martin Luther: Selections from His Writings*, ed. J. Dillenberger (New York: Anchor Books, 1962), pp. 207–40.
32   Murdoch makes this claim following Weil near the end of "The Sovereignty of Good Over Other Concepts." Augustine's most forceful statement of his position is of course in the *Confessions*. A more precise argument linking it to a distinctly Christian conception of God is found in his *On the Trinity*.
33   On the idea of "real joy" see William Schweiker, *Theological Ethics and Global Dynamics: In the Time of Many Worlds* (Oxford: Blackwell, 2004).
34   There is another strand of thought that seeks to avoid both of these sources. Schopenhauer, whom Murdoch so deeply engages, finds remnants of Eastern thought, especially Hinduism, in the Perennial philosophy of some Western thinkers. He sees this as Asiatic and even Aryan and so the real legacy of the West. I cannot engage this option in the present chapter. On this see Arthur Schopenhauer, *The Basis of Morality*, 2nd edn, trans. A. B. Bullock (Mineola, NY: Dover, 2005).
35   Elsewhere I have called this a form of "moral madness." See Schweiker, *Theological Ethics and Global Dynamics*.

Chapter 9

Reverence for Life – The Spirit of Life*

Whether humanity *ought* to live, or ought to become extinct, is a question which cannot be answered through the dictates of rational expediency, but only out of a love for life.[1]

1

Some of the chapters in Part I of this book reflected on the idea of "conscience" as important for thinking about our moral lives and religious concerns. Conscience, it was argued, is the moral labor of our lives; it names the capacity to hear the call to responsibility within the very core of our being. But that poses a question. What is the norm and measure of responsible existence? It is not good enough to preach: be conscientious! Throughout the previous chapters I have expressed the norm as "the integrity of life." What does that mean? How does it relate to theological humanism? This chapter and the next one address these questions by engaging two contemporary theologians for whom the theme of "life" has been especially important, namely, Jürgen Moltmann and Knud Løgstrup. By engaging their work, I hope to clarify the meaning of the "integrity of life" for theological humanism.

Jürgen Moltmann is one of the late twentieth century's most renowned Christian theologians. He was especially important for developing the theology of hope and also for advancing political and liberation theology. In his more recent writings, Moltmann has argued that there is a necessary connection between the experience of God and reverence for life. In one book he

* This chapter was first published in a briefer form as "The Spirit of Life and the Reverence for Life," in *God's Life in Trinity*, ed. Miroslav Wolf and Michael Welker (Minneapolis: Fortress Press, 2006), pp. 22–31. Copyright William Schweiker.

writes that because "life comes from 'the source of life' – the creative divine Spirit – and is alive in the Spirit, it must be sanctified. Life is sanctified when we encounter everything living with reverence before God."[2] While Moltmann has not written much on ethics, the idea of the reverence for life enables Christians and theologians interested in ethics to engage Moltmann's work at its most humanly salient point.[3] What is at stake in this engagement is nothing less than the perspective of Christian faith on reality and also the most basic good that can and ought to orient human life and action.

Moltmann is right that a new sensibility for the worth and fragility of life is profoundly needed in an age of global suffering and ecological endangerment. The discourse of "reverence for life" resonates deeply within present moral and religious longings. However, the question is whether or not an "ethics" of the reverence for life articulates the proper expression of Christian moral thinking in our time. On that question, I have profound reservations. What follows, then, are reflections on the *necessity* of the connection between the Spirit of life and an ethics of the reverence for life. In the process I will clarify the meaning of the "integrity of life" as the best way for a theological humanist to speak about the norm and measure for responsible existence.

2

On first glance it might appear that a conviction about the living God would naturally lend itself to an ethics of the reverence for life. The divine life is the power and energy of finite life and also the vibrancy of new life. When reality is viewed in the light of God's coming, then a reverence for life seems necessarily to follow. The sanctification of life on Moltmann's account entails trust in God, respect for others and self, and also reverence for all life. Little wonder, then, that if "life itself is sanctified because it is holy, the conclusion that has to be drawn is an ethics of *reverence for life*. ..."[4] At least that is Moltmann's conclusion.

Despite Moltmann's interest in a theology of life, it is not immediately obvious why Christians concerned about ethics ought to bother themselves with reflection on reverence for life. The ethics of reverence for life is most often associated with Albert Schweitzer's ethical mysticism. "Only by serving every kind of life," he wrote, "do I enter service of that Creative Will whence all life emanates. ... This is the mystical significance of ethics."[5] Most contemporary moral reflection, Christian or otherwise, rejects any connection to mysticism, and, most basically, the metaphysics of Will that Schweitzer's thought presents. Our age, ethically speaking, is anti-metaphysical, anti-mystical, and increasingly anti-universalist or, to say the same thing, particularistic. As shown in Part I of this book, many theologians attack the idea of moral universals in the name of the particular beliefs and practices of the Christian community. Thinkers interested in the mystical return the compliment. Rarely do they make any connection to ethics. They usually renounce moral rationality as effacing the complex texture of the spiritual life. Finally, in a world increasingly under the dominance of global economic forces, the spiritual and moral longings of peoples are often relegated to private thoughts and practices or they find uneasy expression in the inherited religions. For all of these reasons, it is not clear why anyone should reflect on an ethics of reverence for life that too easily floats between vague spirituality and the ardent rationalism of global systems.

Matters are more complex, however. In various ways the idea of *reverence for life* does resonate deeply in the moral and religious sensibilities of peoples around the world. These sensibilities arise in part as a protest to endangerments to life: ecological destruction, global poverty and oppression, the denial of the needs of future generations, the destruction of local cultures and traditional religious forms by means of worldwide political and economic systems, and, most pointedly, a loss of awareness of the inviolability and mystery of life. What is more, the reverence for life is often bound to spiritual awakenings among people both within new religions and spiritualities as well as the fresh vitality seen among forms of the classical, global religions. For example, the Buddhist priest and peace advocate Thich Nhat Hanh has insisted that reverence for life is the first precept of a viable moral and religious outlook for our age.[6] Even new spiritualities, like forms of ecofeminism and holistic theologies of creation, use the language of reverence for life to articulate their moral visions.[7] Conservatives and fundamentalists in the religions, especially among Christians, have embraced "the right to life" and the "sanctity of life" that evoke reverence.

The widespread resonance and rejection of the idea of the reverence for life warrants some reflection. At the heart of Christian conviction is the living God who graciously bestows life, even new and eternal life, on human beings and all reality. The task of Christian existence is to dwell within the power and presence of God. There are many good reasons to engage critically the idea of "reverence for life" within Christian theological and ethical reflection. In order to do so, I will briefly explore Albert Schweitzer's original formulation of an ethics of the reverence for life in order to isolate distinctive features of Moltmann's thought. This strategy of reflection will help us to fill out the meaning of theological humanism.

3

Albert Schweitzer argued that an ethics of the reverence for life is "absolute." It articulates a moral demand and possibility that can never be fully realized in human history. The struggle to fulfill this responsibility deepens human life and mitigates the conflicts of existence. The ethics of the reverence for life also articulates a fundamental conception of reality. In fact, Schweitzer held that the "loss of real civilization is due to our lack of a theory of the universe."[8] An adequate theory, he further held, must be ethical and be affirmative of the world and of life. The idea of an "ethics" of "reverence for life" is meant to meet this twofold demand. How so?

In continuity with eighteenth-century rationalism and especially the reflexive philosophy of René Descartes, Schweitzer seeks to grasp immediate self-consciousness in order to ground his ethics. When one does so, he argued, one comes to realize that the core of consciousness is not the *cogito*, the "I think," as Descartes held. "'What is the immediate fact of my consciousness?' ... 'To what do I always return?' we find the simple fact of consciousness is this, *I will to live.*"[9] If one thinks this awareness through to its conclusion, it is obvious that the will-to-live is a primary feature of the universe, a reality that I affirm, reverence, in myself and must acknowledge in all living things. Yet this insight, this *affirmation of life* as a spiritual act, is hardly piously optimistic.

> The world is a ghastly drama of will-to-live divided against itself. One's existence makes its way at the cost of another; one destroys the other. One will-to-live merely exerts its will against the other, and has no knowledge of it. But in me the will-to-live has come to know about other wills-to-live. There is in it a yearning to arrive at unity with itself, to become universal.[10]

The affirmation of the will-to-live is the first spiritual act of experience, as Schweitzer calls it. However, it is not obvious that an affirmation of my life entails the demand to reverence others' lives. It would be possible to reverence the will-to-life in oneself and not in others.

Schweitzer argued on purely rational grounds that the attitude one can and ought to take toward other life must be consistent with self appraisal. "If I am a thinking being," he writes, "I must regard other life than my own with equal reverence." He endorsed Immanuel Kant's principle of universalizability as the "form" of the ethical. An ethics of the reverence for life means that every type of life is given equal reverence. This led Schweitzer to acknowledge the moral standing of non-human life. Evil, then, is simply what annihilates or hinders or hampers life; good is just the helping or saving or enabling of life to its highest development. So, reverence for life arises from a rational reflection upon and universal extension of the primitive datum of consciousness, the affirmation of the will-to-live. It specifies good and evil in terms of what promotes or destroys life. Further, the ethics is not only universal and rational, it is also activist. It seeks the perfection of the self and also enabling all life to its development. "A man is truly ethical," Schweitzer summarizes, "when he obeys the compulsion to help all life which he is able to assist, and shrinks from injuring anything that lives."[11]

Schweitzer was of course keenly aware that life competes with life. He acknowledged, as already noted, that there is a "division in the will-to-live." That is the ghastly drama of existence. As he notes, it is "a painful enigma for me that I must live with reverence for life in a world which is dominated by creative will which is also destructive will, and destructive will which is also creative."[12] The fullest meaning of an ethical act, any aid given to another living being, is that the will-to-live becomes one with another will-to-live, and, thereby, fleetingly, the division of the will-to-live is put at an end. The destiny of ethical existence is to "choose for my activity the removal of this division in the will-to-live against itself, so far as the influence of my existence can reach." And Schweitzer concludes, "[k]nowing now the one thing needful, I leave on one side the enigma of the universe and of my existence in it."[13]

Schweitzer's ethics embraces as metaphysical fact that the will-to-life is divided against itself. Creative will is destructive will. An absolute ethics of reverence for life does not seek to compromise with this situation, but, rather, to provide an ethical triumph over the truth of reality. In the face of the division in the will-to-life, the ethical person in acts of goodness brings to a momentary end the ghastly drama of reality. When one so acts, Schweitzer insists, one experiences a union, a mystical participation, in the infinite Will in which all are one. That is the mystical significance of ethics and the moral justification of the human adventure. Not surprisingly, the ethics moves then between theism and pantheism. Ethical theism, as Schweitzer called it, "presupposes a God who is an ethical Personality, and who is, therefore, so to speak, outside the world ... [and] it must hold fast the belief that God is the sum total of the forces working in the world – that all that is, is in God."[14]

Schweitzer's ethical theism, metaphysics of Will, and mysticism seem profoundly at odds with Moltmann's arguments about "the coming God." Why then would Moltmann use the discourse of reverence for life? I turn next to Moltmann's eschatological reverence for life, as I will call it.

4

Jürgen Moltmann's most recent books have been part of his "Systematic Contributions to Theology," a project in continuity with the earlier *The Crucified God* and *The Theology of Hope*. The point of continuity is an eschatological perspective, a sustained focus on the coming God. It stands in radical contrast to any apocalyptic outlook centered on a final resolution of ambiguity, suffering, and injustice. "But *Christian* eschatology," Molt-mann writes, "has nothing to do with apocalyptic 'final solutions' of this kind, for its subject is not 'the end' at all. On the contrary, what it is about is the new creation of all things."[15] The end will be the beginning: true creation is to come and thus is ahead of us. The end, the eschaton, is about new life. Moltmann is clear that an eschatological stance and a theology of hope are the fundamental *form* of theology.

Importantly, while hope and eschatology provide the *form* of theology, in recent works Moltmann has been concerned with the *content* of theology. His theology comes to focus on life, new life, and new creation as the necessary content of thinking eschatology otherwise than in apocalyptic terms. If, as he says, theology is "*imagination for the kingdom of God* in the world, and for the world in God's kingdom," then it is centrally concerned with how God comes to dwell in creation.[16] This is, so it appears, the backing for Moltmann's concern for new life.

Consistent with his eschatological focus, Moltmann rejects any account of experience as self-constituting, a claim, already seen, basic to Schweitzer's ethics. One must abandon, as Moltmann says in *The Spirit of Life*, "the narrow reference to the modern concept of 'self-consciousness', so that we can discover transcendence in every experience, not merely in experience of self." This means, further, that the "*experience of God* is not limited to the human subject's experience of self. It is also a constitutive element in the experience of the 'Thou', in the experience of sociality, and in the experience of nature."[17] For Moltmann, the most basic datum of experience is not the will-to-live that one comes to grasp as divided against itself, but, rather, the reality of the living God. More pointedly, the eschatological moment, not self-consciousness, awakens one to the reality of God in all things and all things in God. Moltmann speaks of the Spirit to articulate this divine reality. He conceives of the Spirit as "the divine field of force which permeates us through and through."[18] The Spirit is an environment and also the inward vitality of life. The Spirit's being is the source of life and its worth.

Now, the logic of the ethical argument entailed in these theological claims about the Spirit of Life seems to be this: (1) the divine source of life is the creative Spirit, (2) because of life's source in the Spirit it (i.e., life) must be sanctified, and (3) life is sanctified when *everything* is encountered with reverence before God. Importantly, the correlate argument is (i) that the meaning of reverence is universalized so that one reverences *all* life not because of the rational demands of universalizability but because its source is God, and (ii) the final grounding of the ethic is the Triune life of God rather than the actual dynamics and conflicts of finite life and its ghastly drama. Reverence for life is really about the divine life in all things. The future of history, Moltmann consistently argues, is the coming God, the new creation, God's Sabbath and indwelling in reality. The reverence for life must center on this reality shorn of apocalyptic dread, moral perfectionism, or the attempt through action, as Schweitzer taught, to surmount the division within the will-to-live.

Moltmann is profoundly mindful that death, destruction, and suffering characterize current existence. The distress that drives created being to cry out to God is, he notes, a double distress. "It is distress over the inexorable, progressive destruction of nature by human beings, and it is distress over the destructibility inherent in nature itself: the destructibility that makes this human aggression against nature possible."[19] The tyranny of time and death, he holds, is the condition for human aggression and injustice to human and non-human life, and it is a feature of "nature" as the immanent side of creation longing for redemption. Under the power of time and death, life wars against life in a deadly cycle of violence and oppression. Moltmann thus admits that given present conditions of existence the theological imagination is somewhat limited. It tends to use negative images to speak of the reign of God: when mourning or crying or pain will no longer endure; when death shall be no more (Rev. 21:4). Positive images are possible, too: the kingdom of God, Christ's resurrection, eternal life, and the reign of righteousness and justice.

However, no one presently has a full experience of the kingdom. This is why theology is an imaginative act, according to Moltmann. In anticipation of God's reign, one has to be awakened to the eschatological reality of God's presence in which God suffers with creation seeking to turn creatures from death to life. "Out of hope for eternal life, love for this vulnerable and mortal life is born afresh … [W]e Christians are what Christoph Blumhardt called 'protest-people against death.'"[20] The content of ethics, seemingly, is a hope that warrants protest against death and seeks to sanctify all life before God. What is distinctive about the Christian vision is not specific moral rules, norms, values, or agendas, but, rather, reverence for life born from an eschatological awakening to new creation. It is to live in newness of life in the coming of God. What justifies the continuation of the human project is God's coming that empowers reverence for life.

Moltmann's theology of life can be seen as a negation of Schweitzer's ethics but also an eschatological transformation of a widespread sensibility captured in the discourse of reverence for life. If that is indeed the case, then the orienting question of this chapter returns. Does an "ethics" of the reverence for life, even recast in eschatological terms, articulate the proper expression of Christian moral thinking in our time? I conclude the chapter with that question in mind. My point is not to deny the sensibility of reverence for life as important for this age. It is, much more, to think through carefully the kind of *ethics* we need to embody that sensibility in actual life.

5

Moltmann's theology of life is an advance in thinking about a properly Christian perspective on reality and also the most basic good that can and ought to orient action, rooted, as it was put before, in the remembrance of death and the love of life. It is, thereby, of genuine importance for contemporary theology, and, additionally, an enduring contribution to the worldwide church. Yet, problems remain. It is not at all clear on theological or philosophical grounds that "life" articulates a necessary good that can and ought to be reverenced in all situations. Why should "life" be reverenced? Certainly, a Christian must insist that life is not a second god. Life is a great good, to be sure. It is not the supreme good. To think otherwise is to fail rightly to acknowledge the worth of finite life in its finitude as well as the difference between God and reality. Christians – and certainly Christian theological humanists – love life. Yet even when seen within the life of God, finite life is and will remain radically finite. Its goodness, we must say on theological grounds, is inseparable from its finitude. Anything other than that judgment is a denial of creation which, open to the divine presence, is nevertheless not divine. We are *dust* that breathes, after all.

Moltmann seems to agree on this point. On close reading, he distinguishes between *sanctifying* life and *reverence* for life. To sanctify life, it seems, requires a good or end that one seeks to acknowledge and realize within finite existence. Moltmann writes:

> Harmony with God is called sanctification. Harmony with ourselves as God's image and his children is called happiness. In this sense sanctification leads to true self-realization .... Trust in God, respect for our own lives and the lives of others, as well as reverence for everything living, in which God is present: these are the things which characterize and determine the sanctification of life.[21]

Notice that "reverence" is an attitude, a sensibility, about forms of life that is conceptually distinct from the good to be realized, namely, "harmony" with God, self, others. It is also distinct from other sensibilities, trust and respect. On my reading, there is then in Moltmann's texts the need to distinguish between "reverence" as a *sensibility* related to trust and respect and the *end or good* that can and ought to guide all human actions and relations (harmony/sanctification).

What do we mean by terms like reverence, trust, and respect? It is not possible here to engage in an extended analysis of the meaning of these basic religious and moral concepts. Still, *reverence*, we can summarily say, is the active willingness to acknowledge the moral standing and worth of realms of life, just as *respect* does with self and others, and *trust* characterizes a right relation between people and between people and the living God. The reverence for life is wider than the idea of "respect" insofar as all of life can claim reverence but respect implies some basic moral similarity between those involved in the relation. I can respect the freedom of another person because I have some sense of what that freedom means in their daily life. I can also reverence it. But I can reverence things that do not necessarily evoke respect in me. Trust, conversely, is about a bond of fidelity between agents, divine or human. It is important to keep these ideas distinct, even if they are often related in moral experience. And it is also important to avoid confusing a moral sensibility or feeling (reverence/respect) for what is good. The feelings are *responses* to what is good rather than the good themselves. Just because one feels "reverence" for something does not insure that this thing is actually "good." We can be mistaken – profoundly mistaken – in our moral feelings. It is a grave error to collapse the sensibility of "reverence" and the content of the good, that is, harmony or sanctification. The confusion of a sensibility that motivates action and the good that is the norm and object of the sensibility too often besets an "ethics" like Schweitzer's. What is more, one must insist that human beings bear the responsibility for the use of power at their disposal even when they lack the moral sensibilities one would hope to motivate life. Sometimes duty rather than more refined motivations, like reverence or respect or trust (not to mention love), must have its say.

What then can we do? While the concept of reverence designates an attitude or sensibility about what bears worth, the good that ought to guide and orient conduct is best conceived along lines intimated by Moltmann's argument about *sanctification* and *harmony*. Here too more precision is needed. The idea of "harmony" is hardly obvious, since, for example, it is not clear what is to be harmonized in the self or what would count as a harmonious community. In order to avoid this confusion, I contend that the *integrity of life* best articulates what can and ought to be respected and enhanced in actions and relations. For the sake of precision in moral theory, I am outlining a responsibility ethics that seeks to provide guidance for how one responds to actions and relations in terms of a complex mixed imperative that links duties and ends (we are to *respect* and to *enhance*) with regard to a good related to but distinct from responsible action, the *integrity of life*.[22] To be sure, "integrity" can and must evoke reverence as well as a host of other sensibilities and motivations, as seen in earlier chapters. Yet we make a decided gain in thinking by developing an ethics for the integrity of life thereby avoiding the confusion of sensibility and a conception of the good in an ethics of the reverence for life (Schweitzer) as well as the vagueness of ideas about harmony (Moltmann). I can turn, then, to the *integrity of life* and what it means for a theological ethics while also committed, like Moltmann, to a construal of all things in God and God in all things.

The *integrity of life* means two related but distinct things. First, integrity designates the project of any living being, namely, to integrate or draw together a range of goods sufficient to fulfill basic needs and express capacities necessary for that form of life to continue to exist, to resist non-being.[23] Obviously, the range or kinds of goods differ depending on the form of life considered. A human being, for instance, has needs and capacities for reflection and meaning missing at organic levels of life, even as a human being, no less than a cell or animal, must metabolize energy and interact with its environments. In each case, some "integration" of being is enacted. The analogical use of the concept of "life" across its diverse forms is thereby rooted in the dynamic of integration as a concept for the vitality or power of living. The main threat to any kind of life, accordingly, is disintegration, the weakening of the life process to the point of non-being or death. Even the concept of "death" is analogically predicated on beings owing to the diverse ways they integrate their being. This is why, as Christians have long known, human beings can die in many different ways: physical death, social death through the disintegration of community, existential death in the loss of meaning in life, and even spiritual death or the denial of the spiritual integrity of existence. So too, one can be physically alive and spiritually dead; existentially alive and yet physically dying.

Theologically construed, the power of integration is the presence of the divine spirit, the vitality of life experienced and manifest in the capacity of a being to draw together its being into living expression. This divine power is experienced at diverse levels of life, from the physical to the existential and spiritual in relation to other forms of life. This is why it makes sense to speak, as Moltmann does, of God in things and things in God, or God's spirit as vitality and also environment. The mark of *finite life* is that this capacity for integration at all levels is never complete and thus in time is either destroyed or dissipates to the point of disintegration and thus death. Further, any form of life advances or thwarts the integration of life in itself and others; there is real conflict as well as real concord in reality. What we mean by "good" and "evil" on this meaning of integrity are relations and actions that advance or thwart the integration of existence among beings – and this necessarily includes their environments.[24]

The first point is that by insisting on the "integrity" of life one has a complex understanding of what in fact aids or thwarts any living being and its environments and thereby gains precision in reflecting on how we can and ought to relate to our selves and others. This provides a finer grained conception of goodness than found in the vague idea of "life" that an ethics of the reverence for life hopes to serve. The account helps us to understand the threats to life of greatest moral and religious significance, for instance the conflict between forms of life and forms of death that beset us mortal creatures.

Rather than continue to explore the range of needs that must be met, the capacities exercised, and goods attained for life to be "integrated," we can turn to the second meaning of "integrity" important for reflection on human responsibility. Integrity in this second, but related, sense denotes a unique form of goodness that arises within the life of someone or some community dedicated in action to respect and enhance the integration of life in others as well as oneself. This meaning of integrity specifies the "moral good," a form of goodness that is only attainable, no matter how momentary or fragmentary, through responsible action. A life of moral integrity – the rectitude of conscience – is one that is integrated not simply in terms of the range of goods (natural, bodily, social, reflexive) that meet needs and capacities, but, more radically, through a committed project of respecting and enhancing those goods in, with, and for others. A person of integrity is someone whose strength of conviction is manifest in a specific intentionality and orientation of actions and relations. The integrity of life in this sense denotes the moral vocation of human beings, individuals and communities. It is a unique good of the spiritual core and dynamic of human life.

The idea of moral integrity arises not with the brute awareness of the power to integrate life or even with needs and capacities. It is, rather, an attribute of the exercise of capacities for action in, with, and for others wherein the power to act is deployed to respect and enhance, not demean or destroy, the integrity of others' lives. The truly moral person is one who acts to respect and enhance the integrity of life not just for the sake of integrating her or his own life, but, rather, because that is the hallmark of the responsible life. The same is true for the responsible community, even if, as political realists have always noted, a human community can never attain the level of moral purpose possible for an individual.[25] Put in classical terms, and ones that Moltmann uses, in the genuinely moral act holiness and happiness meet. The amoral person or community abides by the demands of responsibility in order to meet needs and secure wants. The amoral seek happiness and see the demands of holiness, of moral integrity, as a *means* to that happiness. That is the definition of the easy conscience. It makes the spiritual life instrumental to other goods. But what would it profit a man if he gained the whole world and lost his soul (see Mark 8:36)?[26]

Accordingly, the real struggle of human existence, ethically construed, is not the fact that we are subject to time or death, and it is not that we live within a ghastly drama of life divided against life with a profound love of life. Difficulties and conflicts and sorrow abound, of course. Still, the real struggle of existence is to answer the call of conscience to live with moral integrity, to use one's power to respect and enhance the complex array of goods integral to life, having nothing but the hope that happiness will in fact be attained in a life so committed. In communities, it is the response to the demands of justice. The resolution of the challenge has sometimes been called the moral paradox, namely, the insight that "egoism is self-defeating, while self-sacrifice actually leads to a higher form of self-realization."[27] As Christ put it: "He that finds his life shall lose it; and he that loses his life for my sake, shall find it" (Matt. 10:39). The truly moral person or community is one who attenuates immediate and wholesale attention to the needs and capacities required to integrate life in order to have their existence defined by the demands of responsibility. In doing so, a new life is found, a higher kind of being, what is best called "moral integrity." Obviously, this does not mean self-neglect or abasement. Moral integrity is not another name for servitude or the mutilation of one's life by excessive moral demands, but, rather, a proper self-relation mediated by the realm of responsible actions and relations. Accordingly, a range of proximate judgments consistent with the demands of justice guide actions amid the conflicts between forms of life – including love of self – with respect to basic, social, and reflexive goods. The good of moral integrity entails the commitment to respect and enhance the integrity of life in, with, and for others as well as self. It designates the kinds of harmony Moltmann notes. To be more precise, moral integrity articulates the meaning for ethics of perfection in love.[28]

Why then *ought* humanity to continue to exist? That is the question posed in the quote from Moltmann that heads this chapter. Is it to bring to a momentary end the ghastly drama of life against life? Is our moral vocation to live within the eschatological presence of God as people of protest against death? An ethics of responsibility for the integrity of life from the perspective of theological humanism answers that what morally justifies the fateful and costly human adventure can only be found in the fact that through God's gracious renewal of our hearts we can and may and must deploy the power at our disposal in the service of life and thereby enact amid the turmoil of existence the triumph of spirit over force. It is, to put it otherwise, to live out the primal Christian plea to have God's will be done on earth even as it reigns in heaven. The world around us is neither a ghastly drama nor awaiting its true creation, but, fully marked by sorrow and pain and also joy, much more the *agora*, the arena or stadium, of responsibility in which human beings can and may and must cooperate with divine purposes for life.

6

These reflections have thought along with Moltmann about a theology of life. I have tried to clarify why on Christian grounds we can and must develop an ethics of responsibility for the integrity of life. Yet surely what is most crucial is not the precision of concepts or the imaginative depths of a theology. What is most important is the tenor and orientation of our lives in a world riddled with hatred, violence, and sorrow. Our lives and energies must be dedicated to lifting up the lowly by respecting and enhancing the integrity of life. In those acts are to be found testimony to the Spirit of Life.

Notes

1   Jürgen Moltmann, *The Spirit of Life: A Universal Affirmation*, trans. Margaret Kohl (Minneapolis: Fortress Press, 2001), p. xii.
2   Jürgen Moltmann, *The Source of Life: The Holy Spirit and the Theology of Life*, trans. Margaret Kohl (Minneapolis: Fortress Press, 1997), p. 49.
3   On the structure of Moltmann's thought and also the theme of "why there is no ethics" see Geiko Müller-Fahrenholz, *Phantasie Für das Reich Gottes: Die Theologie Jürgen Moltmanns Eine Einfürhung* (Gütersloh: Chr Kaiser/ Gütersloher Verlag, 2000).
4   Moltmann, *The Source of Life*, p. 49.
5   Albert Schweitzer, "The Ethics of Reverence for Life," first published in *Christendom* 1 (1936), 225–39. It is also reprinted in Henry Clark, *The Ethical Mysticism of Albert Schweitzer: A Study of the Sources and Significance of Schweitzer's "Philosophy of Civilization"* (Boston: Beacon Press, 1962), pp. 180–94. It has been printed with the permission of the WWC, at www1. chapman.edu/Schweitzer/sch.reading4.html, p. 13. This and subsequent quotations are from a printed online version.
6   Thich Nhat Hanh, "The First Precept: Reverence for Life," at www.ncf.carleton.ca/rootdir/menus/sigs/religion/buddhist
7   On this see Larry L. Rasmussen, *Earth Community, Earth Ethics* (Maryknoll, NY: Orbis Books, 1998).
8   Albert Schweitzer, *The Philosophy of Civilization*, trans. C. T. Campion (Buffalo, NY: Prometheus Books, 1987), p. xiv.
9   Schweitzer, "The Ethics of Reverence for Life," p. 4. It should be noted, although I cannot explore it here, that after Freud it is difficult to imagine that the immediate datum of consciousness is a will-to-live somehow free from the death instinct. In short, consciousness is more complex, over-determined, and chaotic than Schweitzer seems to have admitted.
10   Schweitzer, *The Philosophy of Civilization*, p. 312.
11   Schweitzer, *The Philosophy of Civilization*, p. 310.
12   Schweitzer, *The Philosophy of Civilization*, p. 312. One should remember that Schweitzer studied Schopenhauer and also Asian traditions, including Jainism. The claim that ultimate reality (Creative Will) is creative and destructive is consistent with these forms of thought.
13   Schweitzer, *The Philosophy of Civilization*, p. 313.
14   Albert Schweitzer, *Christianity and the Religions of the World*, trans. Johanna Powers (New York: Henry Holt, 1939), p. 81. Also see Lois K. Daly,

"Ecofeminism, Reverence for Life, and Feminist Theological Ethics," in *Liberating Life: Contemporary Approaches in Ecological Theology*, ed. Charles Birch, William Eaken, and Jay B. McDaniel (Maryknoll, NY: Orbis Books, 1990), pp. 86–110.

15   Jürgen Moltmann, *The Coming God: Christian Eschatology*, trans. Margaret Kohl (Minneapolis: Fortress Press, 1996), p. xi.

16   Moltmann, *The Coming God*, pp. x–xvii. Also see *Experience in Theology: Ways and Forms of Christian Theology*, trans. Margaret Kohl (Minneapolis: Fortress Press, 2000). For a discussion of the methodology, see Benedict H. B. Kwon, "Moltmann's Method of Theological Construction," in *Sin-Theology and the Thinking of Jürgen Moltmann*, ed. Jürgen Moltmann and Thomas Tseng, *Internationale Theologie* 10 (Frankfurt: Peter Lang, 2004), pp. 1–22.

17   Moltmann, *The Spirit of Life*, p. 34.

18   Moltmann, *The Source of Life*, p. 68.

19   Moltmann, *The Source of Life*, pp. 111–12.

20   Moltmann, *The Source of Life*, p. 124.

21   Moltmann, *The Source of Life*, p. 48.

22   On this argument see my books *Responsibility and Christian Ethics* (Cambridge: Cambridge University Press, 1995) and *Theological Ethics and Global Dynamics: In The Time of Many Worlds* (Oxford: Blackwell, 2004). Also see David E. Klemm and William Schweiker, *Religion and the Human Future: An Essay on Theological Humanism* (Oxford: Wiley-Blackwell, 2008).

23   The claim here is distinct from, but related to, other basic frameworks in theology. Paul Tillich, for instance, argued that being has a polar structure as well as its depth (self-world and the depth of the power of being). Life is the dynamic affirmation of this structure in self amid time and against the threat of non-being. Søren Kierkegaard talked about a self-relating dynamics that is also related to the divine. Hegel spoke of the dialectic of spirit whereas Immanuel Kant and Johann Gottlieb Fichte explored the synthetic power of the transcendental subject. Friedrich Schleiermacher explored consciousness with respect to an oscillation between abiding in self and passing beyond self. The idea, then, that "life" is a dynamic power is hardly new, reaching back, one might say, to ancient ideas about "anima" and soul. My worry about these other positions is that talk about polarities or existential self-relation can be empty and seems driven more by the problem of self-certainty than how to exercise power. The innovation of my argument, if that can be said, is to explore the multiplicity of needs and capacities that must be integrated and how that helps to fill out a conception of goodness. While my argument has resonance with classical and modern ideas, it avoids reducing life to a polar structure or the power of self-relation.

24   H. Richard Niebuhr helpfully called this a "relational theory of value." I have drawn on this idea and yet modified it in order to explore the complexity of the integrity of life at its various levels. On this see H. Richard Niebuhr, *The Responsible Self: An Essay in Christian Moral Philosophy*, intro. James M. Gustafson, foreword William Schweiker, Library of Theological Ethics (Louisville, KY, Westminster John Knox Press, 1999).

25 On this see, most recently, Robin W. Lovin, *Christian Realism and the New Realities* (Cambridge: Cambridge University Press, 2008).

26 The point here is about the distinction between moral and amoral. The amoral person on this account could engage in actions that are in fact responsible but the intentionality of an act would not be truly moral. The question of what is immoral requires for its intelligibility clarity about the domain of the moral, of what is just, right, good, and fitting as well as the proper intentionality of action. On this account, I judge that Kant was simply right and in fact merely articulated a principle of Jewish and Christian thought. The point of the moral life cannot be simply to achieve happiness, as Aristotle thought. The moral life entails an intentionality, a proper maxim of action as Kant put it, and so is bound to the rectitude of will. This is absolutely basic in classical Protestantism. Luther, for instance, always drew the distinction between "doing works of the law" and "fulfilling the law." Only the latter, rooted in grace, is truly "moral" or "spiritual." See Martin Luther, "On the Bondage of the Will," in *Luther and Erasmus: Free Will and Salvation*, ed. E. Gordon Rupp and Philip S. Watson, Library of Christian Classics (Philadelphia: Westminster Press, 1969), esp. pp. 302–18.

27 Reinhold Niebuhr, *An Interpretation of Christian Ethics* (New York: Seabury Press, 1979), p. 33. Many thinkers in various religious traditions have noted this paradox.

28 Interestingly, at several points Moltmann cites John Wesley, especially in *The Spirit of Life*, on the relation between happiness and holiness. My own reflections here are deeply Wesleyan. Importantly, Wesley thought that the Sermon on the Mount, and not natural law and virtues, as with Catholics, or the Decalogue, as among the sixteenth-century Reformers, presented the proper construal of the Christian life. See John Wesley, *Sermons on Several Occasions* (London: Epworth Press, 1975).

Chapter 10

Sovereign Expressions of Life

1

The previous chapter engaged the theology of Jürgen Moltmann around the idea of "reverence for life" in order to clarify the "integrity of life" as the basic norm and value of theological humanism. In this chapter I want to continue the discussion by exploring the work of another thinker especially interested in the theme of life. The Danish philosophical theologian Kund Løgstrup was a major voice, even a daring voice, in twentieth-century theology and philosophy. Well known in Europe, he is little known in the USA. His work was first introduced in the American context by James M. Gustafson, also a seminal figure in contemporary Christian thought. More recently, Løgstrup's ethics has received new attention from philosophers like Alasdair MacIntyre and also British and American theologians.

In what follows I want to examine aspects of Løgstrup's ethics and his claims about the "sovereign expression of life." The focus of my inquiry, to borrow Løgstrup's own questions, is what renders life definite. That is, what gives specific shape, character, and meaning to existence? Is a human life rendered definite by an act of will; is it the narratives we inhabit and the virtues we cultivate, as Christian particularists claim; is it the command of God, as Karl Barth insisted; maybe definiteness is found in love, in *agape* or *caritas*; or, as Løgstrup thinks, is the definiteness of one's life realized in responsibility to the sovereign expressions of life? Each of these options is found in the history of Christian thought. Within each there is also a claim about what empowers or capacitates moral action, say, eternity, the story of God's action in Christ, God's word, the fount of true love, or life in its sovereign expressions. The question about what renders life definite thereby reveals the way a thinker or community understands the connection between religious devotion to the God of Christian faith and moral relations to others.

Dust that Breathes, by William Schweiker © William Schweiker 2010.

However, the importance of this topic is not only a matter for Christians. As thinkers like Zygmunt Bauman have noted, within the whirl of current global dynamics, within liquid modernity as he calls it, it is not clear what is to constitute the seriousness of the moral life.[1] We are more and more aware of the extent of relations to others, but global dynamics can also be morally numbing. Little wonder, then, that a host of different religious and philosophical thinkers have sought to clarify the radical claim the other has on us. They are seeking – we all are seeking – to combat forms of moral flatness or what I have called "overhumanization."[2] Our inquiry thereby cascades into the methodological problem of how theology and philosophy can and ought to interact. That is the case because "God" has, in theistic discourse, been the source of the authority of morality which philosophers theorize on other grounds. We will, accordingly, wrestle with the problem of the relation of theological and philosophical ethics.

Too much is made of the supposed difference between theological ethics and moral philosophy. The distinction between "philosophy" and "theology" holds only if one has stark conceptions of "Reason" and "Revelation," used in each case with a capital "R," and if their truth claims cannot, in principle, overlap with each other. I am not sure who holds those ideas anymore. Some philosophers who engage Løgstrup's thought seem, at least to me, to confuse the question of where one gets one's ideas and the different problem of how one validates an argument. To be sure, Løgstrup draws inspiration from his Christian, and specifically Lutheran, heritage, but that fact, he insists, does not validate his position. Philosophers too, whether they admit it or not, draw from resources, but their drawing, just like the theologian, is not enough for validating. Løgstrup's claim, and it is one that I share, is that theological sources can pay their way by opening insights that can then be validated in open and free discourse. Call that philosophy if you want, or maybe, more properly, Christian moral philosophy. The real issue is whether there is a source of moral empowerment not reducible to but operative within the structures of human being in the world, the issue, recall, explored also in Chapters 6–7.

We can begin to engage Løgstrup's work with matters roughly methodological, then move through the question of what renders life definite, to, finally, the question of life itself and its claim to goodness. Pursuing this line of thought allows contrasts to be drawn between Løgstrup's position and others as well as advancing some thoughts about theological humanism. For Løgstrup, the good of life – that is, why it can and ought to claim consideration in all its vulnerability and yet tenacity – appears in the ethical demand and the idea of sovereignty. The human task is to realize life whose definiteness is beyond our power to control. Why does Løgstrup think that we are to realize our lives already defined by the sovereign expression of life? If we can sort out the reasons Løgstrup speaks of life as he does, then we will have made headway in understanding not only his ethics but also some problems for current thought.

2

From the early work *The Ethical Demand*, which focused on trust and also the silent demand to care for others, to the later work on "sovereign expressions of life," in the volume recently edited by Professor Kees van Kooten Niekerk, Løgstrup's thought moves through an astonishing range of topics, historical and contemporary.[3] The core of the position, as far as I can see, spins on several interlocking ideas. First is the ethical demand. It arises through the primal bond of trust in which human beings open themselves to the care of others, and, correlatively, assume responsibility for the well-being of the other. Insofar as each situation differs, there is no set content to responsible action with and for others. As Løgstrup puts it, "The radical demand says that we are to care for the other person in a way that best serves his or her interest. It says that but nothing more."[4] And this is because we live in a condition of "being already delivered" to the other, and so vulnerable to the other's power and their being vulnerable to our power. We come into the world of moral claims and demands. The idea is that morality is a feature of our being in the world. Certainly, anyone who knows American theology and philosophy will hear resonances of (say) H. Richard Niebuhr's account of faith and loyalty, Josiah Royce on the beloved community, or the classical pragmatists, like John Dewey and William James, on the dynamics of experience. Human existence transpires within bonds of fidelity that are the condition for individual and social lives. Relations are real, as James put it.

In his later work, Løgstrup seems to have grasped, second, that the ethical demand arises within relations needed for life to be sustained and to flourish, the orders or spheres of creation (to use Lutheran language). These constitutive relations are not something we construct; we realize our lives within them and thus they have a certain kind of sovereignty over us. This sovereignty is manifest in various feelings, modes, or dispositions – like fidelity or mercy or trust – these expressions of life determine the moral space of human existence. Yet precisely because they are sovereign, the relations can be violated. One can choose not to realize one's life in responsibility for and with others. The domain of the good, that is, of the sovereign expressions of life, is non-coercive, in that respect. Insofar as that is the case, then the ethical demand in the narrow sense requires responsibility when an agent does not spontaneously further life. The belief, and it is also a Lutheran one, is that true moral action should be spontaneous on behalf of others. Yet for Løgstrup it is life, not a Christian's faith, which is spontaneously active in love. A sense of duty, the call of the ethical demand, is an indication of a rupture in our being. The law is needed when love fails or conscience is dulled.

Finally, Løgstrup was at pains to explore social norms and values needed to order common life, realizing that these change throughout time.[5] Granting the importance of social norms and conventions, the whole point of his ethics is to show that the moral domain is not reducible to convention. Ethics is not politics or social convention. The ethical demand and the sovereign expressions of life are basic, unceasing, categorical, and unconditional features of human existence. Any denial of this point, he thinks, violates discernible aspects of human life and also Christian convictions about the goodness of creation.

In this light it is plain why, methodologically, Løgstrup calls his ethics "ontological" and why he contrasts it with other options in modern moral theory. He was not seeking a return to a classical metaphysical ethics wherein reality is teleologically ordered to some good or God that transcends the world. By using the term "ontological," Løgstrup, along with other twentieth-century thinkers, aimed to specify the *structure* and *meaning* of our being in the world rather than some claim about the whole of reality *simpliciter*.[6] Whatever else might be said about the nature of reality, it is the case that human life in the world finds it structure, it definiteness, and its meaning within an ethical horizon. Moral obligations to care for another are not human inventions or simply a construal of the world based on the stories of our communities, but, conversely, are sovereign over us, demarcate a moral space of life, in which we realize or fail to realize moral goodness. Even the power or capacity to act spontaneously for the other transcends our willing; it is the sovereignty of life. Løgstrup is a moral realist.

This methodological orientation in ethics immediately poses a question. How is the moral texture of life, the ethical demand and life's sovereign expressions, knowable so that we might rightly orient our lives? Løgstrup's method of ontological ethics is broadly phenomenological and also hermeneutical in character. It is phenomenological because he tries to describe those features of existence within which the ethical demand and the sovereign expressions of life appear, are disclosed. The phenomenologist wants to attend carefully to how something presents itself, appears, for understanding. This kind of attention thrusts one into the wild and complex character of reality. The phenomenological attitude is why Løgstrup analyzed trust, mercy, and fidelity. These expressions of life appear within human intersubjective relations and disclose the structure of being in the world that precedes specific actions. The position is also hermeneutical since Løgstrup explores the appearance of sovereign expressions of life in and through the interpretation of cultural artifacts in order to grasp their *meanings.* He explores plays, novels, poems, and biblical stories as well as the history of Christian and philosophical ethics. The hermeneutical cast of mind is one that insists that in order to understand the meaning of something one must *interpret* not simply its givenness but the complex and all too human ways we think, speak, reason, and sense things. In other words, phenomena always appear within some context shaped by cultural forms and thereby require interpretation to grasp their meaning as well as to overcome ambiguity and obscurity. The concern, then, is to grasp the appearance of sovereign expressions of life in meaningful forms and how these forms structure human being in the world.

Through this analysis of trust, mercy, fidelity, and the expressions of life the ontological fact of our being in a world comes to light. It is important, in this respect, that Løgstrup, while influenced by Martin Heidegger and others, decisively alters the understanding of human facticity. The horizon of human existence is not, as for Heidegger, finitude as such. What makes for authenticity is not anticipatory resoluteness in the face of one's ownmost possibility of death. Rather, a human being is in the world, Løgstrup argues, always and already within bonds of trust and other sovereign expressions of life within which she or he can and may and must realize life and the lives of others. Others are also situated in relation to oneself. The shift from the question of authentic existence to that of responsibility is why many contemporary thinkers see a parallel in Løgstrup's thought to that of Emmanuel Levinas. What constitutes subjectivity is not will or resoluteness, but responsibility for and with the other.[7]

However even if one can make good on the ontological claim about the structure of human being in the world, the question still remains about what renders life definite, that is, what brings moral specificity to human existence. Thought must probe deeper into Løgstrup's ethics and also take a comparative turn.

3

In exploring what renders life definite, consider Løgstrup's ethics in comparison to three other positions. Two of these positions, that of Iris Murdoch (Chapter 8) and that of Emmanuel Levinas (Chapter 5), we have engaged before in this book. The other one we have not yet explored. Since Løgstrup was usually at pains to counter Kierkegaard, we can start there and then engage positions which, in a rough typology, move from will through desire to a focus on intersubjective relations as what renders life definite.

Now, for Kierkegaard, at least as Løgstrup reads him, a human life is rendered definite by purity of heart, by willing one thing. In the choice or decision to constitute one's life in relation to the eternal, the self relates itself to itself and also relates to the other, as it is said in *Sickness unto Death*.[8] It is important to note the difference between the eternal, the realm of the God relation, and what is morally universal. For Kierkegaard, response to a universal moral demand cannot render life definite, because persons ought to respond similarly to the demand. Ethically speaking, good people are all alike. What particularizes existence, what renders it definite, is the self's decision to relate to the divine, the eternal, who has entered time in Jesus Christ. This means that it is God who empowers Christian existence; God acts in Christ – eternity enters time. From Løgstrup's perspective, the moral relation to the other seems eclipsed in Kierkegaard's thought. Apparently, there is no way to conceive how God might be encountered or known in and through the conditioned structures and meanings of our being in the world. What is more, it is the act of will which is sovereign in rendering life definite. I stand alone, I exist alone, if I am truly to exist before eternity. The tender bonds of trust, mercy, and so testimonies to the goodness of creation fall out of view.

Other thinkers challenge the existentialist heroism of the solitary individual and in doing so join Løgstrup's cause. They are quite different, however. Iris Murdoch, as noted in Chapter 8, denied the supremacy of will in modern ethics and sought to recover the place of love and attention for the concrete other person.[9] Because of the tyranny of the fat and relentless ego, in order to live rightly a moral agent must direct her or his attention to the other person under the sovereignty of the Good. Love is the perception of the reality of the other that thwarts consoling illusions of the ego. In this respect, what renders life definite is the ascetic practice of attention, that is, tutoring desire by clear and sustained vision of the Good rather than an act of will. Yet the Good does not act; it orients consciousness through its magnetic pull but it is not living. If Kierkegaard concentrates everything on the solitary individual and thus risks the loss of moral relations to others, Murdoch, some worry, effaces the self in love for the other and the sovereign Good. The proper claim of respect for oneself is thereby at risk. Not a transcendence of morality, as with Kierkegaard, but an eclipse of the self before the other seems the case.

Kierkegaard and Murdoch focus on will and consciousness, decision and attention, as what renders life definite. Kierkegaard is a Christian theologian: God in Christ enters and empowers the human self. The sovereignty of Good, for Murdoch, is magnetic and thus only denotes what the old God, as she called it, symbolizes: perfection. The structure, dynamic, and reordering of consciousness is adequate to symbolize the working of the Good. Levinas and Løgstrup, conversely, turn to intersubjective relations. Each man uses the language of responsibility to get at the domain of morality and also what renders life definite. But what do they mean? I have already recounted Løgstrup's position so here we can contrast it with that of Levinas, and the contrast centers ethically on the difference between *command* and *demand*.

Recall from Chapter 5 that according to Levinas what constitutes the moral realm and what defines my life as an ethical subject is the command in the face of the other, a command that can be summarized as "thou shall not murder."[10] It is the infinity of the face of the other, and not the eternity of God, that summons me to absolute obedience and thus is sovereign over me. Responsibility and subjectivity arise simultaneously, or they do not arise at all. The encounter with the other is a virtual Sinai, an utterance of the Most High, in which is to be found a *trace* of God. Levinas is aware, of course, that human life is more complex than face-to-face relations. The realm of the political enters with human plurality and diversity, what he calls the "third." His point is that what renders life definite is the command of the other. Ethics, so defined, is first philosophy. "God's" working is exhaustively denoted by the structures of being in the world, one's responsibility for the other.

I have raced through these positions in order to make a point about Løgstrup's ethics. By insisting on the ethical demand and the sovereign expressions of life he is trying to clarify how human existence is rendered definite in a way that sustains the unconditional character of the ethical and yet also embeds that demand in realms of goodness that claim their own sovereignty. Further, he is making a theological point insofar as the power of life exceeds the structures of our being in the world even if it acts in and through those structures. Neither taken out of the world (Kierkegaard) nor lost in attention to the other (Murdoch) nor subject to infinite responsibility before the command of the face of the other (Levinas), we are in a world saturated with value but also marked by the silent demand of responsibility. Responsibility requires that we labor unceasingly to sustain and build up the world of relations and thus participate in the ongoing work of creation. In Lutheran terms, one's moral vocation is within orders of creation.

On reaching this point, we can move to the deepest level of reflection and ask about life itself as well as the intertwining of theological and philosophical reflection. Løgstrup seems to suggest that an "ontological" ethics in our time must take a turn to the priority of "life," including divine life. What does that suggestion mean?

4

What precisely does Løgstrup mean by "life" and its sovereign expressions? Why does he think that ethics must now take its orientation from that perspective? Actually, the question of perspective is crucial to Løgstrup's entire project. He holds that "characteristic of the epoch in which we live is the fact that the shift from the ethics of custom to morality has become permanent."[11] That is, a shift happened with the rise of modernity in which a moral value or moral norm is true not simply because a community held it as a custom. The modern age, on his reading, moves beyond mere convention in understanding the truth of moral norms and values. This is, I should add in passing, perhaps not quite the case any longer in our so-called postmodern age. As noted in early chapters, a lot of current Christians – and many other communities around the world – hold forms of moral particularism, that is, an ethics of custom or convention, where beliefs, virtues, norms, and values are understood to be true because one's community happens to hold them. Throughout the world, and also in Christian ethics, one witnesses a reversion to and deep longing for traditionalism, the supremacy of custom and convention. Sometimes this is put in terms of the priority of faith over reason or authority over inquiry. Other times it is the triumph of the political over the ethical, sociology over theology, often to very destructive ends. Løgstrup and theological humanists think otherwise.

Løgstrup's point is that in situations where customs and norms are challenged, where an age of reflection has actually dawned, forms of thought can too easily focus on the tension between, on the one hand, an abstract, undetermined self who must define life in an act of thought or will, and, on the other hand, the ethics of custom. He finds that account in Kierkegaard, Kant and Hegel, and others. Against those positions he seeks another option which neither regresses to custom nor to the undetermined subject. "In any given situation," he writes, "before duty can begin to be relevant, the spontaneous expression of life – trust, mercy, sincerity, and so on – is called forth." He continues:

> Not that it is a matter of engaging with the expression of life, as though it were *that* we needed to relate to. So doing would be tantamount to turning it into a duty with the duplication to which duty gives rise, as Hegel and Kierkegaard correctly observe. No, the call to us is to engage with the situation – through the corresponding sovereign expression of life.[12]

Sovereign expressions of life are media of intersubjective relations through which there is free and immediate responsiveness to the other which overwhelms reserve and preempts any attempt to set self and other at odds. Løgstrup sees this, for example, in speech in which we are spontaneously open to the other in face-to-face communication and only break that openness if we resist its force, say, in willful acts of suspicion or genuine animosity. He finds free responsiveness, hermeneutically, in the character of the Good Samaritan, whereas the priest, for example, acts in reserve and so needs to reflect on the motive of mercy transmuted into duty (see Chapter 3). The Samaritan, conversely, acts within the sovereign expression of life so that care never is burdened with duty. Granted, in some situations the ethical demand is needed in order to require responsibility, but those are moments when the sovereignty of life's expressions fails to empower spontaneous action. "Duty enters," he comments, "when I am trying to wriggle out of the situation."[13] Moral norms, ideals, and social obligations are obviously needed in the political order. Yet all of these, as I have said, derive their validity and force from the sovereign expressions of life. They are not the core of the moral life, but its substitute.

We might say, then, that the sovereign expressions of life are "states" in which we have already been delivered to each other, but "states" saturated by the power of spontaneous care for the other in a way that serves his or her interest. The expressions of life have unconditioned agency which cannot be rendered into ideas, in a strict sense, but, rather, into ideals and norms – ideals and norms which change throughout time. The sovereign expressions of life denote a freedom for good before the freedom of the will. This is, then, an ontological ethics because Løgstrup explores fundamental moods or comportments to life (trust, mercy, sincerity) as disclosing the structure and meaning of our being in the world, which also empower, capacitate, genuine life. The method is phenomenological and hermeneutical and, as such, it poses a mighty challenge to those positions, like Heidegger's, Kierkegaard's, or Sartre's (as Løgstrup mentions), which characterize the structure and meaning of being in the world as towards death (Heidegger), eternity (Kierkegaard), or the absurd (Sartre) and thereby seem to drain the finite world of moral significance and empowerment.

What is not clear, given Løgstrup's overriding concern to explore the relation between the sovereign expressions of life, the ethical demand, and social norms, is the meaning of "life" in his ethics. If the meaning of the "individual" for Kierkegaard is the relation via decision between the self and eternity, the meaning of being is "time" disclosed in anticipatory resoluteness towards death, for Heidegger, and subjectivity reveals itself in infinite responsibility for Levinas, what is "life" for Løgstrup? The question of life and why it is central in Løgstrup's ethics is not easy to answer. At this level of reflection – rather than the phenomenology of life's expression or the ethical demand – we find the nub of the problem mentioned above: the relation between theology and philosophy.

My guess is that for Løgstrup life denotes situated openness to and capacity for care of the other, if one can put it that way. In other words, if one phenomenologically reduces the sovereign expressions of life to what they disclose about life – and so brackets specific expressions (fidelity, trust, sincerity, and the like) – what appears? "In all their elementalness and definitiveness, the expressions of life are what normally sustain all human interaction. … All of this comes of the fact that the immediacy of human interaction is sustained by the immediate expressions of life, whose sovereignty is such that they defeat our past experiences and private musings."[14] The inner-meaning of our being in the world, then, is a sustaining immediacy and openness of human interaction and thus the condition and source of every human good. We dwell within a state of definiteness which we do not determine but in which our lives are realized or not in their vulnerability and having been delivered already into the power of others and they to us. More primordial than mistrust is trust, more basic than death is life, more real is good than evil. Theologically construed, this is a claim about God's creative and sustaining activity. There is an agency at work in and through the structures of our being in the world, unconditioned by that structure. We live, move, and have our being within the sovereign expressions of life, to amend St Paul's words at Mars Hill (cf. Acts 17:22–31).

Is this a philosophical or theological claim? Consider the question in two ways. First, it would be an exclusively theological claim if and only if the construal of the meaning of life required for its intelligibility faith in God as creator or sustainer. It would be an exclusively philosophical claim if and only if the meaning of life and its expressions required for its intelligibility the rejection of any theological construal. Løgstrup denies each of those options. Theological discourse can be a way to articulate the meaning of life, but there are other ways. Philosophical reflection cannot refute theological insights when they lead to the same grasp of life and its openness. Theological and philosophical discourses are overlapping and intersecting modes of thought whose distinction is important but not decisive. What matters is that about which we are thinking, namely, the ethical demand and expressions of life. The way we validate claims is via open reflection rather than appeal to religious authorities or sacred texts. The theologian, no less than the philosopher, can interpret and describe, engage in hermeneutics and phenomenology, with an ontological intent.

Second, the relation of philosophy and theology can be considered otherwise. The dividing line between these outlooks is the question of whether or not the good or the right or eternity or life invigorates responsible human life, if it, to speak crudely, "acts," or, conversely, if the good, right, and just stands inactive as a demand on the human will. If you say that, yes, the good acts to invigorate responsible life, then you are a theologian because, come what may, you believe that there is a force other than human will, consciousness, or desire active in the moral universe. If you deny that proposition, then the term philosophy, in the modern sense of the term, seems apt to describe the outlook. On this score, Løgstrup is an unabashed theologian and maybe more so than many current so-called theologians. Løgstrup thinks, thankfully, that we are not alone in the universe. He can concur with a saying of Albert Einstein: "In the service of life sacrifice becomes grace."[15] The purpose of the moral life is to sanctify life within and under its own power.

5

I have pursued my reflections into Løgstrup's ethics in the way I have because I think his work signals a profound advance in thought while also being problematic at its core. The advance is to move theological and philosophical reflection on "life" beyond paradigms of thought focused on the individual, *Geist*, Heideggerian ontology or, we could also add, *Lebensphilosophie* associated with Nietzsche, Bergson and others. Løgstrup has shown how we are already delivered into life with its values and demands. The moral life is nothing else than living at its fullest and most true, profound, and free. This point, and thus the turn to the centrality of the idea of life, is what I want to endorse in the strongest terms possible.

Now the problem comes to light which must be answered. Under the reality of "liquid modernity" it is not the case that life and its expressions are obviously sovereign. The interlocking realms of life, from the genetic code to the global environment and I would add divine life as well, are endangered through the expansion of human power and consumption. Life, it would seem, can no longer sustain us in our wantonness. An overhumanized world cannot endure. In this situation, surely we must endorse the turn to the importance of life in theology and ethics, but we must also fashion an ethics of responsibility for the integrity of life, as I argued in the previous chapter, rather than one that transpires within the supposed spontaneous and immediate givenness of life. On Løgstrup's account, life seems to have a certain inexhaustibility to it; it is unconditioned by the limits of finitude because, we might surmise, it is rooted in God's creative action.

We need, I submit, more precision and differentiation. An ethics for the integrity of life must distinguish and yet relate various interlocking forms of life, ranging from biological through social and reflective to even divine life and new life, if it is to address the forms of endangerment that now beset our world. Much greater care needs to be taken in the use of the term "life" in a theological and ethical construal of the world. Only in this way do we see the complexity of the problems before us but also the real limits that existence imposes on human action. While Løgstrup rightly, in my judgment, rejected the priority of being towards death as what renders life definite, there is, nevertheless, an insight in that position. As mortals in a finite world we can and must reflect on the *limits* to existence and what those mean in responsibility for the integrity of life. Not only spontaneity but also limits must be part of theological as well as ethical reflection (cf. Chapter 2).

Løgstrup's work remains an inspiration and a goad which we must think with and yet also decisively beyond. The new venture in theological ethics will require, I believe, another look at the actual structures and meanings of being in the world as agents who exert and suffer the use of power within the call of conscience to respect and enhance the integrity of life. One can even see the horizon of ethics *before God* and so join Løgstrup in his attempt to navigate the relation and yet distinction between theological and philosophical ethics. Yet all of this, I believe, rests on an interpretation of the present situation markedly different than Løgstrup faced. An account of our situation and the ethics needed to respond adequately to it is obviously beyond the scope of this book. I conclude, then, that what renders life definite in our global times is the faint call of conscience amid the endangerments to life that we ought not to despair, but, rather, to take heart and claim responsibility for the protection and promotion of future life.

Notes

1 Zygmunt Bauman, "The Liquid Modern Adventures of the 'Sovereign Expression of Life,'" in *Concern for the Other*, ed. Svend Andersen and Kees van Kooten Niekerk (Notre Dame, IN: University of Notre Dame Press, 2007), pp. 113–37.

2 See David E. Klemm and William Schweiker, *Religion and the Human Future: An Essay on Theological Humanism* (Oxford: Wiley-Blackwell, 2008).

3 K. E. Løgstrup, *The Ethical Demand*, intro. H. Fink and A. MacIntyre (Notre Dame, IN: University of Notre Dame Press, 1997); and *Beyond the Ethical Demand*, ed. and intro. Kees van Kooten Niekerk (Notre Dame, IN: University of Notre Dame Press, 2007).

4 Løgstrup, *The Ethical Demand*, p. 55.

5 One finds this point made throughout Løgstrup's writings. It allows him to endorse some form of historicism in ethics without falling into relativism.

6 This account of the distinction between metaphysics and ontology was crucial for twentieth-century thinkers like Martin Heidegger and Paul Tillich but also Catholic theologians such as Karl Rahner. In this sense, what is meant by "ontology" is decidedly different from the ontology Levinas attacks or the current revival of interest in metaphysics.

7 One could also contrast it with Karl Barth's claim about responsibility and the permission to live, even though Løgstrup resists a divine command ethics and also the reduction of valid ethics to divine ethics, as Barth called it.

8 Søren Kierkegaard, *Sickness Unto Death*, trans. W. Lowrie (Princeton, NJ: Princeton University Press, 1941).

9 Iris Murdoch, *The Sovereignty of Good* (London: Routledge & Kegan Paul, 1970).

10 See Emmanuel Levinas, *Totality and Infinity*, trans. A. Lingus (Pittsburgh, PA: Duquesne University Press, 1969); and also his *Humanism of the Other*, trans. N. Poller (Urbana: University of Illinois Press, 2003).

11   Løgstrup, *Beyond the Ethical Demand*, p. 75.
12   Løgstrup, *Beyond the Ethical Demand*, p. 76.
13   Løgstrup, *Beyond the Ethical Demand*, p. 76.
14   Løgstrup, *Beyond the Ethical Demand*, pp. 84–5.
15   Albert Einstein, *The World As I See It*, trans. Alan Harris (New York: Citadel Press, 2000), p. 104.

Chapter 11

Ecstatic Humanism*

1

The previous chapters of Part II of this book have engaged current thinkers on topics important for theological humanism drawn from Christian sources. By examining the thought of Iris Murdoch and Paul Ricoeur it was possible to bring greater depth and clarity to basic claims about human existence, that we are, biblically understood, dust that breathes. In both cases, it was crucial to grasp the interweaving of life and death in human existence and how Ricoeur and Murdoch understood the dilemmas of human existence in distinction from the outlook of theological humanism. In Chapters 9 and 10, the focus shifted to thinkers who focus on the theme of life. This allowed me to elaborate the idea of the "integrity of life" as the central good of theological humanism and therefore the norm of conscience. Moltmann and Løgstrup helped us grasp something of the contemporary spiritual situation marked by overhumanization and endangerments to life. In this global situation, Christians and other people of good will have to labor unceasingly to respect and enhance the integrity of life, or so I have argued.

Turning to the final chapters of this book, we engage other currents in contemporary thought but also return to the theme of humanism. The book's last chapter is dedicated to exploring the recent work of John W. de Gruchy, a white, South African liberation theologian who was deeply involved in the struggle against the evils of apartheid. In this chapter I want to explore what Paul Tillich called "ecstatic humanism." This topic is important not only for

---

* This chapter was first published in a different version as "The Theology of Culture and Its Future," in *The Cambridge Companion to Paul Tillich*, ed. Russell Re Manning (Cambridge: Cambridge University Press, 2009), pp. 138–51. Copyright William Schweiker.

Dust that Breathes, by William Schweiker © William Schweiker 2010.

understanding Tillich's theology, but also for the direction of theological humanism in distinction from other recent proposals for what is called "transcendental humanism" which roots spirituality in humanity and not the divine.[1] Tillich's concept of ecstatic humanism just like theological humanism seeks to avoid the supposed conflict between humanity and the divine, a conflict evidently still present in these other accounts of spirituality.

On all accounts, Paul Tillich was one of the great twentieth-century Protestant theologians and philosophers of religion. His interests and writings span an incredible range of topics, from art to technology to psychology to his magisterial systematic theology. He has always been a controversial figure. Many post-liberal theologians, like Stanley Hauerwas, and also Radical Orthodox thinkers openly profess to hate him. Tillich supposedly abandoned the faith. Feminist and liberation theologians think that Tillich is not sufficiently radical or attentive to the social construction of identity. And postmodern theologians cannot make sense of his commitment to a form of "ontology" and strive to distinguish their analysis of culture from his own. Other thinkers – in various religious traditions – find great resource in his work. The diverse response is true when engaging any great mind.

The task here is not to sort through these debates about Tillich's thought, but, rather, to explore his ideas about humanism. More specifically, I want to explore his "theology of culture" mindful of the enduring task of Christian theology and also his conception of religion and human spirit. My constructive claim is that the theology of culture must now be reconceived in light of contemporary global dynamics. In our global age, the theology of culture is best conceived and practiced as "theological humanism."[2] In a time when the religions are shaping worldwide realities, sometimes violently and sometimes peacefully, it is important that they be given humane expression. Similarly, in an age of expanding human power, some ethical direction and limit to that power is needed in order to protect present and future life. These challenges define the future of faith and the task of navigating life responsibly.

2

In order to rejuvenate Christian theology after World War I, Paul Tillich, Karl Barth, Rudolf Bultmann, and others insisted that theology reclaim as its proper object the reality of God. They sought to overcome what they believed was the failure of cultural Protestantism and nineteenth-century liberal theology adequately to distinguish the difference between Christian faith and cultural values. Tillich conceived of the theological task in a distinctive way. God, the object of theological reflection, Tillich held, is the depth, import, or "substance" of all human cultural activities. A theology of culture is thereby distinct from, if still related to, forms of theology, like Karl Barth's, in which the object of reflection is the God of the Bible within the faith of the Church and formulated in dogmas.

Tillich believed that theological reflection on culture was both possible and needed in order to disclose the religious meaning of a secular world and thus to clarify the relevance of Christian faith to contemporary life. He worried that other attempts to rejuvenate theology might too easily return to a pre-modern quasi-supernaturalism because of their appeals to biblical revelation, and, thereby, would be inadequate for the current age. Tillich also believed that the theology of culture was a new type of ethical reflection. The shift from ethics to the theology of culture was needed in order to avoid the possibility of a double ethics, one for believers (Christian ethics) and another for secular society (philosophical ethics). Further, an adequate ethics must escape the dual threat of graceless moralism and normless relativism – the two errors of other forms of ethics, in his opinion.[3] The theology of culture, then, entailed a specific conception of the theological task, sought to speak to the religious situation of modern cultures, and, further, labored to clarify the connection between faith and morality with respect to social and cultural activities. Theology of culture links the theoretical and the practical, the scientific and the moral, by showing that the divine life is the depth of the meaning-giving power in all human activities.

However, Tillich's conception of the theology of culture exceeded reflection on the nature of theology and its various tasks. Any attempt to grasp religious import, those matters of ultimate concern or meaningful depth in human life, must be carried out with respect to an analysis of actual cultural forms. Tillich engaged an astonishing range of cultural expressions and their religious meanings, including painting, the plastic arts, poetry, architecture, and even cultural movements.[4] He held, for instance, that the anxiety of post-World War I Europe found expression in poetry and drama but also in abstract painting. Cultural forms are the self-interpretation of human life in a particular age, and, systematically understood, an expression of human spirit. Therefore, to analyze cultural forms is to probe the particular shape in which the human spirit manifests itself in an age. The theology of culture thus aligns itself with the normative sciences of spirit or the human sciences, as they are called in his 1923 *The System of the Sciences*.[5] Tillich's position creatively weaves together a conception of theology, an account of human spirit, a historically minded analysis of culture, and a theory of religion in relation to spirit and culture. Armed with this agenda, Tillich sought to illuminate the modern situation.

For all of its novelty, Tillich's conception of the theology of culture has roots deep within Christian thought. He acknowledged that the "theology of culture" continued what others, especially Friedrich Schleiermacher and Richard Rothe, called "theological ethics." His work also extended further the historical reflection of Ernst Troeltsch on the embeddedness of Christianity in Western civilization. Tillich engaged the philosopher Friedrich Schelling and like him affirmed the categorical difference between the Unconditioned and human conditioned reality. As a kind of existentialist, he sought to situate reflection within the limits and ambiguities of human existence.[6] With greater historical perspective, the enterprise of the theology of culture also reaches back to the apologists of the early Church. St Augustine's magisterial *The City of God* engaged the wider culture with respect to Christian beliefs about the divine and the highest good. Augustine did so, much like Tillich, in order to clarify the Christian conception of God and thereby to answer human longings. Theology finds expression through social and cultural reflection, but theology is not reduced to sociology. The object of theology is the living God and not human communities, even the Church.

Tillich insisted that his task was to apply the Lutheran and Protestant idea of justification by faith and the theology of the Cross as convictions not just about salvation but also about the shape of theological reflection. Grace is not subject to human whim or control and it often appears under its opposite, the Cross. The religious experience of ultimate reality can and does appear in the shattering of the cultural experience of nothingness. There is, further, a divine and human protest against any absolute claim made for a relative conditioned religious or cultural reality. Tillich called this the Protestant Principle. Most importantly for the theology of culture, Tillich held as a principle Luther's claim that the "finite is capable of the infinite" (*finitum capax infiniti*). Finite reality, including human existence, while under its own autonomous rule and power can nevertheless mediate and disclose the divine ground and power of all things. Reflection under this conviction is "theonomous," that is, "a turning towards the Unconditioned for the sake of the Unconditioned." "Theonomy," he clarifies, "is directed toward being as pure import (*Gehalt*), as the abyss of every thought form."[7] All domains of reality fall within the scope of theological reflection, especially the domains of culture and history. While there were some revisions in this thought, these ideas basic to the theology of culture remained a touchstone throughout Tillich's long career.

Tillich's work inspired thinkers to probe religious meanings in culture and to articulate the relevance of theological claims. In the 1960s, theologians like Langdon Gilkey drew inspiration from Tillich to address the "death of God" in secular culture. Later, Robert Scharlemann and others, in different ways, sought to use the resources of postmodernism and deconstructionism in ways informed by Tillich's thought. Creative Catholic theologians, like David Tracy, used and revised Tillich's method.[8] Additionally, Tillich's attention to specific cultural forms flowered into sustained reflection by many thinkers on the connection between religion, arts, and literature. And today too there are thinkers who reclaim, revise, and extend the direction of the theology of culture and even cross-cultural reflection.[9] Tillich's theology of culture and his conception of systematic theology during the middle and late decades of the twentieth century was the dominant force of progressive theological reflection in the United States and around the world.

Virtually every aspect of Tillich's theology of culture, or any enterprise like it, has in the last decades come under harsh criticism. Some church theologians, as Tillich would call them, insist that any theology of culture formulates Christian beliefs in non-Christian terms. In contrast, the theological task, they believe, is to reflect on the reality of the Church and the story of Christ.[10] Others revise the dogmatic enterprise associated with the work of Karl Barth in terms of the culture of the Christian community.[11] Another version of church theology is so-called Radical Orthodoxy. Theonomous culture, as Tillich calls it, is supposedly inconceivable because it grants validity to the secular world distinct from the Church.[12] The theologian, they contend, must "re-theologize" the world. Still other postmodern thinkers challenge Tillich's ideas about "spirit," "depth," "being," and "religion." These ideas betray their Western origin in giving undue priority to a specific conception of reason, language, and being that too easily enfolds all reality within their reach and thereby effaces what is other, different. Appeal to the "depth" of culture seems problematic when any one culture is in fact internally diverse and contentious and also when contemporary cultural life is focused on the play of media forms rather than anxiety about "meaning."[13] Tillich's definition of religion as "ultimate concern" and the "substance" of culture is also overly abstract and lacking in historical and social precision; by sheer definition it makes every human being and every culture "religious." Finally, liberation as well as ecological theologians find the theology of culture too anthropocentric and lacking sustained attention to praxis, race, gender, and liberation.[14]

With this brief overview of the task, legacies, and also criticisms of the theology of culture, what then about Tillich's actual conception of it?

3

Tillich's idea of a theology of culture centers on a distinctive conception of the relation between religion and culture. He puts it thus:

> Religion as ultimate concern is the meaning-giving substance of culture, and culture is the totality of forms in which the basic concern of religion expresses itself. In abbreviation: religion is the substance of culture, culture is the form of religion. Such a consideration definitely prevents the establishment of a dualism of religion and culture. Every religious act, not only in organized religion, but also in the most intimate movement of the soul, is culturally formed.[15]

In order to grasp Tillich's conception, one must clarify form and "substance," the concern of religion, and also how religion can express itself through cultural forms.[16]

Tillich's initial formulation of the "idea" of a theology of culture was given in a lecture before the Kant Society in 1919. It was his first publication after four years of service as a chaplain in the German army in World War I, during which he experienced the devastation of war. In this lecture, Tillich insisted that religion, as the experience of the unconditioned, is "actual in all domains of spirit."[17] By "spirit" Tillich does not mean a ghostly figure; it is not a reality opposed to "matter." Spirit "is the self-determination of thought within being." And, further, "spirit is neither a mode of thought nor a mode of being. In spite of its dependence upon both of these elements, it is an irreducible mode. Spirit is the mode of existing thought."[18] Further, every domain of human spirit (e.g., science, art, law, ethics, community, religion, etc.) manifests the power of a radical Yes to its being in spite of the experience of the No, radical nothingness. The "basic concern of religion" is this yes to reality in the face of nothingness. And that is the meaning of Tillich's definition of religion as ultimate concern, namely, that what concerns human beings ultimately is being or non-being. Religion is an activity or conduct of spirit (*ein Verhalten des Geistes*) as a *quality* of consciousness (*Bewußtsein*) but not reducible just to consciousness. How then is one to examine religion as the specific object of a theology of culture?

Tillich notes that a theology of culture must consider the relation of form and import (*Form und Gehalt*). Import, or "substance" (*Gehalt*), is different from content (*Inhalt*).[19] Form is the shape or medium for expressing content and import; it might be a painting or a social movement or an organization or an entire culture. Cultural content (*Inhalt*) is the objective meaning raised into expression by a specific form, like the subject of a painting or the ideals of a social movement. Import (*Gehalt*), while brought to expression by form, is the sense (*Sinn*), the spiritual substantiality, which gives form its meaning (*Bedeutung*). Import is meaning-giving power. The distinction between import and content is crucial, Tillich insisted. Content cannot exhaust or exceed its form; the content of a particular painting is presented in the form of the painting. Without form, the content of the painting is not conveyed. With respect to import, the specific "form" can become more and more inadequate to meaning-giving power such that it is shattered by *Gehalt*. The form is broken open to the power that endows it and its content with meaning. Yet this shattering, Tillich claims, itself is, paradoxically, a form, a kind of form-denying form. He thought that the artists of his time were attempting to express the paradox of form that shatters form, say, in expressionist painting or some kinds of architecture and, paradigmatically, in Picasso's *Guernica*. The task of the theology of culture, Tillich says, "is to trace this process in every sphere and creation of culture and to bring it to expression."[20] The enterprise is distinctly theological insofar as the standpoint of reflection is import rather than form; cultural sciences and the arts, conversely, adopt the standpoint of form. Thinking within this shattering of form by import is theology, properly conceived.

The theology of culture articulates the unity of domains of spirit in terms of the power of meaning that conditions and shatters cultural forms. Here too it has a unique standpoint, but now in contrast to philosophy. In philosophical reflection, the unity of culture is found in the categories of thought and being. For the theologian, this unity is conceived with respect to import (*Gehalt*). More precisely, the theologian articulates the religious depth of culture, its import, expressed through cultural forms and the categories of thought and being. A theology of culture explores the shattering of cultural forms by the excess of import insofar as this expresses the basic religious concern. Yet theological reflection is not irrational or suprarational; it is a form of knowledge, because religious import, the meaning-giving power, is the ground of the categories of thought and being and thus the unity of culture. Theology is act of spirit, the mode of existing thought. These distinctions allow the theology of culture to clarify its standpoint, method, and claim to truth. In terms of Tillich's later work, the power of Being and the courage to be in spite of the threat of non-being are available in all domains of human spirit.

Tillich designates in the 1919 lecture the appearance of meaning-giving power, the import, through the shattering of forms of culture that discloses the depth of culture as "theonomy." All domains of spirit and forms of culture retain their characteristics and autonomy, they are not under the domination of a religious institution or other heteronomous authority, and yet they also can manifest the basic religious experience. What is more, he contends "the more form, the more autonomy; the more import, the more theonomy."[21] The modern world, as Max Weber and Ernst Troeltsch had argued, is that reality in which the social spheres function by their own logics, values, and norms free from religious domination. Granting autonomous social domains, Tillich's point is that every domain can express the religious import and in so doing become theonomous, manifest the depth of meaning-giving power in culture.

4

Throughout the remainder of the 1919 lecture Tillich develops the idea of the theology of culture with respect to specific cultural analyses (art; ethics; politics) even as he relates and distinguishes the theology of culture (*Kulturtheologie*) and a theology of the Church (*Kirchentheologie*). Tillich even addresses the question dear to current church theologians: "What is to become of specifically religious culture, of dogma, cultus, sanctification, community, church?"[22] There are, he suggests, three possible attitudes of church theologians towards culture, attitudes found among contemporary thinkers too: opposition to culture in the name of the church and the kingdom of God; a return to supernatural revelation; and the attempt to draw a distinction between the normative religious principle and the actual religious culture, the church. The theologian of culture is not bound by these options. Rather, such a theologian "stands freely within the living cultural movement, open not only to every other form but also to every new spirit."[23] The church is a spiritual community, as Tillich calls it in the *Systematic Theology*, namely, a type of "church within the church" (*ecclesiola in ecclesia*). The task of the church is to gather and concentrate the religious elements of culture in order to make them the most powerful (*kraftvollsten*) cultural factor.

Unlike church theologians, past and present, Tillich rightly sees that the distinction between church and culture is a sign of brokenness, even sin. What is sought is not to vitalize the church against culture, but, rather, to enact theonomous culture in which the religious community is one element. Further, the "world" is not to be absorbed into the church, as post-liberals think, nor is the theologian's job to "re-theologize" the world and thereby deny autonomous cultural forms, despite the claims of Radical Orthodox theologians. The task is to show the relation of autonomy and theonomy and thereby to appreciate the domain of worldly activity but also to grasp its depth and power of meaning in the divine manifest in and through finite form. When the "secular" is open to its depth of meaning, it is secular, but it is also theonomous. The criticisms of Tillich's theology of culture by various church theologians rest on the denial that the "finite is capable of the infinite."

Tillich was at pains to distinguish theology, as a concrete normative science of religion, from metaphysics and also supernatural ideas about revelation. Import, meaning-giving power, is not to be conceived as some being beyond the world, like a supernatural god, nor is it the totality of being, as in classical metaphysics. It is "an actuality of meaning (*Sinnwirklichkeit*) and, indeed, the ultimate and deepest actuality of meaning that shakes everything and constructs everything anew."[24] On this point, just like the question of the church, some current criticisms of the theology of culture seem wide of the mark. Tillich like many postmodernists believed that classical ideas about "being" and metaphysics are no longer tenable. Being is not to be conceived on analogy to "substance" or "thing-ness" and unaided human reason cannot grasp the structure and whole of reality. As he wrote, "rational metaphysics attempts to abolish the theonomous intention and to replace it with the autonomous one – an attempt that necessarily fails."[25] In contemporary terms, any closed system of thought, a complete rational metaphysics, fails insofar as it disallows one to think within the appearance of "otherness," the in-breaking of meaning-giving *Gehalt* of culture, under the power of that appearance. The point of disagreement, then, turns, much like the criticism of the church theologians, on how the appearance of "otherness" is conceived and mediated. Tillich insists *finitum capax infiniti* even as import shatters cultural form. Thinkers who deny theonomous thinking, who question the "depth" of culture, reject this claim, just as church theologians reject finite human culture as a domain of theonomous power.

However, matters are not quite so simple. Scholars discern shifts within Tillich's thought even if they disagree about their number and the reasons for them.[26] The most obvious shift was due to his shock at the horrible crisis brought by Nazism whose forces and ideas he opposed earlier than many theologians. After World War II, Tillich described the cultural situation as nothing less than a "sacred void." In an essay written in 1946, Tillich held that a "present theology of culture is, above all, a theology of the end of culture, not in general terms but in a concrete analysis of the inner void of most of our cultural expressions."[27] Ten years later in a piece ultimately published in his 1959 book *Theology of Culture*, Tillich contends, "Theology must use the immense and profound material of existential analysis in all cultural realms.... But theology cannot use it simply by accepting it. Theology must confront it with the answer implied in the Christian message."[28] Theological analysis of culture no longer seems to be able to answer the religious question from within the *Gehalt* of culture.

The revision can helpfully be conceived in terms of how one understands the capacity of the finite to bear the infinite, namely, the idea of mediation. Tillich's original 1919 account of the theology of culture held that the realms of spirit can be *transparent* to their ground and power, their religious content, and in this respect answer the religious problem, that is, a quest for a "yes" to reality in the face of the threat of nothingness. Following the horror and destruction of the war, Tillich increasingly conceived the theological enterprise as the apologetic task of correlating the answer of the Christian message with questions of human existence. The answer cannot be derived from the question, he said. At best, the domains of human activity which usually conceal their meaning-giving power might become translucent to that import. While the meaning-giving power is at work in the depth of culture and might appear in the shattering of cultural forms, cultural analysis as such, even in existentialist form, cannot validly know that answer to the religious problem.

Given this shift, the analysis of domains of cultural activity cannot provide the necessary and sufficient normative answer to the quest for the power to be in the face of non-being. That is given only in the message of

Jesus as the Christ as the power of New Being. The theological standpoint is conceived not in terms of a concrete normative science of religion, as it was in 1919. The theological standpoint is properly within what he calls the "theological circle," that is, the faith of the Christian message. The theology of culture seemingly isolates the human questions as well as anticipations of the Christian answer but it cannot validly grasp an answer from within culture. The appearance of the power of New Being in the Christ is not in terms of a shattering of cultural forms, an excess of meaning and power that fragments the limitations of form. *"It is the power of being conquering non-being. It is eternity conquering temporality. It is grace conquering sin. It is ultimate reality conquering doubt....* And out of this ground we can get the courage to affirm being, even in the state of doubt, even in anxiety and despair."[29] Tillich still seeks an answer to the religious problem. "God" is not a being alongside other beings; the symbol "God" points to the ground and power of being. Theonomy is the deepest truth of existence. Yet the force of the shift is that, in the face of evil and sin, the finite can indeed "mediate" the infinite, but finitude itself, in its brokenness and doubt and anxiety, must be *conquered* by the power of new being.[30] Theology is decisively God-centered. What then of the theology of culture and the human spirit?

5

In 1958 Tillich delivered a lecture, "Humanität und Religion," on receiving the Hanse-Goethe Award for service to humanity. He wrote: "Where the honoring of God is purchased with the dishonoring of the human, there in truth is God's name dishonored."[31] Tillich insisted, then, that regard for the dignity and worth of human beings, a human-centered perspective, cannot be opposed by a God-centered theological outlook. Further, throughout his theological career Tillich sought to engage the legacy of humanism. The encounter between early Christianity and the Greek and Roman world, he mused, did not create Hellenism so much as "Christian humanism." In "Christian humanism the fate of Christianity and the fate of philosophy are bound together."[32] Yet Tillich also knew that various forms of humanism, especially since the Renaissance, believe in the self-sufficiency of the human spirit. As he noted in the *Systematic Theology*, these kinds of humanism derive "the Christian message from man's natural state." But this means that "everything was said by man, nothing to man." In contrast, the theologian must insist on revelation that "is 'spoken' to man, not man to himself."[33] As dust that breathes, to recall the biblical metaphor, human beings receive their life from God. We are not just dust but dust enlivened by God and therefore open to the divine Word. The shift from a "naturalistic humanism" to a Christian perspective which we have discerned in Tillich's theology of culture is also found in his engagement with humanism. He both continues to insist on the humanistic outlook, forcefully stated in the Hanse-Goethe lecture, while also denying a purely secular or naturalistic humanism. The possibility of this double stance is found in his idea of "ecstatic humanism," an idea crucial to the future of the theology of culture.

"Ecstatic humanism" means human existence grasped by a power beyond itself, a Word spoken to it, which nevertheless does not violate the dignity and free self-determination of human beings in community with others. It is the event of theonomous human existence and is, furthermore, best defined in terms of love (*Agape*). Theonomous existence is both the fulfillment of the moral aim, which Tillich defined as becoming a person in community with persons, and also the overcoming of human estrangement from our own-most unconditioned depths, from the divine. *Agape*, he notes, "points to the transcendent source of the content of the moral imperative" and thereby reunites human actual existence with its essential being.[34] *Agape* shatters the forms of human love (*eros*; *philia*) as itself a form of love. This love draws within itself justice, the proper acknowledgement of the other as a person, and also the power to act, human freedom. *Agape* is, thereby, an answer to graceless morality and also normless relativism. It is a fulfillment of human purposes in and through finite existence by the import or depth of human being as nothing other than divine love. Ecstatic humanism, we can say, is the theonomous aim of the human spirit, and, accordingly, the condition for any actual theology of culture which seeks to retain its theological depths. Insofar as the theology of culture must examine the domains of human spirit, then, properly speaking, it must do so not just in terms of cultural forms or the theological circle defined by Christian faith, but also with respect to this human ecstatic possibility. Only in this way will the reality of religion as the import of culture not be purchased at the cost of human dignity. Stated otherwise, the religious question, the search for a "yes" to reality in the face of its negation, is answered in the domain of culture in terms of ecstatic humanism.

The idea of ecstatic humanism is important in order to make sense of Tillich's convictions and to address another criticism. Recall that Tillich believed the theology of culture was the continuation of theological ethics. As his thought developed, the ethical force of the theology of culture became eclipsed. The effect was to blunt the critical edge of reflection on culture in the face of those forces, including religious forces, which denigrate human and non-human life. Yet we live in a time when, horrifically, human power endangers all forms of life on this planet, and in an age in which the return of virulent religious fundamentalism means the "religious" and the "demonic" too easily cohere one with the other. This age demands a viable norm or standard by which to orient human power and to judge the moral acceptability of religious appeals and religious authorities. To be sure, Tillich decried forces of disintegration and destruction and was often much more aware of their reality than other theologians of his time. He was mindful that religion can become demonic. Nevertheless, the ethical intentionality of the theology of culture must be reclaimed in light of worldwide endangerments to life and demonic impulses in every religion. Three options are then possible to develop a normative theological ethical stance on culture: (1) return to the 1919 formulation of the theology of culture and attempt to derive norms directly from domains of human spirit; (2) shift with Tillich to the norm and answer disclosed in the Christian message alone; or (3) extend the insight about ecstatic humanism as the "aim," rather than ground or message, of thinking about culture and thereby formulate a norm for cultural and religious realities.

The theology of culture, I submit, is most readily and powerfully revised in and through a robust theological humanism which situates human worth, responsibility, and dignity not against but within the wider realms of life on this planet. On this account, a theology of culture would not only reassert the ethical demand on all theological thinking, but would also widen the scope of reflection beyond Western culture and the church to the patterns and processes of life and the interactions among the world's religions. This new agenda, theological humanism, stands in alliance with the intention of Tillich's project. Its possibility is grasped in the realization that for our time the import, the meaning-giving power, of human aspiration, cultural forms, and the wider reach of existence that is the true ethical aim and standard is best conceived as the integrity of life.[35]

6

The previous pages examined the idea, legacies, and criticisms of Tillich's theology of culture. Most of the critics of his work seem to deny what he judged one must affirm and formulate in the idea of theonomy. On this point, the spade is turned: either one believes that finite, fallible human and non-human realities can mediate unconditioned divine power and meaning while not themselves being the source and norm of that import, or one denies that conviction. One believes that the finite can bear the infinite, or one does not. This is a matter of fundamental theological orientation and religious sensibility. On this point everything turns.

Both the affirmation *and* the denial of this conviction about mediation are present in the legacy of Christian thought. As seen in other chapters, much contemporary theology denies this conviction. That is part of the point of those thinkers turning theology into sociology. Only the Church can mediate God's grace and it does so through its structures of practice and authority. The rest of reality is somehow void of the divine. Yet in doing so one risks a veiled supernaturalism, linguistic idealism in which Christian language is to suffice for the living God, or theology becomes ardently secularist. This book is not the place to attempt a defense of the fundamental religious conviction, and, what is more, such "defenses" are usually convincing only to those who already feel some resonance for them. Of course, "felt" resonances have been explored in previous chapters, in spiritual conviction and the love of life, which empower love and responsibility. So, let it be said simply. Any purchase of the divine at cost to the dignity of finite life is a denigration of God even as the celebration of the secular at the cost of the transcendent ultimately demeans finite life. Granting this point of continuity with Tillich's stance on the capacity of the finite for the infinite, the theology of culture must take a new direction from within its own legacy.

That new direction is the enterprise of theological humanism focused on the integrity of life. The quest to overcome estrangement, the problem of religion, as Tillich called it, must be conceived in terms wider than human and cultural ones. What is sought is the power to respect and enhance the integrity – the right integration – of forms of life against forces that demean and destroy existing life. Yet the integrity of life as norm and aim is not a predicate of any one form of life or a condition which only some beings, human or non-human, can enjoy. It is also a concept for the import, the power and meaning, which respects and enhances finite life in its various realms. Because human and non-human life is now vulnerable to human power, what is needed is a humanistic outlook which places responsibility for the fate of life squarely on human beings and yet also transforms the aim of human life to a good that includes but exceeds the human kingdom, that is, the integrity of life. That outlook is captured in the idea of *theological* humanism insofar as it can link theological reflection on cultural domains with the ethical aim of the integrity of life.

The argument works in the other direction as well. Our age is not only endangered by the rampant extension of human power, it is also threatened by the return of virulent religion in demonic form which threatens finite life with promises of supernatural rewards. Thus not only is a theological transformation of humanism needed, the point just made, but also a *humanization* of religion and thus of theology. The theology of culture must articulate its proper norm. And for our age that norm can only be conceived as the integrity of life invigorating the humane transformation of the religions. From this perspective, the theologian not only analyzes and decodes the power of the integrity of life within various cultural domains. The theologian also works to articulate and transform religious existence within specific communities before that very same power and import. Theological humanism, much more than the original conception of the theology of culture, works at the interface of cultural forms and religious traditions as crucial forces which endanger life but also, surprisingly, mediate the power to respect and enhance the integrity of life. In this way, one extends the legacy of the theology of culture in an age in which global realities pose grave and frightening dangers but also further the deepest longings of the human adventure.

Notes

1   On this idea of transcendental humanism see Luc Ferry, *Man Made God: The Meaning of Life*, trans. D. Pellauer (Chicago: University of Chicago Press, 2002). I cannot explore Ferry's argument in this chapter, but it is a position clearly different from the work of theological humanism. As I have argued, theological humanism is not focused, again, on "humanity" or "divinity" but seeks to avoid the logic of the "center" and takes as its norm the "integrity of life." On this see Chapter 2 above.

2   On Tillich's connection to humanism see Raymond F. Bulman, *A Blueprint for Humanity: Paul Tillich's Theology of Culture* (Lewisburg, PA: Bucknell University Press, 1981).

3   See Paul Tillich, *Morality and Beyond*, foreword by William Schweiker (Louisville, KY: Westminster John Knox Press, 1995).

4   See Michael F. Palmer, *Paul Tillich's Theology of Art* (Berlin: Walter de Gruyter, 1983).

5   Paul Tillich, *The System of the Sciences According to Objects and Methods*, trans. Paul Wiebe (Lewisburg, PA: Bucknell University Press, 1981), esp. part 3, pp. 137–216.

6   It should also be noted that Tillich dedicated his *System of the Sciences* to Troeltsch. For an exploration and extension of Tillich's thought see Russell Re Manning, *Theology at the End of Culture: Paul Tillich's Theology of Culture and Art* (Leuven: Peeters, 2005).

7   Tillich, *System of the Sciences*, p. 203.

8   See Langdon B. Gilkey, *Reaping the Whirlwind: A Christian Interpretation of History* (San Francisco: HarperSanFrancisco, 1984); Robert P. Scharlemann, *The Being of God: Theology and the Experience of Truth* (San Francisco: HarperSanFrancisco, 1984); and David Tracy, *Plurality and Ambiguity: Hermeneutics, Religion and Hope* (San Francisco: Harper and Row, 1987).

9   For examples, see Re Manning, *Theology at the End of Culture*; Kelton Cobb, *The Blackwell Guide to Theology and Popular Culture* (Oxford: Blackwell, 2005); Sylvester I. Ihuoma, *Paul Tillich's Theology of Culture in Dialogue with African Theology: A Contextual Analysis*, Tillich-Studien Bd. 11 (Münster: LIT Verlag, 2004); *Secular Theology: American Radical Theological Thought*, ed. Clayton Crockett (London: Routledge, 2001); David E. Klemm, "Introduction: Theology of Culture as Theological Humanism," *Literature and Theology* 18:3 (2004), 239–50; David E. Klemm and William H. Klink, "Constructing and Testing Theological Models," *Zygon* 38:3 (2003), 495–528; and William

Schweiker, *Power, Value and Conviction: Theological Ethics in the Postmodern Age* (Cleveland, OH: Pilgrim Press, 1998).

10 Stanley Hauerwas and William H. Willimon, *Resident Aliens: Life in the Christian Colony* (Nashville, TN: Abingdon Press, 1989).

11 See Kathryn Tanner, *Theories of Culture: A New Agenda for Theology* (Minneapolis: Fortress Press, 1997).

12 See *Radical Orthodoxy: A New Theology*, ed. John Milbank, Catherine Pickstock, and Graham Ward (London: Routledge, 1999).

13 See Mark C. Taylor, *Erring: A Postmodern A/Theology* (Chicago: University of Chicago Press, 1987).

14 See James M. Gustafson, *Ethics from a Theocentric Perspective*, 2 vols (Chicago: University of Chicago Press, 1992); and Dwight W. Hopkins, *Being Human: Race, Culture and Religion* (Minneapolis: Augsburg Fortress, 2005).

15 Paul Tillich, "Aspects of a Religious Analysis of Culture," in *Theology of Culture*, ed. Robert C. Kimball (Oxford: Oxford University Press, 1959), p. 42.

16 For a treatment of the triads that structure Tillich's thought (form-content-import; culture-religion-religiosity; autonomy-heteronomy-theonomy) see Peter Haigia, *Im Horizont der Zeit: Paul Tillich Project einer Theologie der Kultur* (Marburg: N. G. Elwert Verlag, 1998).

17 Paul Tillich, "On the Idea of a Theology of Culture," in Victor Nuovo, *Visionary Science: A Translation of Tillich's "On the Idea of a Theology of Culture" with an Interpretive Essay* (Detroit: Wayne State University Press, 1987), p. 24. Also see Paul Tillich, "Ueber die Idee einer Theologie der Kultur," in *Religionsphilosophie der Kultur*, 2nd edn (Darmstadt: Wissenschaftliche Buchgesellschaft, 1968), pp. 29–52. The English translation is problematic at points and, therefore, I will amend it and include the German. This passage reads: "Sondern das Religiöse ist aktuell in allen Provinzen des Geistigen" (p. 34).

18 Tillich, *System of the Sciences*, p. 137.

19 The translation of "Gehalt" as "substance," while found in earlier English renderings of his work, is misleading insofar as Tillich never conceived of the divine or the power of being as "thing-like," the impression given by the word substance. Recent translations use the term "import" and, additionally, I will also render "Gehalt" as meaning-giving power.

20 Tillich, "On the Idea of a Theology of Culture," p. 26; "Ueber die Idee einer Theologie der Kultur," p. 37.

21 Tillich, "On the Idea of a Theology of Culture," p. 26; "Ueber die Idee einer Theologie der Kultur," p. 37.

22 Tillich, "On the Idea of a Theology of Culture," p. 35; "Ueber die Idee einer Theologie der Kultur," p. 47.

23 Tillich, "On the Idea of a Theology of Culture," p. 37; "Ueber die Idee einer Theologie der Kultur," p. 50.

24 Tillich, "On the Idea of a Theology of Culture," p. 25; "Ueber die Idee einer Theologie der Kultur," p. 36: "eine Sinnwirklichkeit handelt, and zwar um die letzte, tiefste, alles reschütternde und alles new bauende Sinnwirklichkeit."

25 Tillich, *System of the Sciences*, p. 210.

26   On this see John P. Clayton, *The Concept of Correlation: Paul Tillich and the Possibility of a Mediating Theology* (Berlin: Walter de Gruyter, 1980); Kelton Cobb, "Reconsidering the Status of Popular Culture in Tillich's Theology of Culture," *Journal of the American Academy of Religion* 63 (1995), 53–84; Michael Palmer, "Paul Tillich's Theology of Culture," in Paul Tillich, *Writings in the Philosophy of Culture* (Berlin: Walter de Gruyter, 1990), pp. 1–31; Jean Richard, "Theology of Culture and Systematic Theology in Paul Tillich," *Êglishe et Théologie* 17 (1986), 223–32; and Robert P. Scharlemann, "Demons, Idols, and the Symbol of Symbols in Tillich's Theology of Politics," in *Religion et Culture: Actes du colloque international du centenaire Paul Tillich Université Laval, Québec, 18–22 août 1986*, ed. M. Despland, J.-C. Petit, and J. Richard (Québec: Les Presses de l'Université Laval/Les Éditions du Cerf, 1987), pp. 377–92. Cobb provides a fine discussion.

27   Paul Tillich, "Religion and Secular Culture," in *The Protestant Era*, trans. James Luther Adams (Chicago: University of Chicago Press, 1957), p. 60.

28   Paul Tillich, *Theology of Culture*, ed. R. C. Kimball (Oxford: Oxford University Press, 1959), p. 49.

29   Paul Tillich, "Communicating the Christian Message: A Question to Christian Ministers and Teachers," in *Theology of Culture*, p. 213.

30   See Langdon B. Gilkey, *Gilkey on Tillich* (New York: Crossroads, 1990).

31   Paul Tillich, "Humanität und Religion," in *Gesammelte Werke*, ed. R. Albrecht, 14 vols (Stuttgart: Evangelisches Verlagwerk, 1959–1975), vol. 9, p. 114. "Wo die Ehre Gottes mit der Entehrung des Menschen erkauft is, da ist in Wahrheit Gottes Name entehrt."

32   Paul Tillich, "Fate and Philosophy," in *The Protestant Era*, p. 9.

33   Paul Tillich, *Systematic Theology*, 3 vols (Chicago: University of Chicago Press, 1951–1963), vol. I, p. 65.

34   Tillich, *Morality and Beyond*, p. 40.

35   See William Schweiker, *Responsibility and Christian Ethics* (Cambridge: Cambridge University Press, 1995).

Chapter 12

On Christian and Theological Humanism*

1

John W. de Gruchy, a contemporary South African liberation theologian, has written a book in which he outlines a new form of Christian humanism. If Christians hold that the truth will set one free and, further, that this freedom takes shape in the love of and struggle for others, then de Gruchy's life and work rooted in the struggle for liberation and against the evil of apartheid in South Africa is one long testimony to those convictions. His book is an apt account of that vision of faith and life. No doubt many readers will be surprised to learn that he has decided to don the robes of Christian humanism, and, further, that de Gruchy clarifies those revisions he believes are needed within the legacy of Christian humanism for our global times. But why? Insofar as I have been developing theological humanism from Christian sources, I can only cheer about his book. The banner of Christian faith and humanism which de Gruchy and I champion in our own distinctive ways seeks to formulate a vision of life rooted in God's love for the world mindful of the joy and folly of the human adventure.

This chapter engages de Gruchy's text in order to isolate some of the salient reasons why I think it best to speak of theological humanism drawn from Christian sources. The chapter returns us to the specifics of Christian humanism, explored before in Chapter 6. But we make this return in relation to de Gruchy's revisions to the legacy of Christian humanism. Some of these reasons why I insist on theological humanism, rather than, like de Gruchy, simply calling the outlook Christian humanism, are due to a

---

* This chapter was first published as "Freedom within Religion: On John W. De Gruchy's Confessions of a Christian Humanist," *Conversations in Religion and Theology* 6:1 (2008), 100–19. Copyright William Schweiker. See the original version and also de Gruchy's helpful response to it.

---

commitment to public theological reflection and theological inquiry into culture. Other reasons, explored in early chapters of the book, are rooted in a conception of religious identity and also moral responsibility for the integrity of life. Ruminating on de Gruchy's recent work allows me to make a case for theological humanism but also, as he has noted in print and to me personally, to show that our positions are seeking to advance similar concerns within the wide compass of Christian faith and action.[1] And yet there are important differences between de Gruchy's version of Christian humanism and theological humanism drawn from Christian sources. At least that is what I want to show in this chapter. These are of course "variations" on the question of how rightly to relate Christian faith and the new humanism. In the end I hope to clarify that despite the enduring importance of de Gruchy's work, it is time that Christians and other people of faith and good will embrace within their traditions the outlook and task of theological humanism.

2

Rich in historical detail and subtle in its presentation of the Christian faith, *Confessions of a Christian Humanist* is partly a narrative of de Gruchy's own life of faith in and through which are laced reflections on the full scope of the Christian witness. While not a "systematic theology" in any technical sense of the word, nevertheless between the covers of this book one finds in outline form a wide-reaching presentation of Christian faith. At the heart of the vision is the conviction that Christian faith rightly understood is about becoming fully human in and through faith in Christ and for the liberation of others and the glory of God. Especially notable is the interweaving of biblical, historical, and socio-cultural reflections which, again, reflect the author's own life and thought but which also provide theological content to the intersections that constitute the book's vision of faith.

This point about the interweaving of sources is seen in the very structure of the book. After a prologue in which the author reviews some of the history of Christian humanism, the volume is divided into two major movements of thought. The first "movement" runs through chapters on being human, religious, and secular which provide a reading of the sign of the times on matters reaching from human birth and death to scientism and depersonalized religion. The second movement of the book recapitulates this structure in terms of what it means to be a believer, a Christian, and, finally, a Christian humanist. In these chapters, de Gruchy provides his response, as it were, to our times as depicted in the first movement of the book. In this double structure one sees a classical form of thought first developed by St Augustine in his *Confessions* and also *Civitas Dei*. Christian thinking begins by engaging the religious situation on its own terms, "remoto Christi" (without Christ) as Anselm once put it, and then, in a second reflexive movement, re-engages the situation within the full compass of the Christian witness. By doing so, that is, in making this double move of an initial bracketing of claims about Christ and then lifting those very same brackets, the import and relevance of the Christian confession is illuminated.

The importance of de Gruchy's book for contemporary Christians can hardly be doubted, as well as this "style" of theological thinking. We live in a time when Christian faith and theology are taking various expressions. In some places around the world Christian faith is a tool of violence, oppression, and ignorance. The hard-won advances of the human mind that have relieved disease and advanced human flourishing are too often dismissed in the rancor about "evolution" and "modern Western science." The struggle for human dignity through toleration of sexual difference as well as advocacy of sexual health, especially among women and the poor, is too easily sidelined through appeals to the "bible" and rather vague ideas about the "sanctity of life." The wild apocalyptic speculations of some Christians too easily and too often detract from the struggle and the possibility to live in the present beyond the law of sin and death, a promise and possibility at the core of the Gospel. Further, within theological circles what calls itself "radical," "orthodox," and "postmodern" is in fact too often a strategy to immunize Christian conviction from critical assessment, to draw hard and fast boundaries among peoples, and, what is more, to reinstitute authoritarian and hierarchal ecclesial structures under the appearance of being counter-cultural. In the obsession with "identity" battle lines are being drawn that divide the world into the neat and tidy conceptual boxes called "church" and "world" where (astonishingly) the church is supposedly the domain of peace and the world is the realm of violence. Yet what is especially lost in these theological outlooks is the possibility that the truth might exceed a distinctly Christian community, that the bonds of human solidarity trump ecclesial exclusion, and that in Christ God reconciled the *world* unto himself.

De Gruchy's "confession" is a much needed counter-proposal to these dominant trends and it should be welcomed by Christians of various stripes despite their denominational or confessional differences. His book navigates forces that now blow around the world. His tactic, like Augustine's or Anselm's (two prominent voices in his text), is to engage forms of thought on their own terms and thereby to provide a humane outlook that thankfully stands in contrast to the overly dogmatic and strident forms of too much current theology. In short, de Gruchy has written a hopeful and sane account of Christian conviction which is nevertheless marked by prophetic force and moral passion. Seeking a mature worldliness of humanity fully alive as the very glory of God, to use Ireneaus' famous idea, this book liberates Christian theology from its captivity to the esoteric discourse of "postmodernism" and the sterility of wooden orthodoxy in order to provide a vibrant vision of faith and life.

Beyond the summary just offered, the question becomes this, at least for me: how best to engage the book? The question is a complex one. Certainly the customary form of an academic "writing" is some engagement with complex arguments ending with a flurry of criticism. That does not seem appropriate in this case. It is far better and certainly more suitable for me to adopt another style. Consider then, dear reader, that what follows are my "ruminations" on the book, the attempt on my part to consider, appropriate, and then re-consider an important text. And after a good deal of thought, I have decided to engage the book in several steps circling around matters of genre, conceptual distinctions among kinds of humanism, and, finally, a point of possible difference among us. So, I turn to my first point of rumination, the genre of confession.

3

However wide one casts the net in terms of who counts as a "Christian Humanist," it remains the case that thinkers of this ilk have always been interested in the various ways thought and faith are communicated. Humanists have been notoriously interested in questions of literary "genre" because, just like history, language is the domain of human strivings and meanings. Erasmus, surely one of the greatest of classical Christian humanists, wrote sermons, treatises, translations (of the Bible and classical thinkers), an enchiridion, the great Colloquies, and of course satire, *Praise of Folly*. Other humanists, from Rabelais to Thomas Merton and others, have done the same thing, adopting an astonishing range of literary forms to get at the wealth and poverty of the human adventure. (Again, reader, we have engaged some of these forms before, and note as well that a scholarly review is its own literary and rhetorical form. It is one that I have set aside in order to adopt yet another form.)[2]

It is important, I believe, that de Gruchy has written a "confession." Part of any engagement with the book must wrestle with his choice of genre and the multiple meanings of that concept in its literary form. What is a confession, after all? At least three meanings of confession seem present in this book, some of which are long associated with humanistic inquiry, Christian and non-Christian. It is absolutely crucial to de Gruchy's vision, as far as I can see, that these confessions with their different meanings are ordered in a specific way, one of them providing the frame or space for the other two.

First, the text draws on the semantic force of a "confession," that is, to profess one's own most basic convictions and thus to annunciate one's life-defining commitments. This use of confession, I recall, reaches from St Augustine, the virtual creator of the genre, through time to Rousseau, Tolstoy, and others. A second and related meaning is the confession of sin; an act by a speaker/author that reveals to her or his interlocutor – and even to God – the depth of fault. The hope, of course, is that confession in this sense is part of the possible transformation of life, the invigoration of the will and the healing of human woe. And here too, it seems to me, de Gruchy avails himself of this meaning of confession. In marked difference from theologians who rest secure in their convictions about the Church, de Gruchy courageously admits his faults but also the many ways in which the churches have failed to live humanly in God's grace.

A third and final meaning of confession that resonates throughout the pages of this book comes to mind. It is the communal act of Christian confession of faith, especially in those great declarations of the twentieth century that fought the idolatry of fascism (the Barmen Declaration) and apartheid (the Belhar Declaration). In this sense, Christian confession creates the context, the space of reasons, within which the other two senses of "confession" find their meanings and their purposes in Christian discourse. In this light, it is hardly surprising, now that I consider it again, that the very structure of this book hinges, in chapter 5, on what it means to be a believer before then ascending to the meaning of "Christian humanism." The hinge, in other words, turns on Christ as a way to re-engage the signs of our times and thereby to unfold the meaning of Christian conviction. This is also why, again on my reading, de Gruchy is moved to interweave personal narrative, theological and even dogmatic reflection, with social and cultural engagement in making his case for Christian humanism.

I mention the point about "genre" in order to grasp something deeper about the structure and nuance of the book, but for other reasons as well. First, it is vitally important to understand what the genre of confession allows an author to avoid, at least rhetorically speaking. A contrast will make this point, one that I hope will not strike my readers as self-serving on my part. In my recent book, co-written with David E. Klemm, *Religion and the Human Future*, we subtitled the book "An Essay on Theological Humanism."[3] Coined by Michel de Montaigne, an "essay" in its original sense meant a trial, a testing, of oneself and one's perceptions and convictions. The genre has much of the same personal and humane resonance as a "confession," but an essay stresses the demand to make a case, to provide reasons, for the positions adopted. De Gruchy's confession, it seems to me, can assume precisely what an "essay" on theological humanism drawn from Christian sources cannot assume, namely, that the confession is sufficient testimony to the veracity of the faith expressed. Stated otherwise, the genre of confession allows de Gruchy to remain within the confines of Christian proclamation, to revise the faith in terms of the faith, rather than putting faith on trial with the demand to make a case for convictions. For a theological humanist, the resources of a faith tradition are necessary but not sufficient for determining the truth of those convictions. In this sense, the tactic of arguing "remoto Christi" is never as innocent as a theologian like de Gruchy would like it to appear. The confession of Christ is always and already present. I will return to this in the final step of these ruminations.

In terms of rhetorical genre de Gruchy's book is an example of a chastened and wisened ecclesial theology rather than the kind of theology demanded by an "essay." Now, I hope, and, yes, pray, that these two genres (confession; essay) can travel in tandem. Any good humanist should try his or her hand at each of them – and many other forms of writing and speaking as well. Yet it is important to see that this book is written for an ecclesial audience, at least in terms of genre. Its claims to truth presuppose the creedal confession that forms the space of reasons for the other layers of confession de Gruchy practices. That is part of what would make it difficult to "review" the book since the terms of engagement are set. This fact has required that I adopt a different form of reflection.

The other reason I mention the question of genre beyond the point about the structure of the book is a bit more complex. The decision to set a personal confession within the context of the confession of the Church is to judge that the most appropriate "form" for Christian thinking is defined by the historic consensus of the Church about its creedal affirmation. Whereas an essay or a handbook or a satire or a letter (other humanist genres) attenuate the authority of creedal formulations, the confessional genre, at least as de Gruchy has deployed it, works otherwise. This means, as I read the text, that the book is less adventurous in probing the meaning of Christian convictions from a humanistic outlook and much more concerned to show the enduring relevance of traditional Christian claims for our time.

My first engagement with the book, then, is to note that de Gruchy's text is a subtle interweaving of ideas about "confession." This interweaving structures the book and also makes it somewhat difficult to assess. Who can challenge a confession? The book is also set within a specific creedal context which underscores the connection of confession and truth in the very core of the idea of Christian humanism. Yet I have also begun to suggest that other thinkers who also want to work humanistically with Christian sources – thinkers like me – might have reasons for adopting different genres in order to carry out their reflection on the turmoil and joy of the human adventure Christianly construed. I want now to deepen that suggestion and thus to return to the points just made, to re-engage them along the pathway of these ruminations. I must shift from matters of genre to conceptual distinctions between types of religious humanism. I hope to show that these distinctions are important for understanding de Gruchy's work.

4

Much to the delight of many and to the horror of others, we are in the midst of a resurgence of interest in humanistic thought. This resurgence probably has many causes, given the rough and tumble of things human. It might be due, for instance, to the force of anti-humanistic and authoritarian social forms around the world and thus the awakening of many thinkers to the need to defend basic humanistic principles and values. It might be a matter of the usual flux and flow of intellectual work. The resurgence of interest in humanism could be due to a deep, if too often inarticulate, awareness that human power – especially through genetic technologies – now endangers the human species itself. The interest could be explained as the attempt to re-think the connection between human beings and other forms of life on our shared planet in a time when many, like Peter Singer, want to "unsanctify human life." It could be, as it was for Pope John Paul II, a worry about the possible triumph of a "culture of death." Or the interest in humanism might spring from a sense that the very idea of a human "nature" has come to an end in our time; as Bill McKibben and others put it, there is an "end of nature."[4] Whatever the reason, it is in fact the case that there is new interest in and criticism of humanism, religious and otherwise. De Gruchy's work needs to be seen in this context as well and not just through the analysis of rhetorical form. In order to do so, we can draw distinctions, only some of which he mentions.

De Gruchy rightly notes some of the history and figures that we have charted throughout this book. Classical humanism is often associated with the Italian Renaissance, although there are some important differences between those thinkers and what is known as the Northern Renaissance, especially about Christian faith.[5] As popularly understood, Renaissance "humanists" of various stripes proclaimed that human beings, and humans alone, are ends-in-themselves, possessing intrinsic worth and supreme importance. All other forms of life (natural or divine) are appraised in relation to human well-being. As Tzvetan Todorov notes, humanism "refers to the doctrines according to which man is the point of departure and the point of reference for human action. These doctrines are 'anthropocentric' doctrines, just as others are theocentric, and still others put nature or tradition in this central place."[6] The end or good of human life for traditional humanism is the free, productive, and creative exercise of human capacities for the sake of human flourishing. "The distinctive feature of modernity," Todorov writes, "is constitutive of humanism: man *alone* (and not only nature or God) decides his fate. In addition, it implies that the ultimate end of these acts is a human being, not suprahuman entities (God, goodness, justice) or infrahuman ones (pleasures, money, power)."[7] Humanism holds that the right orientation of human life is the *creative* exercise of power to shape one's existence and to seek flourishing.

Humanism in its various types (scientific, secular, religious) presents different outlooks and orientations on life.[8] What every humanist agrees upon is that human beings possess intrinsic worth. Put most simply, humanists affirm the dignity of individual life, a cosmopolitan scope of moral concerns that exceeds the boundaries of race or creed or sex or religion, and, finally, human beings as ends-in-themselves. The most basic difference among humanists, as Tony Davies notes, is whether "'Man' denotes an essential *starting point* ... or as a *destination*, less a given set of intrinsic qualities than the goal of an epochal and never-to-be completed process."[9] "Man" as *origin* and "man" as *end* provide related but starkly different orientations in life and also outlooks on existence. Does one live from one's humanity in fullness or does one struggle to bring one's humanity into being? Christian humanists have it both ways: human dignity is rooted in the incarnation of God in Christ but is also a destiny into which one lives in the glory of God. As dust that breathes, human beings, for Christians, are oriented towards finitude but also towards God.

For de Gruchy, I recall, this tension at the heart of a humanistic account of "man" is found in two images that traverse the book beginning with page one. One image is the picture of Dietrich Bonhoeffer that hangs over his desk and from whom de Gruchy draws the insight that God treasures not superhuman perfection but the "man for others." Conjointly, the other image is the famous drawing by da Vinci that represents the Renaissance picture of perfect man, "The Vitruvian Man." *Confessions of a Christian Humanist* weaves its way between these two contrasting images of the "human." In doing so, the text enfolds a tension found throughout humanistic discourse.

What is sometimes called "anti-humanism" in religious and non-religious forms is simply the negation of these features of humanism. That is to say, an anti-humanist typically denies the distinctive worth and dignity of human beings; often, in order to honor the deity or nature or history or society, she or he denies that human beings are real makers of history (that is left to providence or supra-human social systems), and she or he seeks a good that not only exceeds but also counters the human good. Anti-humanists are not necessarily against human beings; they merely assert that a humanistic conception of life is untenable and may be morally dangerous. It is safe to say that anti-humanism has a long legacy in the West ranging from the Stoics (on some accounts) to certain radical forms of theocentrism and also the current focus on biological or global social systems as the real "agents" in the world. Neither my ruminations in these pages nor de Gruchy's book takes up the challenge of anti-humanism.[10] More salient for the sake of these reflections is another distinction important for understanding the current resurgence of humanism.

On my understanding what has happened with the current resurgence of humanism is a shift or turn taken by a variety of thinkers who have attempted to address in various ways the challenges of anti-humanism as well as other criticisms of classical thought. Usually called "neohumanists," these thinkers, as we have seen in previous chapters, adopt a wild array of positions but seem to agree on two basic points. The first point of agreement is that with too much classical humanism in its non-religious forms the center of focus was on the development and perfection of the individual. The Virtuvian Man was not only an icon of perfection but he – and it was always "he" – was a rather solitary being. Perfection meant becoming god-like, on a classical metaphysical vision of deity: unchanging in the fullness of being. One recalls, for instance, Pico's great *Oration on the Dignity of Man*. This classical perspective seems too individualistic, too focused on the self, for contemporary sensibilities. Surely it is not just the self that is an end, a good, in itself; surely the other, the "you," as Todorov puts it, also makes a claim to finality, to ultimate respect and care. If that is true, then a shift in the conception of what counts as the human "good" must be conceived beyond the ideal of individual perfection and much more in terms of respect and care for the other. In this way – but never tell them – many secular thinkers have just learned from Christians about the radical claim of the other, the neighbor and even the enemy.

In a related way, classical humanism in its religious guise seemed too ready to understand the scope of human transcendence to reach beyond the domain of the human and into the divine. The point of life, the perfection of the human project, is then other-worldly. If that is the case, then the love of God seems to eclipse the love of others and transgress the proper limitation of human capacities. As Friedrich Nietzsche – a kind of anti/neohumanist – put it, man will only become man when he is not siphoned off into the gods. Without denying the possibility of religious sensibility, contemporary neohumanists insist that the range of human transcendence is lateral, that is, oriented towards the human other. Neohumanism is then a reconceptualization of the reach and range of human transcendence. In this way, Christian theologians – but never tell them – have learned from their "secular" colleagues.

As noted, neohumanism takes a variety of forms. In previous chapters I have explored Todorov's non-religious form of thought and contrasted it with Levinas, Ricoeur, and Murdoch, each of whom re-conceives a relation to the divine or to the "religious." In all cases, what is crucial to distinctly neohumanistic modes of thought is an emphasis on the other, the finality of the you (as Todorov puts it) and thus some conception of lateral transcendence. It is precisely on these points, we will see shortly, that de Gruchy's Christian humanism both accepts the neohumanist turn, as did Bonhoeffer, and yet also challenges it, as did Bonhoeffer. The same will be the case with theological humanism drawn from Christian sources. In order to understand that point, still another set of distinctions is in order.[11]

There are two basic forms of *religious humanism* – two ways of combining humanism with religion. Members of both forms believe that genuine flourishing comes from learning, cultivating, and enacting basic human qualities. They are different, however, in the way they relate to the historical religions. The first form is the *humanism of organized religions*. Within Buddhism, Islam, Christianity, and so forth, there have always been those who hold that human dignity and happiness are foremost among the benefits of right conviction and practice within their own religion. Under this conception, religious humanism appears only in the specific guise of a "Jewish humanism," a "Christian humanism," an "Islamic humanism," and so on; there is no generic version of religious humanism. The convictions of one's religion are viewed as the necessary and sufficient conditions for being truly humanistic. Here de Gruchy stands and can do no other. For these people, the aim of religion is to bring people close to God or the divine *so that* humans may flourish in their own lives. Pleasing the gods at the expense of human happiness, or seeking redemption from this worldly vale of tears in an other-worldly heaven, nirvana, or place of eternal bliss are not the primary goals of this kind of religious humanist.

One finds this form of religious humanism within Eastern and Western Christianity when theologians speak of the "humanity of God." The purpose of Christian humanism is to show how beliefs about God's incarnation as a human being in Jesus Christ provide the backing and the aim of an authentically humanistic outlook. Because God became human in Jesus Christ, Christian faith is then the truest expression of a humanistic view of the world. As Thomas Merton once wrote, "True Christian humanism is the full flowering of the theology of the Incarnation."[12] Or, again, as Irenaeus put it long ago, "The glory of God is man fully alive." The grounds of this outlook and its goal, like every similar kind of religious humanism, remain within the confines of a specific religion.[13]

The second form of religious humanism can be called *spiritual or speculative humanism*.[14] In this form, the humanistic impulse focuses on common spiritual qualities abstracted from the particularities of religious traditions. This form of religious humanism comprises a family or spectrum of approaches with a shared conviction that whereas religions are many, the human spirit is one. They seek the spiritual unity that underlies the diversity of religions and cultures. Spiritual or speculative humanists tend to believe people can become too attached to their inherited religions and fail to see what is common in the spiritual quest. The future of humanity, they would say, depends on plumbing the depths of the human spirit and articulating its shared principles, practices, and common longings. In contrast to the humanists of organized religions, the spiritual-speculative humanists find the necessary and sufficient conditions for being truly humanistic in analyzing and interpreting human being as such and never solely in the convictions of one specific religion.

Humanists of this kind may have either a spiritualistic or a speculative bent. The former take the religions of the world as repositories of profound insights and experiences. In spite of differences, each religion in its core comprehends the heart of human being in relation to the divine.[15] Their aim is to identify the common structures and universal forms underlying every religion. The spiritualist sees that the modern person is privileged to behold the big picture of religious diversity within a globalized world and is no longer confined within the boundaries of one religion. They define the spiritual task of modernity as the effort to distill into systematic form the human wisdom that abides in different degrees within all religions.[16]

Speculative-leaning religious humanists look for universal truths about human being in relation to what is of ultimate importance and reality in the great philosophical systems, and not so much among the historical religions. Platonism or Hegelianism have been interpreted in humanistic terms to show how an understanding of the Form of the Good or the Absolute Idea may be intrinsic to the human spirit. These and other philosophies have religious roots on close examination, but they purport to rise above them into speculative heights. Recently constructed philosophies related to existentialism, phenomenology, and even postmodern deconstructionism are used to articulate the meaning of human being as open to and receptive of the divine in the fabric of human life.

Too often humanists within organized religions (Christian humanists, etc.) undervalue important efforts outside their own traditions to understand the common shape of the human drive for meaning, value, and worth. They usually prefer to remain within the interpretive circles of particular narratives, symbols, and theological formulae; they do not seek to ascend from their traditions to a more cosmopolitan point of view. Likewise, spiritual-speculative humanists tend to underestimate the degree to which their thinking, which aspires to universality, is nonetheless embedded within historical traditions of language, culture, and religion. No one is religious or even a human being in general. Human thought, precisely as human and thus limited, is situated within particular social and cultural legacies, like the legacies of distinctive religions. The writings of any speculative humanist concerning universal human meanings can be localized within particular cultural trajectories. Even humanistic philosophers live within (loosely) organized historical communities.

That is perhaps enough by way of summary of forms of humanism to make a rather simple point, but a point that would make little sense without the summary. As I read and ruminate on de Gruchy's text, I see that the three forms of "confession" he has woven into whole cloth express a distinctive kind of neohumanism of an organized religion. It is, first, a *Christian* humanism since the confession of the Church provides, rhetorically and conceptually, the space of reasons, as I have called them, within which to consider both human well-being and his own confession. Yet it is a Christian *humanism*, since de Gruchy happily links the resources of classic humanism with his own reading of the Gospel. And finally it is, I submit, a kind of Christian *neohumanism* since his own struggles in South Africa, his reading of Bonhoeffer, and his confession of the sins of the Church in its complicity with evil moves towards the priority of the other and so the moral and political meanings of Christian faith. The rhetoric of the confession, then, also denotes the kind of religious humanism we find in the pages of this book. That is, I suggest, a source of its insight and power.

What then? Should I end my ruminations with this summary analysis of the rhetoric and structure of the text? Is it enough to say, Amen? (That is, truth be told, surely something I believe every reader of this book should utter after finishing it.) A few more words are in order, I suppose. They return us to the point about rhetoric and the warrant of theological humanism.

5

With some sense of the flow and force of de Gruchy's account of Christian humanism, it now seems appropriate to isolate a possible point for further reflection and argument. On one level this might seem incidental. De Gruchy and I both write and try to live as Christians; both of us draw on a variety of resources to advance our claims; both of us are committed to a neohumanistic expression of faith and life. Yet for a variety of reasons, what I call "theological humanism" does not fit neatly into the present forms of "religious humanism." It differs from a religious humanism of an organized religion, like de Gruchy's Christian humanism. How so?

I am convinced that in our times the confession of faith can no longer serve as sufficient warrant for the truth of that faith. This is why I have advocated in earlier chapters of this book the public character of theology and also the need to engage culture. In a world in which religions and cultures interact and reflexively shape each other, for good or ill and peaceably or not, there is the demand for judgments about the veracity of claims, especially moral and political claims, which exceed the resources of any one tradition. There is the need for some orienting good which can be used to test claims to truth by members of any religious community, a good that focuses attention on the interdependence and vulnerability of forms of life, human and non-human. I call this good "the integrity of life" and I believe that the requirements of responsibility are to respect and enhance that good (see Chapters 9–10). The content of and knowledge about this good, I further contend, is not the possession of any one community or tradition. It is human property. And it can be used to test and criticize traditions when they take expression in forms, actions, and policies that demean and destroy the integrity of life. While finding deep agreement with de Gruchy's vision of Christian humanism, I believe that precisely by being a humanist one is committed to the public adjudication of claims under widely accessible goods and norms.[17]

While a theological humanist always inhabits some religious tradition, he or she does so in ways different than someone who believes her or his tradition's convictions are the necessary and sufficient condition of humanistic and theological commitments. A theological humanist believes that the resources of his or her religious community are *distinctive* among the many ways of being religious and human on this planet. Those resources are nevertheless not utterly *unique*. One's religious tradition can be compared with other religious outlooks, criticized, revised, even rejected in the light of interactions with others who also seek integrity in life. One's tradition is a necessary but not sufficient warrant for the truth of claims and a vision of life. So, theological humanism entails a *critical* relation to one's own religious community and its beliefs and practices. The critique arises from shared insight and not just from within the resources of the Christian confession.

This point might raise the hackles of some Christian theologians and maybe even de Gruchy. They might think that I am veering towards a speculative or spiritual form of religious humanism. I can imagine them musing that on my account everyone supposedly is linked in the great web of the integrity of life in which the spiritual depth of existence is to be found and which reason can probe for valid moral and political forms. I can assure you I am not humming "Circle of Life" from the *Lion King* while writing these ruminations nor am I racing towards some kind of reverence for life as the panacea for our social and religious ills. Given the finitude of human thought, the rootedness of our lives in time and matter, we do not, I believe, have the capacity to grasp the whole, the all. We are dust that breathes – to say it yet again. At best we use the conceptual and symbolic forms of specific traditions coupled with the hard labor of the imagination in order to discover meanings about our lot in life and to provide orientation to existence. Human beings understand by interpreting. We are creatures who seek understanding and orientation and traverse cultural domains and yet also live amid an ocean of ignorance we will never completely control or cross. Humility – the awareness that we are formed of earth and so dust – means that speculative claims are not reports on ultimate reality but imaginative outposts on the way to hard-won understanding.

A theological humanist insists that there is no ahistorical access to a universal structure of the human spirit, such that the influence of historical life marked by diversity somehow drops away. Humans live within histori-cal traditions; each of us is shaped by a host of cultural and religious symbols, narratives, rituals, and the stream of their interpretations that exert powerful influence on thinking. Theological humanism is mindful of the entanglement in all dimensions of historical religion and culture. It intends to fathom these influences, rather than to become stuck in or to flee from them, rooted in the conviction that the finite can bear the infinite. The norm theological humanism applies in its critical reflections on traditions is, again, the *integrity of life*. The integrity of life is not revealed from on high or grasped in a flash of speculative wonder. It is an idea and norm that arises from dogged reflection on human individual and social existence in its diversity within the wider compass of life on this planet. We approach that idea only in and through the uses of distinctive cultural and religious resources. Another way to make this point is to say that theological human-ism agrees with thinkers like Kwame Anthony Appiah who write about "rooted cosmopolitans."[18] One adopts a vision of the human adventure, an inclusive concern for human and non-human life, but rooted in some dis-tinctive cultural, social, and religious resources. This is why I explored before the idea of the cosmopolitan conscience (Chapters 3–4).

If one takes these points together, then it becomes clear why a theological humanist is more given to writing essays and ruminations rather than con-fessions or manifestos. One uses resources at hand in order to seek under-standing about how responsibly to orient life but always under the demand to respect and enhance the integrity of life. I draw my theological humanism from Christian sources, but those sources must also be "essayed," that is tested in the unending work of interpretation and rumination aimed at understanding. Stated otherwise, the outer frame, the conceptual space of reasons, is not defined by the Christian confession qua confession, as de Gruchy's marvelous book is, but, rather, the horizon to which Christian faith is dedicated, the integrity of life and even new life in Christ. One imagines that faithful people of good will in other communities might say the same thing about the aim of their convictions. In fact, one hopes that is precisely what they will say and how they will live. In other words, a genuine theological humanist tests theological and humanistic claims by a good, a standard, that is the sole attribute of either the divine or the human, namely, the integrity of life. It is this move, I believe, that distinguishes the purposes of theological humanism, itself a version of a Christian neohumanism, from the kind of Christian humanism outlined and advocated in de Gruchy's book.

6

These ruminations have run their course. I trust that it is obvious how deeply I appreciate de Gruchy's work, the profundity and subtlety of the book, and also how, in my judgment, it poses just the right questions. In the final analysis, I am not even sure how much difference there is between his position and the one I have intimated in these pages. In a real sense, the differences do not matter. What does matter is that finally and thankfully Christians are committing themselves to provide intelligent and humane expressions of their faith in an age when the world is weary, hope is flagging, and the religions are too often at war. The demand of the age – and it is God's demand at root – is to take a stand on behalf of what furthers human well-being and the future of our world. The demand before us wells up from the dust and from all breathing things. It is the demand to respond to the call of conscience in our time and thus to turn into the winds of the Spirit for the service of the integrity of life.

Notes

1 More recently we have joined together with others to explore new forms of Christian and non-Christian humanism first in the African context and then elsewhere. I have greatly benefited from the discussions held at various points and especially at STIAS, the Stellenbosch Institute for Advanced Study at Stellenbosch University in South Africa, directed by Hendrik Geyer.

2 On rhetorical form see for instance Edward W. Said, *Humanism and Democratic Criticism* (New York: Columbia University Press, 2004); and also Ernesto Grassi, *Rhetoric as Philosophy: The Humanist Tradition* (University Park: Pennsylvania University Press, 1980).

3 David E. Klemm and William Schweiker, *Religion and the Human Future: An Essay on Theological Humanism* (Oxford: Blackwell, 2008).

4 Bill McKibben, *The End of Nature* (New York: Random House, 1989).

5 See Margaret Mann Phillips, *Erasmus and the Northern Renaissance* (New York: Macmillan Co., 1950).

6 Tzvetan Todorov, *Imperfect Garden: The Legacy of Humanism*, trans. Carol Cosman (Princeton, NJ: Princeton University Press, 2002), p. 6.

7 Todorov, *Imperfect Garden*, p. 30.

8 For examples see Timothy G. McCarthy, *Christianity and Humanism* (Chicago: Loyola Press, 1996); Salvatore Puledda, *On Being Human: Interpretation of Humanism from the Renaissance to the Present*, trans. A. Hurley (San Diego,

CA: Latitude Press, 1997); and Corliss Lamont, *The Philosophy of Humanism*, 5th edn (New York: Frederick Ungar, 1967).

9 Tony Davies, *Humanism* (London: Routledge, 1996), p. 31. Emphasis mine.

10 See Kate Soper, *Humanism and Anti-Humanism* (La Salle, IL: Open Court, 1986).

11 In what follows I am drawing extensively on Klemm and Schweiker, *Religion and the Human Future*.

12 Thomas Merton, "Virginity and Humanism in the Western Fathers," in *Mystics and Zen Masters* (New York: Farrar, Straus & Giroux, 1967), p. 114. For a statement of this outlook in Protestant theology see Karl Barth, *The Humanity of God*, trans. John Newton Thomas and Thomas Wieser (Richmond, VA: John Knox Press, 1960); and in Russian theology see Paul Valliere, *Modern Russian Theology: Bukharev, Soloviev, Bulgakov: Orthodox Theology in a New Key* (Grand Rapids, MI: Eerdmans, 2000); and for a helpful general discussion of this point see R. William Franklin and Joseph Shaw, *The Case of Christian Humanism* (Grand Rapids, MI: Eerdmans, 1991).

13 Interestingly, there are even post-theistic forms of humanism in organized religion. One thinks, for instance, of the Society for Humanistic Judaism. Sherwin Wine, its founder, formed a congregation which eliminated references to God in worship services and proclaimed, "We revere the best in man." In certain Unitarian Universalist congregations there is also a denial of "God" and yet an assertion of humanism within the religion. Other examples could be cited.

14 Examples are as far-ranging as the philosophical deduction of "natural religion" by Jean-Jacques Rousseau in *Émile*, trans. Barbara Foxley (London: Everyman's Library, 1989), and the set of universal "spiritual" qualities (especially "concern for others' well-being" born of "love and compassion, patience, tolerance, forgiveness, contentment, a sense of responsibility, a sense of harmony") as articulated by the Dalai Lama in *Ethics for the New Millennium* (New York: Riverhead Books, 1999), pp. 22–3.

15 The religious phenomenology of Mircea Eliade, for instance, interprets the meanings of myths and symbols to display the universal archetypes of *homo religiosus*. The point could be made by reference to any number of thinkers, such as Gerardus van der Leeuw, Carl Jung, and others.

16 Hermann Hesse, *Die Einheit hinter den Gegensätzen* (Frankfurt am Main: Suhrkamp, 1986).

17 I have tried to make this argument in *Responsibility and Christian Ethics* (Cambridge: Cambridge University Press, 1995).

18 Kwame Anthony Appiah, *Cosmopolitanism: Ethics in a World of Strangers* (New York: Norton, 2006).

Index